This study is based on three years of fieldwork with ninety-nine active gang members and twenty-four family members. The book describes the attractiveness of gangs, the process of joining, the chaotic and loose organization of gangs, and gang members' predominant activities – mostly hanging out, drinking, and using drugs. The authors also discuss gang members' rather slapdash involvement in major property crime, their disorganized participation in drug traffic, and the often fatal consequences of their violent lifestyle.

Although the book focuses on the individual, organizational, and institutional aspects of gang membership, it also explores gang members' involvement with other school and neighborhood structures. Extensive interviews with family members provided groundbreaking insights into gang members' lives. Throughout the book, however, the authors keep the perspective of the gang member in the foreground. As much as possible, the story is told in gang members' own words.

Life in the Gang

Cambridge Criminology Series

Editors
Alfred Blumstein, Carnegie Mellon University
David Farrington, University of Cambridge

This new series publishes high quality research monographs of either theoretical or empirical emphasis in all areas of criminology, including measurement of offending, explanations of offending, police, courts, incapacitation, corrections, sentencing, deterrence, rehabilitation, and other related topics. It is intended to be both interdisciplinary and international in scope.

Other titles in the series
J. David Hawkins, editor, *Delinquency and Crime: Current Theories*

Simon I. Singer, *Recriminalizing Delinquency: Violent Juvenile Crime and Juvenile Justice Reform*

Life in the Gang

Family, Friends, and Violence

SCOTT H. DECKER
BARRIK VAN WINKLE

CAMBRIDGE
UNIVERSITY PRESS

Published by the Press Syndicate of the University of Cambridge
The Pitt Building, Trumpington Street, Cambridge CB2 1RP
40 West 20th Street, New York, NY 10011-4211, USA
10 Stamford Road, Oakleigh, Melbourne 3166, Australia

First published 1996

Printed in the United States of America

Library of Congress Cataloging-in-Publication Data

Decker, Scott H.
    Life in the gang : family, friends, and violence / Scott H. Decker,
Barrik Van Winkle.
      p. cm.
    Includes bibliographical references.
    ISBN 0-521-56292-9. – ISBN 0-521-56566-9 (pbk.)
    1. Gang members – Missouri – St. Louis – Case studies. 2. Gangs –
Missouri – St. Louis – Case studies 3. Group identity – Missouri –
St. Louis – Case studies 4. Juvenile delinquency – Missouri – St.
Louis – Case studies. I. Van Winkle, Barrik. II. Title.
HV6439.U7S723 1997
364.1'06'60977866 – dc20   96-7896

A catalog record for this book is available from the British Library

ISBN 0-521-56292-9 hardback
       0-521-56566-9

Contents

Acknowledgments   vii

Preface   ix

Chapter One
Life in the Gang: Family, Friends, and Violence   1

Chapter Two
"Are You Claiming?" Methods of Study   27

Chapter Three
"I'm Down with the Bloods, What's up Cuz?" Membership Issues   56

Chapter Four
"We Ain't No Worldwide Thing or Nothing": Gang Structure and
    Relationships   85

Chapter Five
"Where You Hanging? Let's Go Banging": What Gang
    Members Do   117

Chapter Six
"I Love to Bang": Serious Crime by Gang Members   144

Chapter Seven
"Doing Time" in School and Elsewhere: Gang Members
    and Social Institutions   187

Chapter Eight
"My Mom Doesn't Know": Gang Members and Their Families   230

Chapter Nine
"There's Only Two Ways to Leave the Gang, Die or Move":
    Responding to Gangs   261

Notes   281

References   287

Index of Gang Members, Relatives, and Ex-Members   293

Subject Index   297

Acknowledgments

LIKE MOST FIELD research, our project required the efforts of a large number of people. Funds to support the fieldwork came from a grant, 90CL-1076, from the Family Youth Service Bureau, Administration of Children and Families, U.S. Department of Health and Human Services. Maria Candamil was our initial project officer for the grant and has remained a friend and colleague throughout the process of completing this book. They should take her picture and put it beside the description of what an ideal project officer should be. Terry Lewis and Alice Bettencourt, also of the ACF staff, provided valuable assistance. In addition, Terry Jones, dean of the College of Arts and Sciences at UM-St. Louis, provided a leave for the fall 1994 semester that greatly aided in the completion of the analysis.

We are grateful for the cooperation of the St. Louis Metropolitan Police Department throughout our study. Colonel Clarence Harmon, then chief of police, gave us his assurance that the department would support our project and not interfere with its day-to-day operation. As always, he was true to his word. Mike Nichols, a sergeant in the "Gang Squad," was a frequent source of advice and consultation. And Lieutenant Tom Malacek, former commander of the Juvenile Division, was ready to help us when we needed it.

Two gang researchers faithfully read and commented on the study plan and the manuscript. Cheryl Maxson of the Social Science Research Institute, University of Southern California, provided a good deal of assistance in helping to place our study in the context of other gang research. She remains a trusted friend and colleague. David Curry, now a colleague in the Criminology and Criminal Justice Department at UM-St. Louis, provided important consultation throughout the study, helping to keep it focused on mainstream issues. The book is better for their input.

We received the assistance of a number of talented and hard-working student assistants throughout the project. Steve Manley helped to pretest the questionnaire, code interviews, and organize the preanalysis. Yolanda Gant provided valuable assistance in coding interviews and handling field relations, especially with female gang members and family members. Diana Kimes helped to clean up some of the analytical aspects of the book after the data had been collected. Chris Reichard and Richard Rabe created the tables and figures for this book. And Joy Chatman did a remarkable job transforming interview answers into numbers.

Cathy McNeal helped to shepherd the project in a variety of ways. As always, her assistance was very much appreciated. Laurie Mitchell transcribed every interview for our project. Her diligent efforts, going over interview tapes again and again, made a major contribution to whatever success our project may have enjoyed. Richard Wright (professor of Criminology and Criminal Justice at UM-St.Louis) provided assistance on a number of important matters. His aid with questionnaire construction, analytical framework, and editing the manuscript were valuable to our efforts. Richard deserves special thanks for his prompt and insightful criticisms of the manuscript.

Dietrich Lester Smith was our field ethnographer for this project. His job was to contact potential subjects in the field, screen them for eligibility, and convince them to participate in the project. Such a job calls for an unusual individual and Dietrich is indeed such a person. His knowledge of the streets and the gang members who dominate them was invaluable to the project. We are grateful for his efforts and his friendship.

Finally, we wish to offer thanks to our families for putting up with the days and nights away from home to conduct this project. JoAnn, Sara, Laura, and Elizabeth Decker were patient, curious, and supportive throughout the process. Polly Strong and Katie and Tina Van Winkle were a constant source of cheer, help, patience, and prompting over years of work.

Preface

THIS IS A STUDY of the gang member's perspective. Our goal is to embed the group process and values of the gang within social institutions. Thus, we seek to provide an institutional and cultural context for gang values and activities. Our observations are based on three years of intensive fieldwork and interviews with gang members on the streets of St. Louis. Our study sheds light on the ways gangs grow in cities where there is no recent history of gangs. We do this by directly examining the perspective of active gang members and the family members of active gang members. It is our belief that attempts to understand gangs and gang members are enhanced by this approach and that programs designed to prevent gang membership or enable gang members to remove themselves from the gang can learn from such a study.

Our commitment to highlighting the gang member's perspective is informed by several convictions. The first of these is our belief that the best way to study gangs is to do so on their own turf. To accomplish this, we employed the services of an experienced field-worker, familiar with the St. Louis community and its neighborhoods. Based on contacts with nearly five hundred gang members, we were able to generate a sample of ninety-nine active gang members and twenty-four relatives of active gang members. These contacts were built over a period of several years' involvement in doing field research with active offenders. A second distinguishing feature of our research is that we relied only on field contacts to recruit the members of our sample. None of the subjects in our study were found through official agencies such as the police, courts or social service agencies. It was our belief that what we learned from gang members may well be influenced by the way in which we had made contacts with them. Making contacts in the field does not come without its own biases; however, it did provide us with a method of getting in touch with and interviewing gang members directly. Finally, while we did use a questionnaire, ample opportunity was provided for each participant in the study to tell us their story in their own words.

Our interest in recruiting and studying gang members in the field is linked to our desire to explore the broad range of activities in which gangs and gang members engage. A sample drawn from a criminal justice population or some other institutional setting (such as a school) would undoubtedly focus on activities related to that institution. Our commitment to understanding the gang member's perspective leads us to consider both gang and nongang activities, beliefs, and relationships. Since even the most "hard-core" gang member spends a considerable amount of time outside the gang, we feel that our approach is well suited to uncovering such activities. We also examined relationships among subgroups of gang members that didn't involve the entire gang, or that mixed gang and nongang members. A field study is particularly compatible with such goals.

This orientation places our work in a long and rich tradition of field studies of gangs. Thrasher's (1927) pathbreaking work with 1,313 gangs in Chicago in the 1920s is perhaps the best known of these. In the last decade, a number of field studies of gangs and gang members have been conducted (Moore 1978, 1991; Vigil 1988; Sanchez-Jankowski 1991; Hagedorn 1988; Padilla 1992; Sanders 1994; Campbell 1984). Our work is distinguished from these in a variety of ways. First, we have chosen to study gangs in a city with an emerging gang problem. Unlike Chicago and Los Angeles, gangs in St. Louis have reemerged since the middle 1980s. By using a study site where gangs lack the intergenerational quality found in some cities (Chicano gangs in Los Angeles or black gangs in Chicago, for instance), we can examine the factors responsible for the rapid growth in gang membership. As a city with an emerging gang problem, results from St. Louis may provide insights into the growth of gangs in dozens of cities across the country (Spergel and Curry 1993; Curry, Ball, and Fox 1994). A second distinguishing feature of our work is the choice of the study site. St. Louis is plagued by many of the social conditions that characterize large cities across the country – rapid depopulation, chronic unemployment, a declining industrial employment base, an aging housing stock – yet is still a manageable enough size in which to conduct such a study. An additional feature of our study is its focus on a greater number of gangs than is generally found in field studies. Padilla (1992), Moore (1978, 1991) and Vigil (1988) conducted intensive studies of a small number of gangs. In contrast, our work spans a much larger number of gangs, choosing instead to focus on the diversity across gangs and gang members.

The most unique feature of our work, however, is its focus on the links between gang members and their families. This relationship has received limited attention in past research and is critical to understanding the activities and perspective of most gang members, especially teenaged members. We could not hope to understand this relationship by studying gang members alone, since a relationship implies that there are at least two parties. By contrasting the perspectives of gang members with family members, we hope to reveal more about the link between families and youth who become involved in gangs.

CHAPTER ONE

Life in the Gang: Family, Friends, and Violence

I'ma die for my colors, that's the first thing they say, I'ma die for my colors. What a color? A color that somebody done painted, red and blue. Say for instance I might be walking down the street and some Crips see me and it may be about five Crips, I'm the one Blood, just walking.

Jump that color, I heard.

They gonna walk up to me and they gonna take me out, yeah, what's up with that color, they talking about they gonna burn me, then we start doing that [pounding on his chest], you know, that mean they finna kill you. (Male #001, "Mike Mike," twenty-year-old Thundercat)[1]

THE COLORS red and blue are the symbols of street gangs, especially the Bloods and Crips. And as this quote from a leader of the "Thundercats" illustrates, colors can have lethal consequences. These gangs, and others like them, have captured the public imagination in the United States, fueling concerns about violence and drug sales. Much of this awareness is generated by the media; movies, television, radio, and newspaper stories are the primary sources of knowledge about gangs for most Americans. However, the picture of gangs and gang members painted by these images misses much that is of central importance to understanding gangs. Without such understanding, our ability to respond effectively to the threats gangs create or the criminality their members engage in will be severely limited.

Interest in gangs is not new. They have been an object of study for at least the last century, and their consideration by journalists and novelists extends well beyond that. Surges of academic and public interest in gangs occurred in the 1890s, 1920s, 1960s and late 1980s into the 1990s.

1

Changes in four social and demographic characteristics link interest in gangs in each of these periods: (1) immigration, (2) urbanization, (3) ethnicity, and (4) poverty. Each of these decades corresponds to rapid changes in the composition of city populations and economies. Working together, these factors produced conditions that make the formation and growth of gangs more likely. Yet economic and population variables alone cannot explain the growth of gangs or the nature of gang activities. Other insights are needed, particularly those that come from gang members themselves, because these insights can inform us about the values and group processes that lie at the heart of gang behavior.

There is controversy about the first use of the term "gang" to refer to an aggregation of relatively organized offenders. Sanchez-Jankowski argues that the term was first applied to "outlaws" in the 1800s. However, Bursik (1993) cites evidence from Johnson regarding groups in Philadelphia and from Haskins for New York City that gangs existed in cities before they did in more rural Western outposts. Sheldon (1898) is generally credited with the first academic use of the term "gang" (see Yablonsky 1962, 73). His description of gangs stems from a broader interest in the group activities of children, particularly games. In observing youthful social associations, he found that "spontaneous societies" seemed to emerge from the everyday activities of young people. Of particular interest were the predatory organizations involved in violent and property crimes, which he labeled gangs. Despite the involvement of these groups in illegal activities, he found considerable overlap between their characteristics and those of social clubs. The role of imitation was given prominent status in accounting for the behavior of these groups.

Throughout its history, the term "gang" has enjoyed a diverse usage, being linked to outlaws in the "wild west" and organized crime groups, among others. And the use of the term has not been confined to North America; "swing kids" in Nazi Germany were often named as gang members (Bessel 1987), and recent news reports have identified gangs in Russia (Raab 1994), Sarajevo (Burns 1993), and El Salvador (O'Connor 1994). The diversity of groups the term has been applied to provides evidence of the dilemmas in responding to the "gang problem." On the one hand, since so much adolescent activity takes place in groups, it is important to distinguish legitimate adolescent group activity from that which has a consistent illegal character. On the other hand, it is useful to distinguish groups of juveniles who engage in street crimes from their more organized adult counterparts, typically known as organized criminals. The lack of a consistent definition of gangs creates problems, not the least of which is the ability to compare information about gangs across cities and across different periods of times. For example, many of the groups regarded as gangs in the 1890s would not be so identified at the current time. Since not all of the illegal group activity of young people has a similar motivation or character, it is useful to have a less rigid definition of gangs. In this way, the term can capture variations across time, cities, ethnic, and age groups. However, the lack of a consistent definition of gangs creates problems for public officials who must formulate a response to what is perceived as the "gang problem." Without a clear concept of what is a gang and who is a gang member, public officials find themselves responding to an amorphous, ill-defined problem. This often leads, on the one hand, to denial that gangs exist or, on the other hand, to the overidentification of gangs (Huff 1991).

In this book, we present the results of three years of studying gangs in a declining Midwestern rust belt city, St. Louis, Missouri. Working the street, we recruited, interviewed, and observed active gang members and their families. Our study corresponded to a period of rapid growth in both the number of gangs and gang members in St. Louis, enabling us to provide insights about the origins and expansion of gangs.

Our Study in Perspective

Our work fits into a long tradition of examining gangs and gang members. We see its historical roots in the work of Thrasher in Chicago in the 1920s and draw considerable theoretical inspiration from the work of Short and Strodtbeck on group process, Klein on gang structure, and Yablonsky on violence. The work of Moore, Vigil, Padilla, and Hagedorn has helped guide our perspective on gang structure, gang activities, and the expansion of gangs. What makes our work distinctive, however, is its dependence on the gang member's perspective in a city with an emerging gang problem.

Early Gang Studies. The themes of immigration, urbanization, ethnicity, and poverty are most evident in examinations of gangs in the 1890s and at the turn of the century. The majority of such accounts were journalistic in nature. Faced with waves of immigrants from western Europe, New York found itself with a considerable level of gang activity in the late 1890s, much of it involving Irish immigrants. According to Riis (1892, 1902) young Irish (and later Italian) immigrants found integration into the economy to be difficult. Lacking activities to occupy their time, they formed gangs to provide for social and material needs. His descriptions of the gang focused on the myriad social conditions faced by the children of immigrants: poverty, poor education, poor housing, dirt, and the lack of wholesome activities. Gang life was a natural outcome for such youth:

> So trained for the responsibility of citizenship, robbed of home and of childhood, with every prop knocked from under him, all the elements that make for strength and character trodden out in the making of the boy, all the high ambition of youth caricatured by the slum and become base passions, – so equipped he comes into the business of life. As a "kid" he hunted with the pack in the street. As a young man he trains with the gang, because it furnishes the means of gratifying his inordinate vanity; that is the slum's counterfeit of self-esteem. (Riis 1902, 236–237)

The response to such problems was rather straightforward; occupy the time of these individuals and they will cease to be involved in gang activity. Activities such as athletics were recommended as "safety-valves" (Riis 1892, 131) for youthful energies.

The role of immigration in gang formation provided an important foundation for later examinations of gangs. Asbury (1928) studied gangs in New York City, especially in the Five Points area populated largely by recent Irish immigrants yet to move out of the economic underclass. He provided encyclopedic descriptions of the variety of gangs and their activities. The primary activities for these gangs were fighting, with each other as well as rival gangs. Asbury was careful to make the distinction between those who grow up in a gang and criminals who organize to perform illegal acts more effectively. He highlighted with considerable detail the colorful names used by these gangs, names that included the Roach Guards, Pug Uglies, Shirt Tails, and Dead Rabbits. It is an important historical footnote that red and blue, the colors adopted by the contemporary Bloods and Crips respectively, were the colors used by the Irish gangs of New York City in the 1920s. The Roach Guards used blue as their color, and the Dead Rabbits used red as their symbol. This underscores one feature common to most American gangs throughout history, the use of symbols to identify members. Asbury also described numerous small gangs with affiliations to a larger gang, suggesting that most gang activity was concentrated around the neighborhood among a small group of friends well-known to each other.

Thrasher's Study of Gangs. Thrasher's pioneering work appeared in 1927, the first serious academic treatment of gangs. Working within the sociological paradigm of the Chicago School, Thrasher gave gangs a cultural and ecological context. Using the concepts of culture and neighborhood ecology, he sought to explain gang transmission (the intergenerational character of gangs in neighborhoods and subcultures) as part of a process of collective behavior. Gangs in Chicago were found primarily in interstitial areas. These areas were characterized by three consistent ecological features: (1) deteriorating neighborhoods, (2) shifting populations, and (3) mobility and disorganization of the slum. The "ganging process" was dynamic and produced organizations that were constantly undergoing change. In this context, Thrasher saw gangs as

> the spontaneous effort of boys to create a society for themselves where none adequate to their needs exists. What boys get out of such association that they do not get otherwise under the conditions that adult society imposes is the thrill and zest of participation in common interest, more especially in corporate action, in hunting, capture, conflict, flight and escape. Conflict with other gangs and the world about them furnishes the occasion for many of their exciting group activities. (1927, 37)

Thrasher found considerable variation in the definition of gangs but also noted that gangs played a variety of functions, further complicating efforts to define them in precise ways. In his view, gangs originated from the spontaneous group activity of adolescents and were strengthened by conflict. This process consists of three stages. In its earliest stage, the gang is diffuse, little leadership exists, and the gang may be short lived. Some gangs progress to the next stage, where they become solidified. Conflict with other gangs plays a notable role in this process, helping to define group boundaries and strengthen the ties between members, uniting them in the face of a common threat. The final step in the evolution of the gang occurs when it becomes conventionalized and members assume legitimate roles in society. For those groups that fail to make this transition, delinquent or criminal activity becomes the dominant focus of the group. Among Thrasher's great strengths is his description of the process by which groups form, solidify, and disintegrate. He portrayed the relationship between gangs and other forms of social organization in a figure that traces the natural history of the gang. Most notable about this figure are the poignant reminders that social associations characterize most adolescent activities, and the majority of activities are law abiding.

Activities within the gang, according to Thrasher, were diverse and motivated by typical youthful concerns, such as thrills and excitement. A number of predatory activities were observed, with stealing being the most common. Many gangs were characterized by Thrasher as conflict groups that developed out of disputes and flourished in the presence of threats from rival groups. Fighting was the preeminent activity, and clashes with members of one's own gang were as likely as those with members of rival gangs. For gang members, violence served both to unite them and to speed the adaptation of the gang to its environment. In this way, violence played an especially important function in the integration of members into the group. The threat presented by rival gangs served to intensify solidarity within the gang, especially for new members. Despite their involvement in criminal or delinquent activity, most gang members were assimilated into legitimate social activities, most often athletics.

Gangs are isolated from mainstream society both by geography and lack of access to legitimate institutional roles. This isolation contributes to the within-group solidarity so critical to Thrasher's account of gangs, but it also plays another role. It helps to explain the lack of integration into the economic, educational, and social structure of cities and serves to prevent many gang members from giving up their gang affiliations for activities of a more law abiding nature. The isolated nature of the gang also allows it to enforce its rules (such as they may be) in a manner largely unimpeded by other institutions. Order is maintained through informal mechanisms as well, particularly "collective representations" (297) such as symbols, signs, and group argot. The power of the collective is seen in its role in "mutual excitation" (299), promoting behavior among gang members that they would not normally engage in. Despite the attention given to the larger collective of the gang, Thrasher notes the importance of subgroups within the gang.

> The two- and three-boy relationship is often much more important to the individual boy than his relationship to the gang. In such cases a boy would doubtless forego the gang before he would give up his special pal or pair of pals. (322)

It is important to note that these subgroups exist in all parts of the city, regardless of whether they are affiliated with larger gangs.

Despite the fact that Thrasher's observations of gangs are nearly seventy years old, and that the demographic characteristics of cities have changed profoundly since then, many of his conclusions have important implications for the contemporary study of gangs. The central questions he addressed – gang transmission, growth of gangs, sources of cohesion among gang members, the role of threats, the importance of collective behavior, distinguishing adolescent group behavior from gang behavior, and most importantly the role of culture in understanding gangs – remain important today. And many of his observations, especially about the role of structural variables and group process within gangs, remain critical issues for the contemporary study of gangs.

Gangs in the Sixties

The advent of the Depression and World War II induced a decline in gangs and the attention paid to them. However, the conclusion of World War II brought rapid social change to American cities, as the American economy struggled to adapt to peacetime. At the same time, northern cities experienced a massive migration of southern blacks moving to the "promised land" (Lerman 1991) of jobs and greater opportunity. In many ways, this migration mirrored earlier waves of European immigrants who had moved to the industrial cities of the northeast and Midwest seeking employment. And like many of their European counterparts who came before them, southern blacks often found their new homes to be less than hospitable places.

Theory Development. Gangs began to reemerge in cities in the 1950s and spawned a new generation of gang research, theory, and policy. Attention paid to gangs by criminologists in the 1950s and 1960s yielded important theoretical insights and policy recommendations. Building on the theoretical traditions of Emile Durkheim and Robert Merton, Albert Cohen (1955) developed the theory of status frustration to explain the process by which boys become involved in delinquent activities and gangs. Because they are judged by middle-class standards that many are ill equipped to meet, working-class and lower-class boys develop frustrations about achieving status goals. As a means of resolving these status concerns, they turn to delinquent activities and to the group affiliation of the gang. Richard Cloward and Lloyd Ohlin (1960) also built on the Mertonian tradition of emphasizing the role of shared cultural success goals and institutional means of achieving those goals. Rather than emphasizing status concerns, they focused on the blocked opportunities for achieving legitimate success faced by most working-class and lower-class boys. Because the opportunities for success were differentially distributed by neighborhood, some boys found that they lacked the access to achieving the goals society defined as important. The result was three forms of adaptations; conflict gangs, property gangs, or retreatist gangs.

The adaptations resulted from the level of available opportunities and the extent to which boys were integrated in the neighborhood.

Not all commentators on gangs and youth delinquency concurred with the premise that a single set of cultural values permeated American society. For the theories of Cohen and Cloward and Ohlin, it is critical that this be the case, because the commitment to a common set of values causes status frustration (for Cohen) or blocked opportunities (for Cloward and Ohlin) and leads to delinquency. Walter Miller (1958) theorized that a far different set of values permeated lower-class culture, values that naturally lead to increased levels of delinquent and gang involvement. For Miller, six "focal concerns" defined life for lower-class boys: fate, autonomy, smartness, toughness, excitement, and trouble. Commitment to these values, as opposed to those of the dominant culture, need not be explained by lack of access to legitimate success roles. Lower-class boys learned these values as a consequence of living in their own neighborhoods where such values were dominant. Miller's approach emphasized the role of a subculture in the creation and maintenance of delinquent groups and gangs.

An important development in theory and research occurred with the appearance of Lewis Yablonsky's (1962) work on the violent gang. Drawing on Thrasher, he identified three types of gangs – delinquent gangs, violent gangs, and social gangs – indicating that the violent gang was the most persistent and problematic for society. Not unexpectedly, the role of violence looms large in every aspect of this gang. The violent gang forms in response to threats against safety, and thus represents a form of protection for its members. It has a loose structure and little formal character; for example, leaders in this gang "emerge" and membership within gang subgroups in many cases is more important than the larger gang. Violence, the defining event for members of these types of gangs, can arise over seemingly senseless matters but most often occurs in response to perceived threats against gang territory. Membership fulfills a number of needs; most importantly, it meets the psychological needs of boys incapable of finding such fulfillment in the larger society. Because of its lack of organization, Yablonsky identifies the violent gang as a "near group" (272); a "collective structure" situated somewhere between totally disorganized aggregates (like mobs) and well-organized aggregates (like delinquent or social gangs).

Action Research. Much criminological work takes place in a policy vacuum; that is, the research is seldom closely coordinated with ongoing policy or programmatic initiatives. A remarkable exception to this is found in the work of four researchers: Spergel (1966), Klein (1971), and Short and Strodtbeck (1974). Each of these projects evaluated a gang intervention program that was premised on theories about gangs and gang behavior. And in each the researchers used the evaluation to revisit theories about gangs and delinquency, an occasion too rare in our field. We examine each of these because they helped to set the tone for the gang research that was to follow.

While Spergel, Klein, and Short and Strodtbeck all examined active gang and delinquency prevention programs, Spergel's work was most concerned with the practical matters of working with gangs. He analyzed the approach to gang intervention that had become popular, the detached worker. At its heart, detached street work is problem-oriented, group social work, an approach with a long history, especially in Chicago, where the Chicago Area Projects had used it for some time. In part, this approach depended on the social structure of the neighborhood or community in which it operated. Spergel argued that successful work with gang members depended on an understanding of four factors: (1) the delinquent subculture (beliefs, norms and values) within the neighborhood, (2) the delinquent group itself, (3) the individual delinquent, and (4) the agency worker. Spergel highlighted the role of delinquency theory, particularly that of Cloward and Ohlin, and argued that street work *practice* must be determined by *theoretical explanations* of delinquent groups. Spergel's work had a prescriptive orientation, offering program and intervention suggestions for street workers addressing gang and delinquent behavior.

Klein (1971) assumed both a more theoretical and analytic approach to dealing with gangs, though his analysis emerged from the "action context" of evaluating gang intervention programs. Two programs, the Group Guidance Project and the Ladino Hills Project (which operated from 1962 through 1968) formed the basis of his analysis. He notes the programmatic efforts of Mobilization for Youth in New York, the Los Angeles Youth Project, the Chicago Area Projects, and Youth for Service in San Francisco. Each of these projects held many features in common, especially the detached worker approach that took programming into the community and encouraged street workers to fully involve themselves in the gang and gang activities. Klein's theoretical antecedents include Cohen, Cloward and Ohlin, Miller, and Bloch and Niederhoffer.

Klein arrived at the unsettling conclusion that the Group Guidance Project may have increased delinquency among gang members. Specifically, he found that delinquency increased among gang members who received the most services and that solidarity among gang members seemed to increase as a result of the attention paid to the gang by street workers. This led Klein to the conclusion that gang intervention programs may have the latent consequence of contributing to the attractiveness of gangs, thereby enhancing their solidarity and promoting more violence. He paid considerable attention to issues of gang structure, particularly solidarity among gang members. He concluded that most characteristics of gang structure were difficult to differentiate from other features of adolescent street culture and that members of gangs shared most in common with other (nongang) adolescents. His conclusions that gangs and gang members contained large variation within their respective ranks reinforced his earlier observation that gangs were not monolithic.

Klein's views of leadership and the sources of cohesion within gangs were consistent with his definition of gangs and gang membership. In his view, leadership was largely age related and was not so much a specific office as it was a mixture of functions. This reinforced the notion that gangs resembled other features of youth culture (disorganized, spontaneous, short term) more than they did more formal adult structures. Further support for this contention was found in the consistent report by gang members that their primary activity was "hanging out" with other members on the street. And their delinquency was described as "cafeteria style" (125) rather than a purposive, well-organized specialization. Cohesiveness, the force that keeps gangs together, was more a product of external than internal sources. That is, the bonds of gang membership do not become stronger in response to internal mechanisms (meetings, codes, signs, activities) but rather as a response to external pressures. In general, Klein found that few gang goals existed outside of those generated by external pressures, and the few internal gang norms that did exist were weak and transient. The external sources of cohesion were structural (poverty, unemployment, and weak family socialization) but also included pressures that resulted from interaction with other gangs as well as members of one's own gang. In particular, the threat of violence from another gang increased solidarity within the gang. One effect of this is that most victims of gang violence were other gang members. Of particular concern to Klein was the role membership interaction played in strengthening gang cohesiveness. The more gang members met and the more important their gang was perceived to be in the community, the stronger the bonds were between gang members. Against this backdrop,

Klein saw the intervention of detached workers and gang programs enhancing gang cohesiveness, making the dissolution of the gang a greater challenge.

The Ladino Hills Project gave Klein the opportunity to build on findings from the Group Guidance Project. A specific effort was made to avoid increasing gang solidarity, an outcome that would make the gang more attractive, increase membership, and expand delinquent activities. A working premise of this approach was that programmatic "attention" paid to gangs by such institutions as the police, social workers, and the schools had the latent consequence of making the gang more attractive and should be avoided. In addition, organized gang events were discouraged. The results were encouraging in many respects, as gang cohesiveness declined during the project. Despite this, the rate of delinquency increased, particularly for more serious crimes. However, the amount of delinquency overall declined, a decline that was concentrated among "companionship" offenses. The withdrawal of adults from gang activities diminished both gang cohesion and delinquency.

Short and Strodtbeck (1974) began their analysis with a premise similar to Klein's, specifically that the War on Poverty may have increased gang solidarity. Based on research in Chicago, their conclusions are similar to those of Klein, particularly with regard to gang structure, cohesion, and activities. Short and Strodtbeck adopted an approach consistent with the poverty area research of Shaw and McKay and the group delinquency perspective found in the theories of Cohen, Cloward and Ohlin, and Thrasher. They found, however, that it was difficult to locate gangs that correspond to those described in most theories. This led them to examine in greater depth the *processes and values* that lead to gang delinquency. Indeed, they use the concept of values to link the social status (especially social class) of gang members to their illegitimate behavior.

Short and Strodtbeck paint a picture of gangs, gang members, and gang activities remarkably similar to that drawn earlier by Klein. Like their Los Angeles counterparts, gang members in Chicago reported that the activity that consumed the greatest amount of their time was "hanging out" on the street. Short and Strodtbeck found five specific indices of gang activity: (1) conflict, (2) institutional social activities, (3) sexual behavior, hanging out, and selling alcohol, (4) homosexuality, fathering illegitimate children, and common-law marriages, and (5) involvement in minor car related crimes, conflict, and alcohol use. They observed that these behaviors are not greatly dissimilar from the more routine activities of adolescent males. Stated differently, these analysts were unable to find activities that consistently differentiated gang members from their non-gang peers. Gangs had a shifting membership and structure, with allegiances vacillating over time. Leadership seldom had power and generally was incapable of exacting discipline from members. Concomitantly, few strong group norms laid claims on the behavior of individual gang members.

Status plays a central role in Short and Strodtbeck's explanation of gang formation and activities. Threats to the status of the gang were particularly important, and conflict emerged from disputes about the reputation of the gang. But status threats also operate at the individual level for Short and Strodtbeck. They regard threats, especially to individual status, as fundamental to understanding the origin of gangs. Three systems external to the gang provide the major sources of (and threats to) individual status: (1) adult institutions such as school and jobs, (2) community institutions in the areas that generate gangs, especially street culture, and (3) gang culture. In the course of maintaining relationships with each of these systems, gang members experience threats to their status as individuals. For Short and Strodtbeck, the gang emerges as a collective solution to status threats posed by these relationships. This solution, however, is of short duration.

As America attempted to deal with demands by racial and ethnic minorities for an increased share of economic and social justice, attention to the gangs of the 1950s and early 1960s waned. Gangs faded from public concern in the sixties, replaced by broader concerns over race, increasing crime, and urban unrest. Perhaps the decline in interest over gangs confirmed what Klein and Short and Strodtbeck had reported; gangs had little permanence and stability and, if left alone, may well fade away. Whether the attention paid to other problems caused the decline in gangs, or whether gangs simply faded from the urban scene remains an open question. Regardless of the explanation, social scientists, social workers, policymakers, and the public turned their attention to other matters. This may reflect a change in the funding priorities of the federal government, as resources for studying youth gangs were no longer available (Howoritz 1983).

Recent Field Studies of Gangs

Moore (1978; 1991) has conducted the longest ongoing field research with gangs. Her work is the result of collaboration between academics, Chicano ex-convicts (referred to as Pintos), and gang members in the

Mexican American neighborhoods of East Los Angeles. Moore's research places primary importance on the role of Chicano culture and the position of Mexican Americans within the cultural and institutional life of East Los Angeles in explaining gang formation and activities. Her work underscores the isolation of the barrio from mainstream life in Los Angeles, particularly its political and economic detachment. In her earlier work (1978), gangs from three barrios (White Fence, Hoyo Maravilla, and San Fernando) were studied through the use of Pintos as research associates.

Moore and her associates isolated three distinctive characteristics of Chicano gangs: (1) they were territorially based, (2) they had a strong age-graded structure resulting in "klikas," or cohort groups, and (3) fighting occupied a central role in Chicano gang life. After fighting, drugs played a prominent role in the life of gangs. Contrary to Klein's earlier work, Moore emphasized the life-long role that gangs played for their members and communities. Adult gang members were plentiful in number and performed a role in the intergenerational transmission of gang membership within neighborhoods. The strong ethnic culture of Chicanos also helped to shape the structure and activities of Chicano gangs through its emphasis on individual status. In part, this occurred as a result of the high rate of imprisonment of Chicano gang members. While in prison, ethnic gangs attracted and socialized inmates from their neighborhood not previously involved in gang activity. Thus, a prison gang culture was formed; and gang culture ultimately found a role on the street. Moore argued that the continuities between Chicano prison gangs and those on the street are strong because the experiences in the prison and neighborhood are similar. That is, Chicanos are not included in the mainstream of the economy or political structure in either setting. This enhances ethnic solidarity and produces the pressures that cause increased cohesion among gang members.

Field researchers rarely get the opportunity to return to their subjects and setting years after an initial analysis. Yet such a procedure is essential for documenting changes over time. Moore (1991) accomplished this by going back to two of the neighborhoods she studied earlier (White Fence and Hoyo Maravilla). She was able to develop a list of gang members from her earlier work, from which a random sample of 156 men and women were chosen for in-depth interviews. Her findings underscored the effect that the growth of the urban underclass has had on gangs and their activities. In addition to the evaporation of many employment opportunities, the decline of housing, and schools and dramatic population changes (movement of the middle and working class from traditional neighborhoods) created conditions that altered the nature of the barrio and its gangs.

Early gangs began as "friendship groups" (31) with informal structures, which claimed a territory as their own. Members were committed to protecting themselves and their neighborhood. These gangs had a strong age-graded structure; cliques within the gang of boys and girls of the same age were the primary source of gang activity. Moore considered two explanations for the growth of these gangs: (1) resistance theory and (2) illicit opportunity theory. Resistance theory postulates that gangs form out of a conscious effort of their members to reject the legitimacy of the existing political order. As such, they are viewed as "revolutionary." Illicit opportunity theory, on the other hand, argues that gangs serves as "training grounds" for adult criminality (42). Moore found that neither approach accurately described the changes that took place in the gangs of the two neighborhoods she studied. Over time, gangs became more institutionalized in their neighborhoods, exerted greater influence over the lives of their members, and became more deviant. This was a consequence of the growth of the underclass. In addition, gangs neutralized the socialization power of other institutions in the neighborhood, further enhancing their ability to grow stronger.

Reflecting their territorial nature, most gang members came from the same neighborhood. There was little evidence that adolescents were "forced" into joining the gang; rather it was a normal outcome of hanging out with a certain group of friends. Gang members spent most of their time "hanging around" the neighborhood. The major change from gangs in the 1950s to the present was the increase in aggression. Little evidence was found to support the contention that gang members had defective personalities or disproportionately came from families with problems. Moore found that work, a productive job, was the single most important strategy for "making it" in the barrio.

Three additional field studies of Chicano and Hispanic gangs are important to place our own work into perspective. Diego Vigil (1988) examined Chicano gangs in Los Angeles in the late seventies. Ruth Horowitz (1983) studied a gang in a Chicano community in Chicago during the late seventies, and Felix Padilla (1992) studied a Puerto Rican gang in Chicago in the eighties. These researchers situated their analyses of gangs and gang members in the context of Hispanic culture and the marginality of ethnic groups in the larger culture.

Horowitz (1983) spent time in the early 1970s studying the "Lions," a

Chicano gang in Chicago. By returning in the late 1970s, she was able to observe the Lions as they made the transition from teenagers to adults. Her analysis focused on the often competing demands for *honor* made by local culture and the expectations of the American Dream that emanated from the dominant culture. The subculture of the gang represented one solution to the demands of *honor*, demands that placed a high premium on self-respect and character, both individual characteristics. Despite the allegiance to these values, the American Dream, emphasizing educational attainment and work, had powerful sway over the young men and women of 32nd Street.

The Lions had existed on 32nd Street since the 1950s. The gang was comprised primarily of male Chicano residents and was a considerable presence on the streets of the neighborhood. Most young men joined the gang at some point in their life, though typically for only a short time. Most members were between twelve and seventeen years of age, and strong age-grading existed within gangs. Approximately fifteen to forty members belonged to each age grouping. While there were some rules of membership and a vague leadership structure, Horowitz characterized the gang as having considerable flexibility. Despite this, she observed collective goals, different roles, and membership stability. Violence was a regular feature of gang life, and members had to be prepared to respond to assailants at any time. Ceremonial events generally accompanied initiation or exit from the gang. Gang status followed individuals long after they had left the gang, as old antagonisms and reputations often died more slowly than gang allegiance. Despite many maturational pressures and opportunities to leave the gang, a number of members remained into their early twenties.

Vigil (1988), who worked with the Pinto project from 1976 through 1978, spent three years in the field compiling sixty-seven life histories of gang members in Los Angeles. Like Moore, he emphasized the unique nature of Chicano culture in the formation of gangs. In particular, he identified "choloization," the process by which Chicano youth are "marginalized" from mainstream society. From Vigil's perspective, Chicano youth are in a position of multiple marginality, that is, they are marginal to several aspects of mainstream culture and institutional life. This is true at the macro level (social institutions), the meso level (families), and the micro level (individuals). The street provides an alternative socialization path for these youths, most of whom are excluded from participation in mainstream institutional activities and lack families capable of providing alternatives to street socialization. Because gang members share many negative experiences in common – family stress, school failure, and lack of interest in legitimate activities – the gang provides a collective solution to the problem of identity.

Chicano gangs are comprised primarily of males between the ages of thirteen and twenty-five for whom neighborhood identification is strong. Most members start in the gang at a young age. Gangs ranged in size from ten to one hundred, though the average size was thirty-six. The primary reason for joining was to be with one's friends, though direct physical confrontations propelled some youths into gangs. Consistent with most other observations, few gang members were pressured to join. While an age-graded structure was present, little formal heirarchy and rule structure was observed by Vigil. Violence was a constant feature of gang life, though it was threatened more often than it occurred. Property crime generally was not committed as a gang act, rather it took place because individuals acting outside of the gang decided to engage in such activities.

Padilla (1992) spent over a year studying the "Diamonds," a Puerto Rican youth gang in Chicago. Gang members were second generation immigrants contacted through social service agencies and "key informants." Interviews and observations were the primary means of data collection. The gang was predominantly an "ethnic enterprise" (3) involved in street drug sales. Adopting the approach chosen by Moore and Vigil, Padilla attempted to understand the gang by focusing on the ethnic experiences of Puerto Rican youth in Anglo culture. Critical to this perspective was the view that these individuals have experienced cultural rejection and, as a consequence, found little hope for inclusion in its institutions.

Despite their active involvement in street-level drug dealing, the primary gang activity was "hanging out"; playing basketball and attending parties comprised two of the other major ways gang members spent their time. Hanging out performed an important role in the gang because it represented the way that gang members "marked" their turf and protected it from infringement from rival gangs attempting to "move in" on the Diamonds' turf. Gang members were "beaten in" as their initiation ritual, also referred to as "turning" or "V"-in. That violence plays a significant role in the first gang activity (initiation) is no accident; violence, and its threat, plays an important symbolic role in gang life. Violence communicates a message to gang members and nongang members alike; violence is a regular part of the gang life, and gang members are unafraid to use it or receive it. Violence also serves to reinforce the solidarity among gang members and accentuate the boundaries between gang and nongang members. For most of the Diamonds, joining the gang was an affirmative decision, not a matter of coercion. Not surprisingly, this occurred most often through the influence of friends; it makes sense that adolescents choose to belong to groups their friends already belong to. Interestingly, being labeled as a gang member by a rival gang led other boys to join the gang. In this way, they joined the gang "out of necessity," seeking the protection of their neighborhood gang from gangs in rival neighborhoods. This underscores the sometimes "contagious" nature of gang membership, merely being identified as a potential gang member by rivals leads individuals to affiliate with a gang, even if they otherwise would not do so.

Drug dealing was the primary activity of the gang, and many gang members referred to it as "work" in the same way they referred to legitimate jobs. However, street drug sales was by no means monolithic. There was considerable variation in the types of drugs sold, how they were sold, uses for drug profits, and the roles involved in drug sales. Large amounts of capital were seldom accumulated; rather the proceeds most often went for more typical adolescent pursuits such as partying, food, clothes, and dating. The gang was a good vehicle to facilitate street drug sales because the collectivism generated by the gang was functional for the business side of drug dealing. Unlike the gangs described by Klein and Short and Strodtbeck, there were clear roles in drug selling and a clear organizational structure. "Pee Wees," thirteen- to fifteen-year-olds, demonstrated their cunning and willingness to take risks by stealing. If successful, they could become runners or "mules" who moved drugs by the time they reached the age of sixteen. The most successful runners sold drugs directly on the streets. For Padilla's gang members, these represented sequential steps in the career development of gang members.

While many gang members hoped to get "respectable" jobs and raise families, the gang reinforced their marginality in society. Being identified as a gang member restricted opportunities that were available to nongang members. In this way, gang membership had the latent consequence of hardening the lines between gang members and other individuals in their community. Padilla recounts several instances in which even low-paying, low-status jobs were denied to gang members because the employer feared their status in the gang would negatively affect business. He describes membership in the Diamonds as "rational" for its members because it "solves" many of the problems of being marginal experienced by ethnic youth, specifically problems stemming from their negative experiences with conventional society. Gang participation insulates members from the negative assessments of their worth offered by schools, neighborhood groups, and even their own families.

Most studies of gangs characterize female gangs and female gang members as satellites of male gangs. Klein (1971) found that gangs were mostly comprised of males but that the number of female gangs and gang members was growing. Despite this, he concluded that most female gangs "grew out of" male gangs. Moore (1991) argued a contrary point. She concluded that many female barrio gangs operated independently of male gangs as well as independently of the barrio turf. But these observations stemmed from examinations largely of male gangs. Few studies of gangs have focused specifically on female gangs. Two exceptions to this are Quicker's (1983) study of Chicana gangs in East Los Angeles and Campbell's (1984) field study of three different female gangs in New York City. Quicker used field techniques to document the activities of thirteen female gang members. All the female gangs he examined were affiliates to male gangs and had less structure and fewer leadership roles than did the male gangs to which they were satellites. The lack of independence of female gangs from male gangs has been a consistent theme in examinations of female participation in gang activities.

Campbell's (1984) fieldwork with three female gangs in New York City is among the most expansive examinations of female gang activities. She spent six months with each of three different types of female gangs: (1) a street gang, (2) a biker gang, and (3) a "religio-cultural" gang. By focusing on one girl in each gang, she provided a study more akin to the "life histories" of Shaw and McKay in the 1920s. Campbell argued that female gangs and their members could only be understood against the backdrop of their life conditions as young women in poor neighborhoods. She reminds us that female gangs are not new; indeed there is evidence of female gangs in the early 1900s. However, her work calls into question the stereotypical portrayal of female gang members as either "marginal" members of society or "parasitical" attachments to male gangs. While noting that these characterizations could be applied accurately to a large number of female gangs, the diversity of female gangs prohibited their blanket acceptance.

Campbell discusses two predominant roles that female gang members play, as sex objects or tomboys. Sex objects are viewed in a proprietary fashion by male gang members, and females in this role are submissive to the will of male gang members. Such females often are marginal gang members and may not form a gang separate from the male gang. Tomboys, however, emulate and engage in more typically "male" gang activities such as fighting, committing crimes, and "hanging out." In each of the three female gangs she observed, Campbell found some evidence of leadership roles and gang structure, though typically less than in the male gangs to which the females gangs were satellized. The girls in Campbell's gangs had a much larger life outside the gang than did their male counterparts, for the most part because of their familial responsibilities. The duties of housekeeping, baby-sitting younger brothers and sisters, and rearing their own children fell disproportionately on the shoulders of female gang members. In a sense, these responsibilities insulated them from further gang involvement. Campbell's work found that female gangs seldom operate beyond the shadow of a male gang.

The growth of the urban underclass has been linked to an increase in gangs. This perspective finds its most outspoken advocate in the work of Hagedorn (1988), who interviewed forty-seven gang members (identified as the founders) of nineteen of Milwaukee's largest gangs. He argued that local factors, especially economic and demographic ones, were the most important variables in explaining the emergence and nature of gangs. Hagedorn is especially interested in explaining the *origins* of gangs. He observed that many Milwaukee gangs took the names used by gangs in Chicago, but there was little evidence that gangs from Chicago had come to Milwaukee to form "satellites." Rather, most gangs in his city emerged on a more or less spontaneous basis from "corner groups," young men who hung out together in their neighborhoods. Others emerged from "dancing" groups that experienced physical threats and fighting, strengthening their alliances, ultimately resulting in gang formation. Taking as his central problem the development of gangs in "satellite" cities, Hagedorn observes that three things must be studied: (1) local conditions, (2) gang traditions from big cities, and (3) the proximity of big cities.

Many similarities exist between the gangs of Thrasher in 1920 Chicago and of Short and Strodtbeck in Chicago in the 1960s and those described by Hagedorn. One difference was, like Moore, he found that gangs are not strictly comprised of adolescents; rather they underwent a "natural splintering process" (5) as gang members aged and moved into different roles within the gangs. Gangs exhibited little formal organization, had few roles or responsibilities, and activities were more likely to originate from subsets within the gang than from the entire gang acting as a unit. Crime was a small part of the overall activities gang members engaged in; like their nongang adolescent counterparts, hanging out, partying, and sports occupied most of a gang member's time. For Hagedorn, the gang served as a family-like organization and in many cases provided a means of survival. Traditional social controls had a weak effect on the behavior of gang members, in part because gang members are isolated from mainstream society. While gang members sold drugs, drug sales were not well organized and provided only a modest level of income. Violence was an integral part of life in the gang, and gang members were expected to use violence against rival gang members.

The work of Sanchez-Jankowski (1991) was among the more ambitious field studies of gangs. Over a ten-year period, he conducted an ethnographic study of gangs in New York, Boston, and Los Angeles. During this time, he was a participant observer of thirty-seven randomly selected gangs representing eight different ethnic groups (Chicano, Dominican, Puerto Rican, Central American, African American, and Irish). His work, based on "living the gang life," provides a radically different view of gangs than its predecessors. He describes gang members as "defiant individualists" who possess several distinctive character traits including competitiveness, wariness, self-reliance, social isolation, strong survival instincts, and a "social Darwinist view of the world." Despite this, he views gangs as "formal-rational" organizations, having strong organizational structures, well-defined roles, rules that guide member activities, penalties for rule violations, an ideology, and well-defined means for generating both legal and illegal income. Sanchez-Jankowski observes that gangs function much like private governments. He also maintains that many gangs have positive relationships with people in their neighborhoods, often performing essential functions such as looking out for the well-being of the community in which they live. These functions include such things as protection against unscrupulous businesses as well as organized crime. He labelled the links between gangs and their neighborhoods as a form of "local patriotism" (199). Further, all of the gangs he studied attempted to develop ties to organized crime syndicates in their city.

A Theoretical Framework: The Role of Threat

This review of field studies of gangs raises important questions about the origins of gangs and the process by which individuals come to join the gang. The framework we use to explain both the origin of gangs and the decisions of individuals to join a gang focuses on the role of *threat*.

Threats of physical violence, whether real or perceived, have important consequences for these questions.

Threat describes a process in which perceptions and interactions work together to produce behavior. But this process does not occur in a vacuum; indeed, it takes place in a context shaped by the labor market, political forces, and other neighborhood opportunity structures. These structural forces, working together, produce external constraints that limit the options and opportunities available to young men and women in the neighborhood. It is within this context that threats emerge and flourish. As Anderson (1994) observed, street culture is a response to the underclass conditions within which gangs operate. This culture has produced a "code of the streets" (86) in which "nerve," "retaliation," and opposition to mainstream social institutions have become the norm. The sources of such a culture are largely institutional: the evaporation of factory jobs, increasing residential segregation, disinvestment in and by neighborhood social institutions such as schools and neighborhood groups, and the resultant alienation and disenfranchisement of young people. Taken together, these forces create a neighborhood context within which threats are not effectively controlled, either by formal or informal social control processes.

The key element in this process is violence. Violence and fighting have been integral to gangs since their origins. Thrasher observed that gangs developed through strife and flourished on conflict. According to Klein (1971, 85) violence provides a "predominant 'myth system'" among gang members and is constantly present. For these reasons, we emphasize the role of physical threat in gang formation, individual decisions to join the gang, and gang activities.

Threat plays an important role in accounting for the origins of gangs. Within many neighborhoods, groups form for protection against outside groups. Sometimes these groups are formed around ethnic lines, though it is often the case that territorial concerns guide their formation, providing support for Katz' notion that gangs seek to "own the street" through a variety of actions. Hagedorn (1988) found that conflicts between the police and young men "hanging out" on the corner led to more formalized structures that ultimately became gangs. Suttles (1972, 98) underscored the natural progression from a neighborhood group to a gang, particularly in the face of "adversarial relations" with outside groups. Many splinter gangs can be traced to the escalation of violence within larger gangs and the corresponding threat that the larger gang comes to represent to certain territorial or age-graded subgroups.

Another area in which threat accounts for gang process is in stimulating the growth of such groups. First, threats of physical violence, whether real or perceived, increase the solidarity or cohesiveness of gangs within neighborhoods as well as across neighborhoods. Klein (1971) identified the source of gang cohesion as primarily external to the gang, an observation also made by Hagedorn. For Klein, gang cohesion grows in proportion to the perceived threat represented by rival gangs. Padilla (1992) also underscored this notion, noting the role of threat in maintaining boundaries between the gang and other groups. This strengthens the ties among gang members, increasing their commitment to each other and the gang. The bonds between gang members allow them to overcome any initial reluctance about joining the gang, and ultimately enable them to overcome constraints against violence. Thus, the threat of a gang in a geographically proximate neighborhood serves to increase the solidarity of the gang, compels more young men to join their neighborhood gang, and enables them to engage in acts of violence they may not otherwise have committed.

A second part of the growth in gangs and gang violence contains an element of what Loftin (1984) calls "contagion." Violence, or its threat, is the mechanism that drives the spread of gangs from one neighborhood to another, as well as causes them to grow in size. From Loftin's perspective, the concept of contagion can be used to explain the rapid growth or "spikes" that occur in violent crime. Three conditions must be present for contagion to occur: (1) a spatial concentration of assaultive violence, (2) a reciprocal nature to assaultive violence, and (3) escalations in assaultive violence. These conditions also apply to our use of the concept of threat. Gangs have a strong spatial structure; they claim particular turf as their own and are committed to its "defense" against outsiders. The specter of a rival gang "invading" their turf to violate its sanctity is likely to evoke a violent response from a gang. In addition, gang violence shows a strong spatial character, as it is almost exclusively directed against rival gang members on gang turf. The reciprocal nature of gang violence, in part, accounts for the initial formation of gangs, as well as how they increase in size and how ties are strengthened among members. The need to engage in retaliatory violence also helps us understand the demand for increasingly sophisticated weapons on the part of gang members. As Horowitz observed (1983), gang members arm themselves in the belief that their rivals have guns; they seek to increase the sophistication of their weaponry in the hopes that they will not be left short, that is, caught in a shootout with less firepower than their rival. The proliferation of guns and shootings by gang members escalates violence by creating the demand for armaments among rival gangs.

The knowledge that youths in a proximate neighborhood are organized and may attack creates the need for an association to promote mutual protection. In this context, Klein (1971) has underscored the "mythic" nature of violence in gang life. The threat of attack by a group of organized youths from another neighborhood is part of the gang "myth" or belief system and helps to create the need for protection as well as to generate organization among a previously unorganized group of neighborhood youths. Vigil (1988) observed that the need for protection against rival gangs is a primary motivation for many youths to join the gang. An attack or threat of attack by a rival gang also increases the solidarity of gang members, reinforcing their membership ties. The threat of violence also "enables" gang members to engage in violent acts (especially retaliatory violence) they may not have chosen under other circumstances, particularly in response to the threat posed by groups in other neighborhoods. In part, this occurs because the gang creates an expanded pool of victim targets by assigning collective liability to rival gangs. In this way, belief in the importance of self-protection grows as a central tenet of gang culture. The need to respond effectively to the violence of a rival gang escalates weaponry and the "tension" that often precedes violent encounters between gangs. Many gang members reported to Padilla (1992) that they joined their gang out of fear of violence at the hands of rival gangs. The concern that a rival gang is considering an attack often compels a preemptive strike (particularly drive-by shootings) from the gang that considers itself under threat. Loftin's (1984) third element of contagion, rapid escalation of violence, is consistent with the sudden peaks of gang violence. Attacks by one gang against another quickly lead to retaliatory strikes. These spikes can be accounted for in part by the retaliatory nature of gang violence.

Threat has a third function. Because gangs and gang members are perceived as engaging in acts of violence that defy rational explanation (such as drive-by shootings), they are viewed as threatening by other (nongang) groups and individuals in society. Eventually, because of the threats they face (and pose), gang members become increasingly isolated from legitimate social institutions such as schools and the labor market. As gang members are involved in violent events, both as perpetrators and victims, members of the community attempt to distance themselves from relationships and contacts with gang members. It is within this context that life in the gang must be understood. Life in the gang is an existence characterized by estrangement from social institutions, many neighborhood groups, and, ultimately, conforming peers and adults.

Isolation from mainstream activities, in turn, prevents gang members from engaging in the very activities and relationships that may reintegrate them into legitimate roles. Gang members become further marginalized because their membership poses a threat to other family members, schools, neighbors, and social institutions. This marginalization extends beyond identified gang members and also includes "symbolic" members, for example, people who fit the rough stereotype of what a gang member is. This makes it particularly difficult to leave the gang, because even after doing so, many individuals continue to be treated as if they were still members and often are blocked from desirable conventional roles. Such stereotypes have negative consequences for people who operate at the margins of society, especially poor, urban, minority males, and may weaken the ties between these individuals and legitimate activities and social institutions. This process makes them even more vulnerable to gang membership, creating a neighborhood context in which gang members become increasingly detached from the very institutions that may play a role in neighborhood social control.

It is important to emphasize that gang members are not merely reactive. While it is clear that much gang violence occurs in response to threats from rival gangs, gangs also act proactively to create threats. Incursions into rival territory, harassing competing drug sellers, asserting their dominance over their own turf, and striking menacing poses are all methods of creating threat. Such acts often have an exaggerated or excessive character to them, generating what Katz (1988) identified as "dread," and enhancing their threat to rival gangs and members of the community.

Much of gang violence reflects elements of collective behavior. Indeed, as Thrasher (1927) and Short (1974) observed, collective behavior processes operate within the gang and can account for the emergence of group violence. The concept of contagion provides the vehicle through which such processes may work. Gang membership creates a collective responsibility for retaliating against threats or wrongs to fellow gang members, whether those wrongs were real or perceived. Threats from rival gangs expand the number of participants in violent encounters, increase cohesion among gang members and enable them to engage in violence they may otherwise have chosen to avoid. Thus it is group processes, reinforced by norms that encourage the use of violence, that enable gang members to engage in violence that often appears excessive, wanton, or senseless. And as Bursik and Grasmick (1993) observed, the gang provides a structure within which collective actions achieve a longer life. That is, absent the gang, the "life course" of a violent encounter may be short lived. The gang provides a mechanism that extends violence over longer periods of time and to larger numbers of participants.

Figure 1.1 illustrates how the concept of threat provides a theoretical perspective that accounts for group and individual activities within and outside of the gang. This framework will be used throughout the book to account for both the individual and the group activities of gang members.

The neighborhood gang provides both instrumental and social benefits to its members. The instrumental advantages include such things as money from drug sales, robbery, or property crime, as well as protection. The threat from the neighborhood gang aids in attracting new members. The social benefits of the gang include power, prestige, or thrills associated with gang membership. In addition, the gang provides a place to "hang out" with friends, something to do. These benefits "pull" neigh-

Figure 1.1

borhood men and women to the gang. Outside gangs provide threats that "push" neighborhood men and women into the gang, seeking protection. Threats from rival gangs escalate violence and weaponry. Both the social and instrumental benefits of membership serve to isolate gang members from social institutions such as the family, school, and labor market. Thus, as a consequence of threat, gang members become segregated from social institutions, adults, and peers, increasing the probability of violence.

Research Questions

This review leads us to a number of questions that frame our analysis. We are concerned with determining the *origins* of gangs and gang membership, the activities gang members engage in, and their *relationships*, both individually and collectively, with social institutions. We will focus first on membership issues, exploring the way gangs originated, as well as the motivations for joining gangs. In addition, we will describe the social processes that keep gangs together and enhance their growth. We will then move to an examination of the activities gang members engage in, both legal and illegal. This will be followed by an analysis of the relationships between gangs (and gang members) and a number of social institutions, including the school, neighborhood, social agencies, and the criminal justice system. We then devote separate attention to the views of gang members toward their family and the views of families toward gang members. The book concludes with a series of policy recommendations.

"Are You Claiming?" Methods of Study

The Research Strategy

A SINGLE PREMISE guided our study; the best information about gangs and gang activity would come from gang members contacted directly in the field. We chose to contact gang members directly, without the intervention of social service or criminal justice agencies, for two reasons. First, we were concerned that individuals referred by agencies may be different from those contacted on the street. Social service agencies may be more likely to see tangential gang members, those who were on the fringe of gangs and gang activity. Thus referrals from such sources may not provide us with contacts with older individuals more deeply involved in gang activity. In addition, we refrained from using police contacts because of a concern that our study might be identified with law enforcement. This too would have inhibited our ability to reach leaders or hard-core gang members. The second reason we chose to use field-based techniques to contact gang members can be traced to our concern that the answers we received may be colored by the process through which subjects were recruited for the study. We recognize, however, that each method of contacting respondents carries its own liabilities. Simply because gang members were contacted by an experienced field ethnographer respected by individuals in the neighborhood is no guarantee that they were honest with us. The issues of response validity and reliability are important, and we pay close attention to them throughout the study.

A sample of gang members recruited from the street without official agency contacts may miss certain key groups or types of individuals.

However, we concur with Hagedorn (1991) that the most effective way to integrate the perspective of individual gang members into a study of their activities is by contacting them in their natural environment, the streets and neighborhoods where they live. Our initial conviction was that we should make direct contact with gang members and their families and let them tell their stories to us in their own words. We remained true to this conviction, though there were times during the study that we were tempted to abandon this approach to increase our sample size.

The use of fieldwork techniques to study gangs is one of the oldest traditions in criminology. Frederick Thrasher used a field-based strategy to carry out his classic study of gangs in Chicago. Since that time, this approach has been adapted for research on gangs in a variety of cities. Whyte's (1943) field work with "streetcorner boys" illuminated the potent forces that led boys to congregate on the corner in an ethnic slum. Hagedorn (1988) spent considerable time interviewing the "people and folks" of gangs in Milwaukee. Vigil's study of Hispanic gangs in Los Angeles (1988), Padilla's work with Puerto Rican gangs in Chicago (1992), and Sanchez-Jankowski's work with gangs in three cities (1991) all used fieldwork approaches. This tradition enjoys its longest standing application in Los Angeles, where Joan Moore has spent over two decades studying the "homeboys" of the Hispanic barrios (1978; 1991). The fieldwork approach employed in all of these studies (and our own) is characterized by three distinct features (Emerson 1983). First, it requires researchers to be present in the community and neighborhood where gangs under study operate. It is not enough to conduct interviews with individuals *outside* of their neighborhoods. Rather, frequent contact with gang members on their own turf is essential to this approach. A second requirement is to take account of the actor's perspective. Thus, understanding the view of the world (or neighborhood) held by those in the gang must become the primary goal of the study. From this perspective, we tried to understand the meaning that activities and symbols held for the gang and individual gang members. The third requirement of a field-based approach is that it employs the use of native terms and categories. Since the goal of such work is to let the perspective of those being studied serve as a guide to understanding their actions, the use of native terms and categories is essential. Each of these features also played a central role in our research.

McCall (1978) has identified two methods of data collection within field studies, direct observation and ethnographic interviewing. We employed both of these techniques in our efforts to better understand the activities and relationships of gangs and gang members. The field ethnographer was primarily responsible for observational issues. Over a three-year period, he spent the majority of each day "on the streets" observing primary and secondary gang activity (graffiti and other symbols), making field notes of where and why gang members congregated, and so on. To retain a sense of the field, we rode with him throughout the period of study to make observations of gang activity and graffiti. His field notes also reveal a good deal about the process of contacting offenders and gaining their trust. As such, they are an important part of this analysis.

The ethnographic interview, however, was the primary means of data collection. We used a lengthy questionnaire to elicit information about issues of specific interest to us: (1) gang membership, (2) gang activities, (3) relationships between gang members (and gangs) and social institutions, (4) perceptions about ways to leave the gang or stop gangs, and (5) relationships between gang members and their families. The questionnaire was developed from two distinct sources. First, we conducted four preliminary, open-ended interviews with active gang members in order to learn more about their perspective and insure that it was integrated into our questionnaire. Because of his knowledge of the streets, the field ethnographer was present for these interviews and his insights were essential to insure that the gang member's perspective was adequately represented in both the questions we asked and the way they were asked. The second source of information for questionnaire construction came from two gang researchers who shared their instruments with us. Dan Waldorf, who is conducting the "homeboy" study for the National Institute on Drug Abuse (NIDA), shared his instrument and grant proposal with us. Jeff Fagan, actively involved in studying gangs, also shared his questionnaire. Both instruments were extremely helpful in arriving at the final version we used. As we sampled two groups – active gang members and family members of gang members – two separate versions of a questionnaire were developed. Each of the questionnaires underwent some change in the early part of the study.

One of the vexing problems in studying gangs is the lack of a clear operational definition of the terms gang and gang member. Indeed, the debate about the proper approach to the definition of gangs and gang members has been the object of considerable discussion in the research literature (Decker and Kempf 1991). Much of this discussion has centered on determining who is and who is not a gang member. These discussions typically have identified levels of gang membership. Thus some distinguish between core and fringe membership, while others talk about active gang members and wannabes (Stephens 1993; Huff 1991).

At another level, the debate has been about whether *cities* have a real gang problem or not. This, in Huff's (1991) estimation, is a false dichotomy that has led some cities to deny that they have any gang problem at all. In other cases, some cities have overrepresented the level and nature of gang activity. The breadth of the debate is illustrated by those who argue that the lack of an accepted definition of gangs is a positive thing because it allows for fuller consideration of the variety of activities and structures represented by gangs (Bookin-Weiner and Horowitz 1983).

Much of the debate over the presence of gangs has focused on the extent to which crime can be attributed to gang activity. Since a large proportion of criminal and delinquent acts committed by juveniles (and a substantial portion of criminal acts carried out by adults) are done in groups, drawing these distinctions is an important and often difficult task. Perhaps the best insight into the difficulty of differentiating between gang and nongang acts is provided by Maxson and Klein (1985) who distinguish between classification schemes that use *gang relatedness* as their defining characteristic and those schemes that use *gang motivation* as the defining characteristic. A less stringent set of criteria are required for a crime to be classified as gang related. To fit this designation, a crime must be committed by someone who is a known gang member, is identified as a gang member by a third party, or is suspected of being a gang member. The classification of acts as gang motivated requires that the crime be motivated specifically by gang activity. In this case, only those acts that have a clear link to the gang, such as retaliation or drive-by shootings, can be classified as gang motivated. As Maxson and Klein (1985) have shown, the gang-related definition attributes about twice as many murders to gangs as does the gang-motivated definition. This is more than an academic debate. The groups called upon to respond to gangs often have a very different understanding of what these concepts mean, meanings that shape their recommendations about the nature and extent of the problem and the most effective responses to it.

Two other definitional issues remain. The first concerns the kinds of groups appropriately labelled as gangs. All observers agree that, at a minimum, a gang is comprised of a group of individuals linked (however loosely) by common interests or activities. Many gangs use symbols to communicate identity as a gang member, and for others "turf" or territory is of central importance. The second issue is closely related to the first and concerns the issue of whether criminal activity is a necessary element for the definition of a gang. Hagedorn (1988) and Moore (1978, 1991) both argue that it is tautological to include involvement in crime as part of the definition of a gang since crime is one of the variables we seek to explain in an analysis of gangs. Others (Maxson and Klein 1985; Huff 1991; Bursik and Grasmick 1993) include criminal activity as an element in their definition of gangs. These individuals argue that involvement in crime is an essential component of the definition of a gang. Without it, the distinction vanishes between gangs and groups like the American Legion or the Biology Club.

Our review of these issues – coupled with the practical need to determine who is eligible to be interviewed and who is not – led us to a working definition of a gang. Our working definition of a gang is an age-graded peer group that exhibits some permanence, engages in criminal activity, and has some symbolic representation of membership. This definition does not include some of the elements common to other definitions such as turf, though turf is very important to most gangs in St. Louis. The definition also skirts the issue of hierarchy and structure, preferring instead to focus on the permanence of the group. We began our project by using a definition that focused on same-sexed peer groups, quickly to discover that such a definition excluded gangs that had both male and female members. As we soon found gangs that integrated the sexes, we revised our approach. This illustrates the advantage of a field-based approach to studying groups whose rules and behavior undergo changes over time. The adaptive nature of a field study enabled us to reflect the dynamic character of gang membership during the period of our study.

Having defined a gang, we needed an operational definition of who was a gang member. Our approach to determining who was a gang member was somewhat more pragmatic than our definition of gangs. As a first step, individuals had to indicate they were a gang member. Self-identification, often determined by the response to the question, "Are you claiming?" was a key "screen" for us in determining who was eligible to be interviewed as a gang member. This approach was evaluated by the field ethnographer who verified, as often as possible, this self-identification with other gang members. We included only those individuals in our sample who had been members for six months or longer. The distinction between the gang or aggregation and the gang member or individual within that aggregation is one of the "tensions" found throughout the analysis of our data (Short 1985). Ideally, one chooses a level of analysis and works within it. However, it is impossible to study gangs without also looking at individual gang members, and similarly it is impossible to look at individual gang members without considering the importance of the collective. Vigil (1988, 65) notes a similar tension in his own work. Indeed, it is one of the common dilemmas found in researching collectives by interviewing individuals.

The Setting for the Study. Because they are profoundly affected by their surroundings, gangs cannot be understood apart from the characteristics of the cities and communities in which they are active. Like most American cities, St. Louis has experienced profound social, demographic, and economic changes over the course of the last four decades. The two most significant changes for the city of St. Louis have been its rapid depopulation and the decline of the city's industrial base. These changes are linked and, taken together, provide an important context for understanding the relationship between city characteristics and the growth of gangs.

St. Louis was the eighth largest city in the United States in 1952, with a population over 850,000. By 1993, the population of St. Louis had fallen under 385,000, and the city ranked thirty-fourth of American cities. So precipitous was the population decline, that the city of St. Louis is now the second smallest central city in the nation relative to the size of its metropolitan statistical area. Population loss occurred primarily in the form of middle-class families – black and white – moving to the suburban "collar" counties, particularly St. Louis and St. Charles counties. The racial distribution of the city's population remained unchanged from 1980 to 1990, being almost equally split between blacks and whites; the percentage of blacks increasing from 45 percent in 1980 to 47 percent in 1990, and the percent white population decreasing slightly from 53 percent to 51 percent. However, the black and white populations had very different age compositions, with the black population being considerably younger than their white counterparts. In addition, racial segregation in the city increased, as a majority of black city residents lived in census tracts whose population was 90 percent (or more) black.

The loss of middle-class residents is of concern to any city; such residents typically invest the most in their neighborhoods. These residents are involved in the kind of neighborhood activities that generate crime control; forming neighborhood groups, participating in school activities, and showing concern for their property and well-being. In short, such families often act to provide an increased sense of community and guardianship in their neighborhoods. The loss of these residents has a profound effect on the crime rate of a city. However, their loss is crucial for another reason. When such middle-class families leave a neighborhood behind, they tend either not to be replaced by new families or to be replaced by those of lower socioeconomic status. Thus, these neighborhoods lose important sources of stability at the same time neighbors with fewer resources replace them.

The second condition that preceded the growth of gangs in St. Louis was the decline of the city's industrial base. The St. Louis economy has been heavily dependent upon the manufacturing sector for employment. The auto and aerospace industries have been most critical in generating jobs. These industries have been especially hard hit by the decreased reliance on manufacturing by the American economy. And a large number of people who formerly worked in such jobs – or expected to do so – found themselves without employment prospects. In 1980, 37,460 city residents were employed in manufacturing jobs, a figure that declined to 24,393 in 1990. The loss of such jobs was particularly devastating for individuals who had not advanced their education beyond high school, the very group left behind in the city. As a consequence, the economic circumstances of city residents had changed dramatically for the worse. In 1990 the unemployment rate for the city was 11 percent, nearly double that for the nation and the rest of the St. Louis Metropolitan region. And nearly one in four city residents (24 percent) lived below the poverty level. One result of these changes was a dramatic increase in rates of violent crime. Rates of homicide, serious assault and robbery for St. Louis are now among the highest of all American cities. In 1993 the St. Louis homicide and robbery rates were third highest of all American cities, and the rate of serious assault was second. With the decline of its industrial base, the city found increased demand for social services even as it found revenues decreasing. The ability of the city to respond effectively to new social problems – including gangs – was challenged at the very time such problems increased.

Like most social changes, the impact of depopulation and loss of industrial jobs was not felt equally in all neighborhoods or by all people in the city. Many neighborhoods where residents had struggled to maintain economic viability were unable to hang on to their economic and social gains. The labor market lost the working-class jobs that had sustained city residents economically, and the jobs that remained in the neighborhoods where population loss had been the greatest could no longer sustain families. These conditions produced the growth of an underclass with few resources to combat the deepening poverty that now dominated these neighborhoods. In addition, where population declines were steepest and where the loss of steady, good-paying jobs was the greatest, crime increased at alarming rates. These social conditions had a profound impact on, among other things, the growth of gangs in the city. Our study focused on gangs in five distinct areas, each affected by the social changes described above. The five areas include four city neighborhoods (the Fairgrounds/O'Fallon Park area, Walnut Park area, Midtown area, Dutchtown North and South) and one that straddles city and county borders (Wells-Goodfellow/Pine Lawn).

We have selected a number of demographic and social indicators for each of the five areas from which gang members were recruited, as well as those for the city of St. Louis. These variables include a measure of racial isolation (the percent of the population that is black), a measure of the level of supervision generally available in a neighborhood (the percent of female-headed households with children), the male unemployment rate in that area, the percent of the area's population living below the poverty level, the percentage of housing units in the area that are vacant, and the rate of serious assaults.

The similarities shared by four of the areas are quite striking. These areas are much alike on the measures of racial composition, female-headed households with children, male unemployment rate, percent poor, and rates of serious assault. And in each case, these neighborhoods exceed overall city levels on these measures, results that are consistent with the argument that many St. Louis neighborhoods have developed an urban underclass. The existence of racial isolation combined with high levels of male unemployment, poverty, and low levels of family formation are variables typically included in depictions of the urban underclass (Wilson 1987; Anderson 1994). These conditions have been credited by some (Hagedorn 1988; Jackson 1991) for spawning the increase in gangs observed across American cities in the 1980s and 1990s. The first four areas included in Table 2.1 certainly conform to the expectation of these researchers about the effect of the underclass. However, the Dutchtown area exhibits characteristics greatly different from these neighborhoods, characteristics not at all consistent with the presence of an urban underclass. Indeed, on each measure, the Dutchtown area has more favorable conditions than does the city of St. Louis as a whole. This challenges the view that links the underclass to the growth of gangs. The Dutchtown area has a large recreation center (Marquette), cheap rental property, and close proximity to the Midtown area. Several large public housing projects in Midtown had closed over the last decade (Laclede Town and the Vaughan Housing Project most prominently), and many residents of these developments sought "safer" areas in which to raise their children. As a consequence, many of the near north-side and

Table 2.1 *Demographic and social indicators of neighborhoods used for gang recruitment*

Area	Racial isolation	% Fem HH w/child	% Male unemployment	% Poor	% Vacant units	Asslt rate
Fairground O'Fallon Park area	98%	25%	21%	32%	17%	3,320
Wells-Goodfellow and Pine Lawn	99%	24%	25%	35%	20%	3,817
Walnut Park area (includes Walnut Park East and West, North Point, and Mark Twain)	96%	19%	19%	26%	10%	2,948
Midtown Area (includes Carr Square, Vande-vanter, St. Louis Place, and Midtown)	89%	21%	25%	50%	28%	3,150
Dutchtown North and South	9%	9%	10%	20%	13%	1,492
City of St. Louis	47%	12%	14%	24%	15%	2,231

Note: Demographic and Social indicators were drawn from Neighborhood Demographic Profiles, Community Development Agency, City of St. Louis, 1993. Crime data come from the Uniform Crime Reports. All data are for the year 1990.

midtown gangs migrated southward toward Dutchtown, an area currently in considerable transition. Thus, the social conditions did not spawn new gangs but provided a new location for existing gangs.

It is against this backdrop that our study takes place. However, the social conditions that occurred in St. Louis did not produce gangs by themselves; rather they created conditions in which gangs could originate and expand.

Gangs in St. Louis. The generation of gangs we studied is certainly not the first in St. Louis. Like other American cities, the presence of gangs has been cyclical, emerging and fading away over time. In each cycle, the emergence of gangs in St. Louis corresponds with the conditions common to their origins in other cities: economic change, rapid population shifts, and changes in the racial and ethnic composition of the city.

The earliest reference to gangs in St. Louis comes from a book written by two "members of the St. Louis Press" (Dacus and Buel 1878). In journalistic fashion, they documented the effect of various developments on the city of St. Louis, paying particular attention to changes in the ethnic composition of the population and the influence of the economy on city life. They observed that certain parts of the city, particularly that area just north of downtown, seemed to be characterized by more intense social problems, such as poverty and low levels of parental supervision. In these areas, groups of young men and women they referred to as "Street Arabs" (Dacus and Buel 1878, 410) banded together in "tribes" or "clans," and these clans had "the language, the propensity, and the skills" (408) that they passed on to other members. A primary objective of such groups was companionship, and their activities included gathering on the street, disturbing neighbors, and engaging in feuds. The feuds often led to fights and retaliation that would last for lengthy periods of time, perhaps as long as several years. These groups were not labeled gangs by Dacus and Buel but certainly resemble the late-nineteenth-century gangs described by Sheldon and Riis in New York City. The emergence of these groups is clearly related to the immigration and industrial patterns in the city.

Thrasher makes reference to a number of gangs operating in St. Louis during the 1920s (1927, 367, 430). While these gangs included juveniles, they were primarily comprised of adults, and tended to be organized. Many gangs filled the demand for alcohol during Prohibition and as a consequence became involved in the political life of the city. Similar to their counterparts of the late nineteenth century, however,

Thrasher noted that most of these gangs could trace their origins to the river district neighborhoods north of the downtown area. During the mid-1920s, a gang war erupted between the two largest and best organized gangs in St. Louis, the Rats and the Jellyrolls. During this period, the Rats accounted for as many as twenty-three murders and dozens of robberies. Other St. Louis gangs included the Cuckoos, White House Gang, McCandles Gang, the Pirate Crew, and the Bottoms Gang. The ethnic composition of these gangs was primarily Irish and German; members of recently arrived immigrant groups. Most of the violence took the form of drive-by shootings and was reciprocal in nature. That is, the violent acts of one gang led to retaliation by another, raising the level of violence. While these gangs were older, more organized, and politically connected, they nevertheless shared much in common with the St. Louis gangs that were to follow them in the 1950s.

Gangs emerged in St. Louis following the end of World War II, in part as a consequence of the rapid changes in size of the population, its ethnic composition, and the economy. While many gangs were comprised of whites, African American gangs emerged for the first time during this period. These gangs had their origins in neighborhoods just north of downtown, where their European predecessors had begun in the late nineteenth century and the 1920s. However, black gangs also were found in the city's western and northwestern neighborhoods. Neighborhood identification was strong among these gangs, and they engaged in legal as well as illegal activities. Most common among the illegal activities were fights (which seldom involved the use of a gun; fists and knives were more typical), property crimes, and neighborhood peace disturbances. Newspaper accounts record that the activities of these gangs put people on edge and led to concern about the lack of "father images" for many young boys in the community. Among others, these gangs included the Barracudas, the Counts, the Turks, the Compton Hill Gang, and the Alston Gang. Felt hats were worn to identify gang members; the most popular colors were blue, brown, and burgundy. Like earlier gangs in St. Louis, these gangs eventually faded from the St. Louis scene.

Finding the Subjects. Snowball or chain referral sampling is a common technique in field studies (Biernacki and Waldorf 1981, 143; Dunlap et al. 1990; Wright et al. 1992). This procedure begins by initiating contacts with individuals close to the issue being studied and "snowballing" out from these initial contacts to include others in their social circle. In theory, this technique should provide a sample that increases proportionately over the course of the research project and eventually expands into a number of networks. Such a sampling strategy should be particularly useful for studying gangs owing to their alleged cohesive nature and interrelationships. The technique is not without difficulties though. We asked about "hidden" behavior, that is, behavior that is generally hidden from formal and informal authorities. A related problem is presented in using snowball sampling to penetrate gangs. While gang membership *itself* was not illegal in Missouri at the time of our study, a code of silence and protection from outsiders prevails about gang membership. Thus, while we may have been able to contact one gang member, there would be no guarantee that they would identify other gang members or put us in touch with them.

Implementing the Strategy

The Sampling Design. Field-based sampling strategies face several important questions; most basic among them is whether to focus intensively on a single network or to branch out in a more extensive way and interview individuals from several different networks. And as Biernacki and Waldorf (1981, 143) have noted, the sample rarely develops at the pace or in the direction that the textbooks would suggest. In their words, snowball or chain referral sampling is seldom "self-contained" or "self-propelled"; it produces many surprises along the way. Our first commitment was to develop a sample of active gang members, and we sought to initiate this process before undertaking any other fieldwork. As this was to be a study of gang members and gangs, we decided to interview individuals from a number of different gangs. In some instances, we were able to interview only a single individual from the gang; in others we interviewed as many as seventeen different members.

The interview was our primary point of contact with members of our sample. This design, the one-shot interview, has some limitations, including the inability to track change within the life of a gang member and perform reliability checks during repeated contacts. However, we attempted to circumvent these problems in a number of ways. The field ethnographer used the ride to and from the interview site to discuss membership issues and gang activities. We attempted to verify, where possible, our interview results with the conversation held during transit. In addition, gang members often had repeated contacts with our field ethnographer, allowing him to gain a sense of the level of gang involvement of a potential subject, as well as to allow the subject to gain trust in him and, ultimately, our project. Finally, we had multiple contacts with a number of the members of our sample. In these ways, we sought to minimize the design problems that occur with studies that have a single, bounded contact with subjects, such as those established through police or social service auspices.

We chose to include family members in our sample as well. The role of the family in urban America has been the subject of considerable controversy, and we were interested in documenting the views of family members about gang membership. We were unaware of any other study of gangs that had specifically focused on family perceptions and relationships with active gang members, making this a unique feature of our work. We also were interested in studying the relatives of gang members because the family represents perhaps the most important social institution in shaping behavior.

Contacting Gang Members. In the course of an earlier fieldwork project (Wright and Decker 1994), we contacted and interviewed 105 active residential burglars. Some of these burglars were quite young and thus we surmised that they might know active gang members. It was with these individuals that our snowball sampling began. In addition, the field ethnographer had developed contacts with several active street criminals engaged in robbery and drug sales. These people were able to give us referrals to active gang members and, equally important, to vouch for our legitimacy. A third line we followed in building the sample was to observe the secondary symbols of gang membership, particularly graffiti. The appearance of graffiti in St. Louis neighborhoods mushroomed during the late 1980s and this provided a trail that the field ethnographer could follow in identifying areas with substantial levels of gang activity.

A fourth way the sample of active members was built occurred quite by accident. We were familiar with a feature writer for the local daily newspaper. In the course of discussions with him about the skyrocketing homicide rate in the city of St. Louis, our conversation turned to gangs. He was anxious to run a story about gang activity but respected our request to remain low key about the details and findings of our study. The reporter suggested instead that he do a story on the field ethnographer, a suggestion we accepted. The field ethnographer had witnessed a shooting ten years earlier and, in turn, was shot by the brother of the man accused of this to keep him from testifying. As a consequence of the shooting, the field ethnographer was paralyzed and used a wheelchair. The reporter found this a compelling story, one which ran on page one of the Sunday newspaper accompanied by a picture of the field ethnographer (Hernon 1990). The field ethnographer carried copies of the story (including his picture) with him wherever he went in the field and used them to convince gang members that our study was legitimate. Throughout the study, media appearances by the field ethnographer (especially on a local television program targeted at the African American community) proved to be a valuable recruitment tool. This strategy was particularly important in the recruitment of the sample of relatives. In several instances the field ethnographer was recognized by persons in the community based on a recent television appearance. On one occasion, he was shopping for produce at a local grocery store when he was recognized by the store security guard. A conversation ensued, and the guard told the field ethnographer about a produce clerk whose daughter was a gang member. The field ethnographer approached the clerk, who related that his daughter had been heavily involved in gang activity. This contact led to interviews with both parents.

Field research on gangs presents different problems than does field research on other forms of deviance. Because gangs are, by definition, self-contained networks with antagonisms toward other networks, we were not always able to "jump" across groups.[1] This meant that we had to "restart" the snowball sampling procedure many times in order to gain access to a large number of gangs. In addition, there were occasions when the snowball sampling strategy did not lead to additional referrals within gangs. Some members were simply reluctant to introduce us to other members of their gang. We attempted to solve the problem of "restarting" the chain referral process by moving to new neighborhoods or looking for new graffiti. Gang members who would be unable or unwilling to refer us to individuals in rival gangs often provided information about where other gangs may hang out or where their turf was located. In some cases we did get referrals between gangs where brothers were members of rival gangs.

Dealing with the obstacles to snowball sampling within gangs called for patience and persistence. The field ethnographer played an essential role in this process, screening potential interview subjects and eliminating many of them from consideration. Over five hundred contacts were made in achieving our final sample of ninety-nine active gang members. The field ethnographer was able to use earlier respondents to "nominate" other gang members as potential interview subjects, and over time, we established ourselves as "legitimate." From the gang members' perspective this meant two things: (1) we were interested in their story and did not impose our own preconceptions of gangs on them, and (2) we weren't connected with law enforcement authorities.[2] One subject expressed misgivings about bringing the leader of his gang in for an interview. His concerns reflect those of many individuals.

INT: Could you get the leader up for us?

MALE #012, "Lance," twenty-year-old West Side Mob member: I would have to talk to him. He might be mad cause I'm here, but I'll let him know. Some of them on papers [probation or parole] and shit and might think there be police involved.

The "vouching" that exists in snowball sampling has an important added benefit; it allows the use of earlier respondents to verify the legitimacy of others as "real" gang members. On more than one occasion, a gang member we had interviewed earlier would caution us against interviewing a certain individual because he was simply "perpetrating," that is, acting like a gang member without really belonging to a gang. Indeed, the issue of verifying eligibility is of central importance to field studies. When they were available, we used referrals to other active gang members provided by members of our sample. But we did not depend on such referrals alone. In addition to asking prospective interviewees if they were claiming and what "set" they belonged to, the field ethnographer asked a number of additional screening questions to verify that individuals who said they were active gang members really were involved in gang activity. These questions covered such topics as the awareness of gang members we knew, recent activities in the neighborhood, and our knowledge of the overall orientation of the gang.[3] This rather conservative strategy (some field research on gangs is wholly dependent on the self-reported status of the interviewee to establish gang membership) probably caused us to decline interviews with individuals who actually were gang members. However, this cautious approach did not insure that everyone we began to interview was an active gang member. On two occasions (#062 and #098 on Table 3.1) interviews were terminated (and their data discarded) when it became clear to the interviewer that the individual was not an active gang member.

One of the most difficult issues in snowball sampling is controlling the pace of the study. In its ideal form an initial contact leads to two new contacts, which each leads to two more; these four contacts should produce eight new ones, and so it goes. The pace of our study is illustrated in

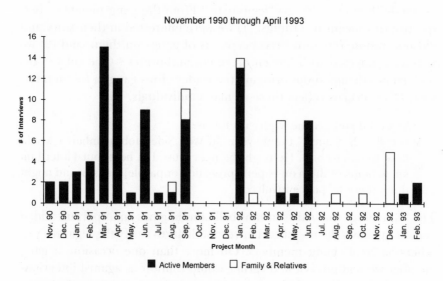

Figure 2.1 Interviews Per Month November 1990 through April 1993

Figure 2.1. This figure makes clear that the pace of our own research was anything but orderly. Indeed, the rate of progress of the study was a series of peaks and valleys. As Wright et al. (1992) have shown, each contact may produce no additional contacts, or it may produce several. Both results produce problems for the pace of a study; one is either restarting the snowball or else dealing with a crush of subjects. Our study was no exception to this pattern. Frequently we were inundated with subjects, while at other times we thought we would never find another gang member regardless of what steps we took.

One development for which we were not prepared occurred during the second year of the study. The project had received some publicity in the media, and we had made several presentations to community groups about gangs in St. Louis. The field-worker gave out business cards printed with his office address and phone numbers to prospective subjects on the streets and to the groups he spoke to in the community. Two young men walked up to our office in the university and announced that they were gang members and wanted to be interviewed for the study. We had determined earlier that contacts had to be initiated through the field-worker, so we referred these individuals to his office to verify their eligibility.

Another problem occurred in following the chain referral process to its logical end. It was difficult to initiate the first few contacts into any new gang. For some gangs, however, once the first interview was conducted, we were inundated with a large number of members of that gang. This was particularly true of the "Rolling 60's," a Crip set, for which the "snowball" quickly got out of control. We cut off this chain of referrals in order to move on to other gangs.

Another issue in implementing the snowball sampling strategy is meeting quotas for subgroups such as race, sex, or type of gang. We were concerned that our study not simply become a study of adolescent black males. This misgiving was grounded in our knowledge that many gang members were females, that not all gang members were minorities, and that the age distribution of gangs in St. Louis runs into the late twenties. This raises the issues of identifying subgroups (Dunlap et al. 1990) and stimulating alternative chains of referrals. We aggressively pursued leads for female gangs and gang members as well as opportunities to locate older and nonblack gang members. These leads were more difficult to find and often caused us to miss chances to interview other gang members. Despite these "missed opportunities," our sample is strengthened in that it more accurately represents the diverse nature of gangs and gang members in St. Louis.

Contacting Family Members. The task of balancing the demands of two different samples proved to be a difficult one. Having successfully initiated the sample of active gang members, we turned our attention to recruiting family members. We hoped to use active gang members to link us to their relatives. In practice, this seldom worked the way we expected. We initially believed that gang members would put us in touch with members of their own families and that we consequently could "pair" the responses. This happened rarely, as most gang members attempted to shield their families from the knowledge of their gang affiliation.[4] This prompted us to adopt a variety of strategies to contact family members. The field ethnographer established relationships with young people at neighborhood centers and recreation complexes. Some of these led to contacts with family members. Other contacts emerged from efforts initiated at places where the family members, especially mothers, were likely to spend time. Laundromats, grocery stores, strip shopping centers, and social service agencies were the primary places we targeted in seeking relatives of gang members. Parents were often reluctant to be interviewed; in general, we found more resistance from relatives than from gang members. Part of this stems from the fact that many parents denied that their children were involved with a gang; in other instances it reflected their ignorance of any such involvement. Clearly, discussing the illegal and life-threatening activities of relatives is an uncomfortable topic most of us would like to avoid. The field-worker's notes are instructive in this regard:

> That pressure can be, I think in a lot of cases we're dealing with people who are going to talk about the criminality within his or her family, we're talking to parents who want to let out of the closet their secret skeletons and this is a very difficult task and it takes time to build each relationship. (November 12, 1992)

Further complicating the process of building this sample is the fact that there are few networks of family members of gang members. While members of the same gang were likely to provide us with referrals to other members of their gang, no such network existed between the family members. Thus in almost every case a family interview was the result of a new search and, as McCall (1978) has noted, the first contact in any network is the most difficult to initiate. The unique nature of the contact chains for parents is illustrated by the process of contacting the parents of a female gang member. This chain began with a presentation made by the principal investigator and field-worker at Children's Hospital in St. Louis. One of the persons present at the talk invited the field-worker to make a presentation to the Barnes Hospital Adolescent unit. A person present at this talk contacted a social worker, who in turn contacted two parents, who contacted the field-worker. Most interviews with relatives involved several intermediaries between the initial contact and the interview. In only three instances were we able to use one family member to refer us to another. Interestingly, in one of these the parent to be interviewed brought along the parent of another active gang member.

The knowledge of gang activity on the part of family members is important to both researchers who would study such relatives and the social service agencies that would provide them with support services. Such information is useful in understanding not only the impact of the family on decisions to join the gang; it lends insights into efforts to reduce gang involvement. Understanding such relationships may place social service agencies in a more advantageous position in designing programs to deal with gangs. Relatives of active gang members who are unaware of that membership are not easily identified for the purposes of a study or interventions.

Field Relations. Contacting gang members in the field was only the first task facing our project. Once contacts were established, the job of maintaining field relations assumed greater importance. There are a number of groups and individuals with whom field relationships must be maintained. Doing so effectively often involves balancing the competing demands of confidentiality, trust, and danger that emerge in a field study of individuals actively engaged in offending.

The key to our study was maintaining good field relations with our subjects. A central element to this process was convincing individuals to come in for an interview. As is often the custom in such research, we paid subjects for their participation in our research. However, this was not the only reason we were able to enlist their participation. Over a number of years the field-worker had established a reputation as "solid" in the community and was able to solicit the services of a number of intermediaries to "vouch" for him in neighborhoods where he was not well known. And in turn, he was able to vouch for us as legitimate, an important concern in the eyes of gang members. We also took steps to boost our own credibility in the eyes of our subjects by learning (as much as possible) the distinctive language and customs of gang members. This was accomplished in part by working closely with the field-worker. More importantly, this process was aided by the orienting premise of our study; learning about gangs and gang members can be best accomplished by hearing the gang member's story directly from the individuals involved. Thus, while we had a questionnaire, we allowed for and encouraged elaboration on the part of our subjects. We went to great lengths to insure that each person we interviewed felt they had received the opportunity to "tell their story in their own words." At the conclusion of the interview, each gang member was asked if there was anything else we should know about gangs. Most members added several points they deemed important, and methods of prohibiting gang violence was a central topic.

We were able to maintain good field relations with our subjects by strictly observing our own commitment to the confidentiality of their statements. Since we interviewed many individuals from the same gang, it was often the case that one member would want to know what an earlier participant had told us. We refused to honor such inquiries, reminding them that the same confidentiality that applied to their own answers also covered those of their fellow gang members. We received numerous requests from gang members to sit in on the interview of a fellow member. These requests were declined as well. The strict confidentiality we were committed to was respected by our subjects, and appeared to enhance our own credibility as "solid" in their eyes.

One of the overriding concerns in our study was violence. In part, gang members were of interest to us because of their involvement in violence. Because of this, we took steps to insure our own safety. One of our guiding principles was to limit the number of people being separately interviewed at the same time and location. In addition, we steadfastly avoided interviewing members of rival gangs at the same time. The field ethnographer carried a portable phone with him at all times, to insure that he could check in with us and we with him. He also checked in with the office on a frequent basis, leaving his current location, intended destination, and an estimated time of arrival. Despite our best efforts, there were occasions when these precautions did not work. The field ethnographer witnessed several drive-by shootings while on the way to pick up interview subjects, and on one occasion, he saw three of our subjects shot while waiting to be picked up for an interview. On another occasion, we were interviewing two gang members, and a member of a rival gang "walked in" to be interviewed. A member of the project steered him out of the building, assuring him that we indeed were interested in talking to him but that it would have to be at a different time. The field ethnographer was frequently identified in the field by gang members when he was transporting another gang member to an interview. Despite entreaties to stop and chat, he never did. And, of course, a cellular phone only works when the battery has been charged or it has been brought along for the day's work; on many occasions the phone simply was not available. Many gang members claimed that they were anxious to show us their willingness to use violence against rival gangs and invited us to be present for a drive-by shooting or to drop them off at a certain location to witness them shooting at rival gang members. We declined all such invitations.[5] Not all exposure to risk of physical danger comes through such obvious means, however. During one interview, when asked whether he owned any guns, a gang member reached into his coat pocket and pulled out a .32 caliber pistol. We assured him that we would have taken his word for it.

While gang members were the primary focus of our research, maintaining good field relations required us to work with a larger circle of groups. Early in the project, we wrote to Colonel Clarence Harmon, chief of police, City of St. Louis, and explained the purpose of our study, asking for his support and a pledge that our study would not be compromised by his officers. Chief Harmon pledged his support for our study and offered us the promise that his officers would not interfere with our work. Such a pledge is important but was never used as we became the subject of only routine traffic enforcement. The lone exception to this occurred when our field-worker became the focus of an undercover investigation by gang and narcotics officers in suburban St. Louis County. The police had received reports that large amounts of cocaine tetrachloride were being sold by a middle-aged black man in a wheelchair. Our field-worker fit this description and, unbeknownst to us, was placed under surveillance for a period of time. The surveillance was called off when one of the officers recalled seeing his picture in the newspaper. We learned about this during a panel presentation to the St. Louis Pediatric Association made with a member of the surveillance team. On another occasion the field-worker was stopped for a routine traffic violation (making an illegal U-turn) after picking up two gang members for an interview. The officer did not issue the ticket, only a warning, and let him go on his way. This story illustrates that gang members "fit" into the community; their presence in the car with an older man (thirty-four) did not arouse the suspicions of law enforcement officials.

The principal investigator met regularly with members of the gang squad of the police department to discuss general issues about gangs. We never divulged specific information about our study, instead providing the gang squad with access to gang research from other scholars. The police respected this commitment on our part and never pressed us for information. For their part, they provided information about trends in gang activity and potential locations we might use to find gang members. In addition, they furnished us with confidential lists of the names of gangs and their estimated sizes. We found close correspondence between their information and our own.

Parents were another group with whom we had to maintain good field relations. This proved to be a delicate job, requiring us to balance the confidentiality we had promised gang members with our desire to interview members of their family. Further complicating this was the fact that few gang members were willing to provide us with access to a family member we could interview. This created a dilemma for the interview process and field relations. Many parents of gang members engaged in what Huff (1991) identified as denial. That is, they were unwilling to recognize or admit that their child was involved in a gang. This called for a considerable amount of tact on the part of the field-worker as well as the interviewers. A number of family members, especially parents, were reluctant to admit that their sons or daughters were actively involved in a gang. Many interviews with parents began with only grudging acknowledgement that their child was involved in a gang, only to conclude with the revelation of colors, guns, gunshot wounds, large amounts of cash, out-of-town trips, and concerns about the friends their child spent time with. Some of the parents we interviewed provided us with access to other parents, encouraging them to participate because "it would make them feel better to have someone to talk to." The fieldworker likened this to "confession" for many parents:

> it seems like confession is good for the soul, once they get a sense that they will be treated with a sense of fair play and know we are doing fair and objective research. And this is the vehicle where parents can probably come and confess their pressures, their stress, not only to their minister or their deacon, but to people who are in the field of understanding crime and then in helping the problem. (December 1, 1992)

The obstacle of denial provided difficulties for subject recruitment. On the one hand, we were committed to respecting both the confidentiality of gang members' stories and the perceptions of parents. On the other hand, it was hard to ignore the objective evidence about the gang involvement many parents were quick to deny. This was made most clear in our attempts to interview the mother of a gang leader who had been slain in a gang-related act of violence. His younger brother was arrested for property destruction; he had spray painted "RIP Darcy" on dozens of locations to memorialize his dead brother's name. Despite the objective evidence to the contrary, their mother denied that either son was ever involved in a gang and was incensed at the suggestion that either son had anything to do with a gang, even though her son's funeral was disrupted by gunfire from rival gang members. The other extreme of this continuum occurred during our interview of a mother whose son had been killed in a drive-by shooting just two weeks before our interview. She admitted that, prior to his killing, she wasn't sure about her son's membership in the gang. However, after his death, several members of his gang confided in her that her son had indeed been a gang member, though he was not the intended target of the shooting. On the way home after the interview, she asked the field-worker to drive her by the site of the killing, as she had yet to see it. When she saw the "RIP" memorializing her son, she told our field worker she felt better about him knowing that his gang members really cared about him. The fieldworker reported that there was still blood on the wall of the garage where he had been shot. By a strange twist of fate, we interviewed the stepmother of the gang member who was the intended victim of this killing two weeks later.

Conducting the Interviews

Having contacted gang members and verified their eligibility, the next step in the research process was to conduct the interviews. Because many of the individuals we interviewed did not have their own transportation and public transportation would have presented yet another hurdle to participation in the study, the field-worker almost always gave subjects a lift to the interview site.[6] While doing so, the field-worker had time to explain further the purpose of the study and the logistics of the interview setting and procedure. This served a dual function. On the one hand, it put our subjects at ease and provided a transitional time between the street (their sphere of activity) and the interview setting (ours). More importantly, many of the subjects discussed their gang activities with the field-worker in the car (before and after the interview), providing us with a means of verifying some of what they discussed with us during the interview. This allowed us to control gang "mythologizing," overblown accounts of bravado and violence, as the field-worker set the tone for the interviews, telling subjects that he only wanted, "the real deal, no bullshit." The field-worker also was able to examine neighborhoods and the groups present at the time of pickup and delivery.

The decision about the appropriate location in which to conduct interviews was relatively straightforward. We wanted to find a place that was viewed as "neutral" by gang members and relatives. We had given consideration early in the project to renting an office but decided that finding a space in a part of the city that was seen as neutral by gangs would prove to be difficult, especially as the gang situation in St. Louis was quite dynamic. In the end, we chose to use vacant offices at the university. There was an intuitive appeal to this choice that we did not realize initially. Conducting interviews at the university reinforced in the minds of gang members that this really was a research project, that we were not connected with the police, and that answers would be held in confidence as we had promised. In addition, minorities were well represented on campus, so interview subjects "fit in," appearing to the casual observer to be students or employees.

While ours is a public university with open access, we decided not to leave the subjects alone on campus. In this way, we could effectively counter any claims that they had caused trouble or were the targets of trouble. This led to a number of unexpected situations; as a consequence of this decision we were required to "baby-sit" subjects on a number of occasions. Frequently a subject only would come for an interview if the person who had referred them agreed to come along. Because we decided not to interview one gang member in the presence of another, we were left with the task of deciding how to handle the person who had made the initial referral and had come along to vouch for us as legitimate. These individuals were "baby-sat" by project staff, and their comments often provided useful insights into their activities as well as those of their partners.

One of the features of field research that has received inadequate attention is controlling the flow of the study. In work such as our own, where the subjects are of interest specifically because of their involvement in violence or their willingness to use violence, controlling the pace of the study assumes critical importance. Initially we had decided that no more than three gang members would be interviewed at the same time and place. It was our belief that this may have posed a danger to the safety of the field ethnographer from rival gangs during the transporting of subjects to the university. In addition, we decided that all interviews had to be scheduled through the field ethnographer. Unless we had a central conduit through which interview scheduling passed, it was possible to have rival gang members in the office at the same time, a situation we were determined to avoid. There were several occasions where our commitment to this principle cost us the opportunity to interview additional subjects, a trade-off we decided to accept. Thus controlling the pace of the study has implications for the quality of the data as well as the safety of the research team.

Early in the project, we attempted to conduct interviews of gang members in groups. While one such interview was successful, we quickly learned that this process was fraught with problems, as the interviewer lost control of the conversation, which drifted toward discussions of social issues. These also proved to be occasions where excess bravado was displayed and discussed. More technically, we could not record answers, and the tape recorded transcript was garbled with the sound of one voice talking over another. A similar problem was reported by Short and Strodbeck (1974) as they attempted to interview twelve gang members at the same time. We abandoned this as an interview strategy but continued to talk with groups of gang members in the field.

Each interview took approximately two hours and, with the permission of each subject, was tape recorded. Seven different individuals conducted interviews over the thirty-nine-month period of study. Three of the interviewers were African Americans, one of whom was a woman. The other four interviewers were white males. We paid careful attention to response bias that may have been introduced as a consequence of the interaction of the race and sex of interviewer and subject to determine whether responses about criminal gang activities, roles, and other gang activities varied by interviewer. In general, few differences on these dimensions were found. In addition, we compared the notes of the field ethnographer to our interview results to determine, as best we could, whether bias had been introduced as a result of this concern. While the possibility exists that such difficulties may have occurred, we are reasonably certain this is not a substantial problem in our data.

Ethical Concerns. Most field studies face a variety of ethical dilemmas, and ours was no exception. Subjects were paid for participating in the study, a practice common to field research. Our initial plan was to provide active gang members with a certificate for clothing at one of the stores popular with young people, and each relative with a certificate for food at a grocery store. Several weeks' experience in the field led us to the conclusion that the best motivator for participation was cash. We decided to set the amount of money at twenty dollars for gang members and fifty dollars for relatives. This level of compensation was high enough to generate interest in participation but not high enough to attract wide-scale interest in the community, allowing us to control the pace of the study. We also set the fee low enough that we were confident that it would not have a criminogenic effect. While twenty dollars is not a small amount of money, it is not sufficient to purchase a gun or bankroll a large drug buy. We are sure that some of our subjects used the money for illegal purposes. But, after all, these were individuals who were regularly engaged in criminal and delinquent acts.

Payment was made at the end of each interview. Owing to university regulations, subjects were required to sign a receipt, though we did not ask them to sign their real names. We also initiated what the field ethnographer came to call the "bird dog fee," a nominal amount of money paid to individuals who provided us with a number of referrals. This payment was instrumental in gaining access to individuals at higher levels of gang hierarchy as well as to parents of gang members. As the university required us to obtain the signature of each person paid to participate in the project, we had to take steps to keep this information confidential. To do so, we came up with a creative solution. Each person we interviewed was assigned a project number. For the purposes of local record keeping, we asked each individual to sign a name (any name) on a sheet next to their project number. They then signed a sheet of paper with their real name and project number on it, folded it and placed it in an envelope that was subsequently mailed to a colleague who lives in a country that does not honor subpoenas for such information from the United States. In this way, we maintained the confidentiality of our subjects and satisfied the requirements of the university.

Because this project was funded by a federal agency (the Administration of Children and Families, United States Department of Health and Human Services) through the university, we were required to obtain the approval of the university Human Subjects Committee. This requirement complicated our desire to maintain the confidentiality of our subjects' identity. We developed an informed-consent form designed to describe the research project as well as to advise subjects of their rights. The committee initially wanted us to obtain the permission of the parents of juvenile gang members. This would have violated our commitment to maintain the confidentiality of each subject, not to mention the ethical and practical difficulties of finding and informing each parent. We told the university Human Subjects Committee that we would not, in effect, tell parents that their child was being interviewed because they were an active gang member, knowledge that the parents may not have had. We reached a compromise in which we found an advocate for each juvenile member of our sample; this person – a university employee – was responsible for making sure that the subject understood (1) their rights to refuse or quit the interview at any time without penalty and (2) the confidential nature of the project. All subjects signed the consent form.

A major concern in doing fieldwork with individuals actively involved in offending is learning about crimes that have been committed. We knew from previous work that we were likely to learn about serious crimes for which an arrest had yet to be made. Our commitment to the confidentiality we promised all subjects helped us to resolve the practical issue of what to do with information we gained about past crimes; we simply would not use the information except in aggregate form to describe the activities of gang members. Of course this meant that we would not inform the authorities (or anyone else, like relatives) of the things we learned. We justify this on numerous grounds. First, we had promised confidentiality to all subjects, and had we violated that promise we would have placed the lives of several individuals (including the field-worker) in jeopardy. Second, it was our job to study gang members, not to catch them. The police are better equipped for that task. Third, the knowledge gained from this study may lead to policies or programs that have an impact on gang activities, resulting in a net reduction in gang-related crime. Finally, most crime goes unreported to the police. We were learning about things that others knew and could have reported were they so inclined. Despite these justifications, we often were troubled by what we learned. We did, however, decide that we did not want to have foreknowledge of a crime, especially a violent crime, and warned subjects of this fact. When a gang member told us he was planning a drive-by shooting or specific retaliation against a rival gang, we told them that such information was not protected by our pledge of confidentiality and that we did not wish to know about it.

Analysis Plan

Data Sources. The primary data for this book comes from the ethnographic interviews conducted with ninety-nine gang members and twenty-four relatives. These data were used for both quantitative and qualitative analysis. The quantitative analysis is rather straightforward and takes the form of simple frequency distributions. Because transcribed interviews could run up to forty typed pages in length, the analysis required a considerable amount of time. In order to simplify the process of data reduction, we employed GOFER, one of the many qualitative software packages available for such purposes.

The software we used is essentially a text retrieval package and allows the use of boolean operators to retrieve, link, and print various segments of an interview. One of the dilemmas faced in the use of such software is whether to employ a coding scheme within the interviews or simply to leave them as unmarked text. We chose the first alternative, embedding conceptual tags at the appropriate points in the text. An example illustrates this process. One of the activities we were concerned with was drug sales. Our first chore (after a thorough reading of all the transcripts) was to use the software to "isolate" all of the transcript sections dealing with drug sales. One way to do this would be to search the transcripts for every instance in which the word "drugs" was used. However, such a strategy would have the disadvantages of providing information of too general a character while often missing important statements about drugs. Searching on the word "drugs" would have produced a file including every time the word was used, whether it was in reference to drug sales, drug use, or drug availability, clearly more information than we were interested in. However, such a search would have failed to find all of the slang used to refer to drugs ("boy" for heroin, "Casper" for crack cocaine) as well as the more common descriptions of drugs, especially rock or crack cocaine. Our solution to this problem was to insert conceptual tags in the text surround by an angle bracket. In this example, the tag < drug sales > was inserted in the text wherever talk of such activity was found. The development of tags was undertaken only after a considerable number (approximately twenty) of interviews had been completed, and the tags correspond closely to items in the questionnaire. This process allowed us to examine all of the statements made by gang members about a single concept, such as drug sales. While this simplified things considerably, further efforts at data reduction were necessary, as many of the tags identified dozens of pages of transcript material.

Research Issues. This study was guided by an important premise; that the best information about the gang member's perspective was likely to come from gang members themselves. There was an important corollary to this premise – we were committed to contacting active gang members in the field. Several key questions formed the basis for the questionnaire and thus provided us with information about that perspective. Our study revolved around a number of activities, both gang and nongang related, that our subjects were likely to engage in. First, we were interested in gang membership. In this context, we wished to learn more about the motivations to join gangs, the process of joining the gang, the symbols of gang membership, the strength of associational ties, the structure or hierarchy within the gang, motivations to stay (or leave) the gang, and how this generation of St. Louis gangs began. The second set of issues concerned the activities gang members engaged in. These included such things as turf protection, drug sales and use, and violence, as well as conventional activities. Throughout our interviews, we detected a tension between gang and nongang activities, and we believe that this dichotomy intersects with the distinction between criminal and noncriminal activities. It is important to note that not all criminality engaged in by gang members occurs within the context of the gang. Similarly, not all gang activity is illegal. An accurate picture of gang members must portray both the nature of their gang involvement and the legal status of their activities. Traditional social institutions play an important role in the lives of gang members. Thus we devote considerable attention to discussing the role of the school, workplace, neighborhood, peers, and criminal justice agencies in the lives of gang members.

A unique feature of our work is its focus on families. There has been little research examining specifically the links between gang members and their family members. For this reason, we have separated the family from our analysis of other social institutions and devote special attention to this relationship. This section of the analysis is facilitated by the interviews conducted with families of gang members and extensive questioning of gang members about the role of their family in relation to the gang. In this context we consider the extent to which gang membership is either encouraged or discouraged by the family, efforts to prevent membership, intergenerational issues in gang transmission, the relative importance of the gang versus the family, and views about gang membership for future generations. Our final section considers the issues of prevention and desistance from gang membership, using the perspective of both active and ex–gang members.

"I'm Down With the Bloods, What's Up Cuz?" Membership Issues

> I don't know. Shit man, there wasn't no joinin' in it and it was a little neighborhood thang you know, just somethin you know, we just grew up like that. We grew up fightin, we just grew up fightin and everybody hangin around so they decided to call they self somethin since we hung around like that, went out doin things and stuff. (Male #002, "Eric," sixteen-year-old Thundercat)

> Girls and money, you get to flash money. You in a gang and girls like a magnet come to you. You get respect from people. Yeah you get respect, girls, money drive around with your friends in fancy cars, saying stuff that nobody else know about. (Male #015, "Karry," fifteen-year-old Crenshaw Gangster Blood)

Why do men and women join gangs? Why do gangs grow and spread into new neighborhoods and cities? This chapter addresses issues related to gang membership using the concept of *threat* outlined in the introductory chapter. Here we consider a number of individual decisions and acts involved in becoming a gang member. The duality of individual decisions and group activities raised in the preceding chapters will be quite evident as membership issues are examined within the group process and context of the gang. Here we present how gang members define a gang, the reasons they joined their gang, how they joined it, what they like about belonging to it, and the symbols of membership. In addition, we explore the issues of race and gender in gangs. In the chapter to follow, we explore the history of the gang, its heirarchy, the strength of association, roles in the gang, goals of the gang, relationships with gangs in other cities, and the growth and spread of gangs.

Individual Issues

Background Characteristics. The characteristics of the individual gang members we interviewed are presented in Table 3.1.[1]

The members of our sample were primarily young African American males. The average age of gang members we interviewed was 16.9 years, with the youngest member being 13, and the oldest 29. Seven of our subjects were females, often recruited in groups of two (see #006 and #007 in Table 3.1) or through their boyfriends. Four of our subjects were white; the remainder were black. The racial composition of our sample merits some comment. We are aware of white gangs in the city of St. Louis that have been in existence for several years. However, we were not able to gain access to members of these gangs through our street contacts. In addition, a number of Asian gangs emerged in the city near the end of the study. We also were unable to gain access to members of these gangs. The nature of our sample, therefore, is not strictly representative of gang members in St. Louis; however, we are confident that we have interviewed within the modal category. These gangs consist of predominantly young black males. Using field methods makes it difficult to generalize from the characteristics of our sample to gangs in other cities, or even to all gangs in St. Louis. However, the characteristics of the gang members we interviewed are generally comparable to those reported in a number of other similar investigations of gangs (Hagedorn 1988; Klein 1971; Short and Strodtbeck 1974) and data made available by the St. Louis police department.

Our subjects represented twenty-nine different gangs. Sixteen of the gangs were affiliated with Crips and include sixty-seven of the ninety-nine members of our sample. The remaining thirteen gangs included thirty-two different members and were affiliated with Bloods. There are six different "constellations" of gangs within our sample. By this, we mean smaller gangs that are affiliated with other gangs for reasons of protection or allegiance. Four of these constellations represent Crip gangs, and two represent Blood gangs.

How Do You Define a Gang? There is considerable debate about what constitutes a gang and who qualifies as a gang member. Bursik and Grasmick (1993) identify two main approaches to defining gang membership; definitions that focus on gang processes (such as formation, recruitment, evolution, transmission) and those that focus on behavior (especially participation in illegal activities). Clearly, the criteria used to

Table 3.1 *Gang member chart*

ID #	Gang name	Gang	Race	Age	Sex	Age joined	Drug sales	Other crimes	# Arrests
001	Mike Mike	Thundercats	B	20	M	14	YES	YES	10
002	Eric	Thundercats	B	16	M	13	YES	YES	6
003	Jerry	Thundercats	B	18	M	12	YES	YES	5
004	Anthony	Thundercats	B	17	M	15	YES	YES	0
005	Antonio	6th Street Hoover Crips	B	19	M	16	NO	YES	4
006	Yolanda	23rd Street Hoover Crips	B	19	F	13	YES	NO	25
007	Tina	Hoover Crips	B	14	F	14	NO	NO	0
008	Robert	Compton Gangsters	B	14	M	13	NO	NO	0
009	Marrien	Compton Gangsters	B	15	M	13	NO	YES	0
010	Jason C.	Compton Gangsters	B	15	M	13	NO	NO	1
011	Lisa	Compton Gangsters	B	15	F	15	NO	YES	0
012	Lance	West Side Mob	B	20	M	17	YES	YES	2
013	Darryl	Bloods	B	29	M	13	YES	YES	100+
014	D. C.	Disciples	B	16	M	12	YES	YES	1
015	Karry	Crenshaw Gangster Blood	B	15	M	13	YES	YES	7
016	John Doe	Crenshaw Mobster Gang	B	15	M	14	YES	YES	3
017	Billy	North Side Crips	B	21	M	14	YES	YES	1
018	Maurice	107 Hoover Crips	B	20	M	17	YES	NO	2
019	Anthony	Crips	B	22	M	15	YES	YES	6
020	Lil Thug	Gangster Disciples	B	16	M	13	YES	YES	10
021	40 Ounce	107 Hoover Gangster Crips	B	16	M	15	YES	YES	10
022	8 Ball	107 Hoover Gangster Crips	B	15	M	14	YES	YES	1
023	Benz	107 Hoover Gangster Crips	B	15	M	13	YES	YES	4
024	Hamilton	107 Hoover Gangster Crips	B	16	M	13	NO	YES	1

Table 3.1 *(cont.)*

ID #	Gang name	Gang	Race	Age	Sex	Age joined	Drug sales	Other crimes	# Arrests
025	Tony	107 Hoover Gangster Crips	B	17	M	16	NO	YES	4
026	Chill	107 Hoover Gangster Crips	B	15	M	14	YES	YES	3
027	G-Loc	Gangster Disciples	B	15	M	10	YES	YES	15
028	Killa 4 Ren	187 Crips	B	15	M	12	YES	YES	6
029	Randell	Thundercats	B	17	M	13	NO	YES	4
030	Kenneth	Thundercats	B	19	M	12	YES	YES	30+
031	John Doe	Thundercats	B	16	M	12	YES	YES	4
032	Skonion	Thundercats	B	17	M	14	YES	YES	2
033	Larry	Thundercats	B	18	M	14	YES	YES	32
034	Lil Gene Mack	19th Street Rolling 60's	B	18	M	13	YES	YES	3
035	Edward	Hoover Gangster Crips	B	20	M	16	YES	YES	15
036	NA	Compton Gangsters BIC	B	18	M	15	YES	YES	13
037	Big Money	Compton Gangsters	B	22	M	20	NO	NO	30
038	G.O.D.	Compton Gangsters	B	19	M	10	YES	YES	10
039	Kaons "BIC"	Compton Gangsters BIC	B	17	M	7	NO	YES	5
040	Knowledge	Compton Gangsters	B	21	M	12	YES	YES	1
041	C. K.	Bloods	B	22	M	20	YES	YES	15
042	Leroy	Rolling 60's Crips	B	17	M	15	YES	YES	2
043	Lee Roy	Rolling 60's Crips	B	16	M	13	YES	YES	1
044	Paincuzz	Rolling 60's Crips	B	16	M	13	NO	NO	0
045	C-Loc	Rolling 60's Crips	B	17	M	16	NO	YES	0
046	Lady Tee	74 Hoover Crips	B	16	F	13	YES	YES	2
047	Baby	Rolling 60's Crips	B	15	F	14	NO	NO	0
048	Corkey	Rolling 60's Crips	B	16	M	15	YES	YES	1
049	Chris	Rolling 60's Crips	B	17	M	15	NO	NO	0
050	John	Rolling 60's Crips	B	19	M	17	NO	YES	1
051	David	Bloods	B	18	M	14	YES	YES	3

Table 3.1 (cont.)

ID #	Gang name	Gang	Race	Age	Sex	Age joined	Drug sales	Other crimes	# Arrests
052	Johathan	107 Hoover Crips	B	15	M	14	YES	YES	1
053	Jimmy	107 Hoover Crips	B	18	M	18	YES	YES	50+
054	Cedric	62 Brim Bloods	B	16	M	13	YES	NO	0
055	Chris	Hoover Crips	B	17	M	14	YES	YES	1
056	Tony	19th Street Hoover Crips	B	17	M	15	YES	YES	3
057	Smith & Wesson	Neighborhood Posse Bloods	B	15	M	14	YES	YES	7
058	Roach	Bloods	B	15	M	11	YES	YES	25
059	Top Gun	Bloods	B	16	M	14	YES	YES	7
060	Bullet	Inglewood Family Gangster Bloods	B	20	M	14	NO	YES	100+
061	K-Red	Inglewood Family Gangster Bloods	B	15	M	14	YES	YES	15
062									
063	Bobtimes	6 Deuce Bloods	B	16	M	14	YES	YES	3
064	Pump	6 Deuce Bloods	B	14	M	12	YES	YES	4
065	BK Kill	North County Crips	B	19	M	18	YES	YES	15
066	Short Dog	Crenshaw Mob Gangsters	B	15	M	11	YES	YES	2
067	$hortDog	Inglewood Family Bloods	B	15	M	13	YES	YES	5
068	CK	Piru 104 Bloods	B	16	M	15	YES	YES	16
069	X-Men	Inglewood Family Gangsters	B	14	M	13	YES	NO	3
070	Lil B-Dog	Inglewood Bounty Hunters	B	15	M	14	YES	YES	3
071	B Daddy	Inglewood Family Gangsters	B	17	M	14	YES	YES	4
072	Blood	Swan Park 59 Bloods	B	17	M	14	YES	YES	7
073	C-Love	Crenshaw Mob Gangsters	B	16	M	15	YES	YES	2
074	Shon	Crenshaw Mob Gangsters	B	16	M	13	YES	YES	2

Table 3.1 (*cont.*)

ID #	Gang name	Gang	Race	Age	Sex	Age joined	Drug sales	Other crimes	# Arrests
075	Tyrell	Bounty Hunter Bloods	B	16	M	14	YES	YES	3
076	Mickey Mouse	Grape Street Crips	B	17	M	16	YES	NO	0
077	Crazy Drakey	8 Drake Gangster Crips	B	18	M	14	YES	YES	2
078	Tina	Treetop Bloods	B	15	F	15	NO	YES	0
079	Hell Bone	Rolling 60's Crips	B	14	M	11	NO	YES	2
080	Coke Cane	Rolling 60's Crips	B	13	M	13	NO	YES	1
081	Half Pint	B Gangster Disciples	B	14	M	13	YES	YES	4
082	Dough Boy	B Gangster Disciples	B	14	M	13	YES	YES	2
083	Winchester	Rolling 60's Crips	B	14	M	13	YES	YES	0
084	Rolo	Rolling 60's Crips	B	15	M	12	YES	YES	0
085	2-Low	Rolling 60's Crips	B	18	M	15	YES	YES	0
086	Gunn	Rolling 60's Crips	B	19	M	10	YES	YES	50+
087	Blue Jay	Rolling 60's Crips	B	18	M	11	YES	YES	0
088	T-Loc	Grape Street Crips	B	21	M	14	YES	YES	1
089	C-Note	88 Street Mob	B	15	M	15	NO	YES	1
090	Rellol	19th Street Long Beach Crips	B	15	M	13	YES	YES	5
091	Paul	107 Hoover Crips	W	18	M	17	YES	YES	4
092	Derone	Rolling 60's Crips	B	21	M	17	YES	YES	8
093	Lil-P	Crenshaw Mob Gangster Bloods	B	16	M	15	YES	YES	2
094	John Doe	107 Hoover Crips	B	14	M	13	NO	NO	0
095	I-Dog	107 Hoover Crips	B	14	M	14	NO	NO	0
096	L. C.	Inglewood Bounty Hunters	B	23	F	20	YES	YES	1
097	Antwan	Insane Gangster Disciples	W	17	M	14	YES	YES	6
098									
099	Joe L.	Insane Gangster Disciples	W	18	M	15	YES	YES	50+
100	J. Bone	Insane Gangster Disciples	W	19	M	16	YES	YES	2
101	Money Love	Insane Gangster Disciples	B	20	M	17	YES	YES	3

distinguish gang activity from nongang activity, gang members from nongang members, and gangs from other forms of adolescent organizations are of critical importance. Our own approach to these issues was presented in Chapter 2. In this section of the book, however, we explore what gang members themselves consider to be the definition of a gang. Interestingly, there is as much diversity of opinion about this matter among gang members as there is among academics and criminal justice personnel.

We received no single answer to the question "What is a gang?" from our subjects. Reflecting the categories offered by Bursik and Grasmick (1993), subjects used both group process and participation in illegal behavior as the defining criteria for gangs. The most common element in definitions of a gang referred to its collective nature, an attribute offered by 92 percent of respondents. This underscores the salience of the group for defining a gang.

> Cause we all hang around each other and there is more than two or three of us and we stick up and hang in there for each other, do whatever for each other. It's a gang, it's a group of us anyway I think. We ain't doing nothing too positive. (Male #012, "Lance," twenty-year-old West Side Mob member)

> A group of individuals who set out to do not necessarily positive things. Just people who didn't do too good in life and are not doing too good now. (Male #042, "Leroy," seventeen-year-old Rolling 60's Crip)

> To my knowledge it's a group of fellas. Not just fellas but ones that can depend on each other that's all down for the same thing. Everybody think a gang ain't nothing but just thinking about being violent. Our gang, we think about working. Yeah, we sit in the parking lot and we drink. We try to get jobs and stay off the streets. We don't want to be known. We want to be known but we don't want to be known in no wrong way. We already got that impression now. We already known the wrong way. (Male #037, "Big Money," twenty-two-year-old Compton Gangster)

While most definitions of this nature began by focusing on the more benign aspects of association, the majority (69 percent) acknowledged the negative aspects of gangs, particularly violence. This was made evident by "Roach" (male #058, fifteen-year-old Blood), who first offered that a gang was "a group" and, when pressed, told us that it was "like family" but finally concluded that it was "Violence, it's violence." The role of threat was underscored in many of the definitions offered of gangs, often by noting the need for protection that the presence of rival gangs created. Indeed, 53 percent of our respondents specifically mentioned the role of threat in defining a gang. Sometimes threat was in the form of "disrespecting" a gang, actions that carried the implicit promise of violence.

> Well we call it a gang I guess because we all stick together and stuff and if somebody disrespect us we just come and retaliate. (Male #049, "Chris," seventeen-year-old Rolling 60's Crip)

> Bunch of us get together, really down for it. It's just like somebody go pick on him so we go after them, just like that. (Male #053, "Jimmy," eighteen-year-old 107 Hoover Crip)

> A large number of people period. Most of the time you with a lot of people you don't gotta worry about getting jumped. (Male #071, "B Daddy," seventeen-year-old Inglewood Family Gangster)

The need for protection took on added importance for those who had been involved in crime, creating enemies as a consequence of their criminal activities.

> The most important reason for me is because I have a lot of people behind me. You never have to watch your back. If you have did a lot of dirt in your life, if you have done a lot of wrong things you have to watch your back cause no telling who want you. (Male #034, "Lil Gene Mack," eighteen-year-old 19th Street Rolling 60's Crip)

These quotes highlight that the threat of being beaten up or shot by rival gangs was a consistent theme in most approaches to defining the gang. This was evident in the responses of individuals whose first characterization of the gang was as a "family." Twelve of the thirteen gang members who characterized their gang in this way indicated that the family character of their gang could be found in the willingness of members to look out for them or offer protection against violent threats from rival gangs.

> It's more like a family away from home. You with your friends, you all stick together. They ain't going to let nothing happen to you, you ain't going to let nothing happen to them. (Male #031, "John Doe," sixteen-year-old Thundercat)

> A gang is something you follow behind the leader. Do different things just like a family. Hang out together, rob, steal cars, fight other gangs like for competition. (Male #017, "Billy," twenty-one-year old North Side Crip)

INT: What is a gang?

FEMALE #047, "Baby," fifteen-year-old Rolling 60's Crip: Like a family in a way. It's like brothers and sisters, like a family. There is more violence than a family.

Finally, there were those who simply defined a gang in terms of its criminal activities. Seventy-four percent of our respondents indicated that this was a reason to define their group as a gang. While violence was primary among these activities, drug sales and other crimes often were mentioned as well.

INT: So the reason you call it a gang basically is why?

MALE #101, "Money Love," twenty-year-old Insane Gangster Disciple: Because I beat up on folks and shoot them. The last person I shot, I was in jail for five years.

A bunch of thugs doing bad stuff. Some people good but they get in trouble and take it out on somebody else. Cause they devilish. They don't think before they do things, they just do things, they don't think. Regular people think. (Male #015, "Karry," fifteen-year-old Crenshaw Gangster Blood)

INT: What makes you all a gang?

WHITE MALE #091, "Paul," eighteen-year-old 107 Hoover Crip: The things we do. Fighting, shooting, selling drugs.

Many features of the debate about what constitutes a gang can be found in the responses of gang members to this question. However, it is clear that the individuals we interviewed focused on the more tangible issues in the debate, often defining their gang in terms of its role vis-à-vis other gangs. The group nature and cohesive aspects of gangs were consistent aspects of their responses. Regardless of how they initially characterized gangs, most subjects (74 percent) quickly focused on criminal activities – especially violence – as the defining feature of their gang. It is interesting to observe that, consistent with Klein (1971) and Short and Moland (1976), no subjects indicated a political orientation or agenda in defining their gang.

Pushed or Pulled into Membership. We now move to consider the reasons offered by gang members for their decision to join the gang. In every instance, joining the gang was the result of a process that evolved over a period of time, typically less than a year. In some cases, the process more closely resembled recruitment, whereby members of a gang would identify a particular individual and "convince" them to join the gang. This, however, accounted for very few of the individuals in our sample, fourteen out of ninety-nine. For the most part, the process of joining the gang was consistent with the formation of neighborhood friendship groups. Twenty of our respondents specifically mentioned that they had grown up in the same neighborhood as other gang members and had done things with them over a lengthy period of time. For these individuals, their gang evolved from these playgroups into a more formal association, in much the same way Thrasher (1927) described gangs in Chicago.

The process of joining the gang has two elements; the first is a series of "pulls" that attract individuals to the gang, the second are the "pushes" that compel individuals to join the gang. The pull or lure of gangs was an opportunity to make money selling drugs (a response offered by 84 percent of our subjects), to increase one's status in the neighborhood (indicated by 60 percent), or both. The primary factor that pushes individuals into gangs is their perceived need for protection. Again and again, our subjects described in considerable detail the threat they were under from rival gangs in nearby neighborhoods. A number of gang members (84 percent) found it impossible to live without some form of protection, typically finding such protection through their association with a gang. It is our argument that, for most members, both pushes and pulls play a role in the decision to join the gang. Four specific reasons were cited for joining the gang. In declining order of importance, they were: (1) protection, (2) the prompting of friends and/or relatives, (3) the desire to make money through drug sales, and (4) the status associated with being a gang member. The desire for protection is an example of a "push" – an external force compelling gang membership. The efforts of friends or relatives to encourage gang membership also represent a push toward gang membership. The other two reasons, desire for money and status, are clearly "pulls," or forces that attract individuals to gangs.

As noted above, most of the individuals we interviewed felt their physical safety was in jeopardy in their neighborhood; for the majority, moving to a safer neighborhood was simply not a viable option as few had the resources to effect such a move. Given these circumstances, most gang members (eighty-three) chose to align themselves with a gang for "protection."

That is the advantage, protection. There wouldn't be all this stuff if certain people wouldn't try to be tough. So they try to be tough, so now we be

Crips. They stay out of our business. Some cats from the city came over, that's how it all started. Jumped my friend. (Male #022, "8 Ball," fifteen-year-old 107 Hoover Gangster Crip)

I thought about it [protection]; every time I walked somewhere people would try to start stuff. Yeah, like one time I got off my bus and these two dudes tried to double pin me. (Male #010, "Jason C.," fifteen-year-old Compton Gangster)

Few gang members acknowledged the fact that affiliating with a gang increased their risk of victimization. Indeed, some went so far as to state that being in a gang insulated them from fighting.

It keeps people from fucking with me. So I don't have no trouble, no fights out on the street and all that. (Female #011, "Lisa," fifteen-year-old Compton Gangster)

And other gang members recognized the dilemma of not being in a gang yet having friends who lived in a neighborhood identified with a particular gang. "Bullet" decided to join his gang since he was seen as a gang member anyway.

Yeah, all your friends Bloods so you don't want to be the odd ball. Say I didn't become a Blood but I was always down with them and when dudes shot at us they was shooting at me too. Any way it goes, I was going to be a gang member. If dudes ride by shooting or whatever they will see me with them. (Male #060, twenty-year-old Inglewood Family Gangster Blood)

Similarly, "Smith & Wesson" reported that already being identified as a rival gang member also played a role in the decision to join.

I got tired of these Crabs saying what's up Fuz and I'm telling them I ain't in no gang. So I got in the gang. See what they do? (Male #057, fifteen-year-old Neighborhood Posse Blood)

Nearly a third (29 percent) of gang members reported that they joined because of the presence of a relative or friend in the gang. The process of recruiting friends and family members into the gang was seldom coercive; indeed most needed only minor forms of encouragement. Many gang members found their way into the gang through emulating a relative (#036) or friend (#054). One reported that he had joined, "Cause my brother was in it mostly" (#031). And another said, "Cause all my friends become one" (#010). Others indicated that it was a natural part of hanging out with friends in the neighborhood.

I ain't going to say it's going to be my life but it was just something that came up to me where I was staying. I was with the fellas and it just happened that I became one of them. I just got in the same stuff they was in. To me I see it as something to do. I can't put it a more better way than that. (Male #020, "Lil Thug," sixteen-year-old Gangster Disciple)

We have identified drug money and status as two of the factors cited most often as attractive features that "pulled" young men and women into gangs. As we document below, drug sales grew in importance once individuals joined their gang. However, only a small fraction (6 percent) were influenced by the opportunity to sell drugs in making the decision to join their gang. Others were more direct, stating that they found the money attractive or that money had initially attracted them to the gang.

My interest was in getting paid, man, strictly getting paid. I had a job at 13. I sold dope, cocaine, but it wasn't a career thing, it was like for extra money. (Male #040, "Knowledge," twenty-one-year-old Compton Gangster)

Girls are a frequent topic among adolescent males, and the opportunity to impress girls through increased status was cited by 40 percent of our subjects as the reason why they joined the gang. In this sense, their motivations closely resemble those of their adolescent peers who were not involved in gangs.

Yeah, you get respect, girls, money, drive around with your friends in fancy cars, saying stuff that nobody else know about. I wanted to be in cause they had the pretty girls and everything. (Male #015, "Karry," fifteen-year-old Crenshaw Gangster Blood)

But status concerns were not confined solely to the pursuit of women.

It make me big, it make me carry guns, it made me like if somebody called and I tell them to come over and they don't come over I get mad cause I'm the big man, he supposed to come to me. I might pop them upside they head or I might pistol whoop them or I just sit back and just dog them out. Many things I can do to a person that they don't ask. (Male #018, "Maurice," twenty-year-old 107 Hoover Gangster Crip)

Process of Entry. Typically, the process of joining the gang was gradual and evolved out of the normal features of street life in the neighborhood. Indeed, the imitative aspects of adolescent life are strong enough to suggest that most gang members affiliated themselves with friends from the neighborhood already involved in the gang. In describing how they came to join their gang, twenty-nine of the fifty-four who offered an answer to this question indicated they joined as a consequence of neighborhood friendships. On average, members of our sample heard about their gang while they were twelve, started hanging out with gang members at thirteen, and had joined before their fourteenth birthday. This suggests a gradual process of affiliation rather than one of active recruitment.

Eleven percent of our respondents began the process of affiliating with their gang by being involved in fights. In these instances, they joined with friends in the neighborhood to fight rival groups in other neighborhoods before formally accepting membership. Violence is a hallmark activity for gangs and serves a variety of latent functions. It strengthens the bonds between existing members, increases the stake of prospective or fringe members in the gang, and serves as a means by which nongang youth come to join the gang.

> It was just when I was being around them they was cool with me and stuff so they just asked them to join in one time. They helped me in a lot of fights and stuff like that. (Male #093, "Lil-P," sixteen-year-old Crenshaw Mob Gangster Bloods)

> I just went on a few posses,[2] I just started hanging around a little bit with them but I was seeing the way things was going and I wanted to join in so I initiated it by the hand signs. (Male #017, "Billy," twenty-one-year-old North Side Crip)

Another route to entering the gang stemmed from normal activities in the neighborhood. As such, becoming part of the gang is a gradual process, often the logical outgrowth of having gang-involved friends in a particular neighborhood.

> The people I hang with are all in it. You know like how you find yourself in a situation. (Female #047, "Baby," fifteen-year-old Rolling 60's Crip)

> I was hanging with them, it was just the area I was in was claimed by them so I just started claiming with them. (Male #025, "Tony," seventeen-year-old 107 Hoover Gangster Crip)

For others, school was the place where entry into the gang occurred. After all, it is not uncommon for friends at school to self-select into the same activities. Viewed in this light, the gang represents a "normal" feature of adolescent life.

Initiation. Becoming a gang member requires more than a decision. Most gangs require prospective members to undergo some sort of an initiation process. Over 90 percent of our sample indicated that they participated in such a ritual.

The initiation ritual fulfills a number of important functions. The first is to determine whether a prospective gang member is indeed tough enough to endure the rigors of violence they will undoubtedly face. After all, members of the gang may have to count on this individual for back up, and someone who turns tail at the first sign of violence is not an effective defender. But the initiation serves other purposes as well. In particular, the initiation increases solidarity among gang members by engaging them in a collective ritual. The initiation reminds active members of their earlier status as a nonmember and gives the new member something in common with individuals who have been with their gang for a longer period of time. Because of these common experiences, the initiation ritual – especially to the extent that it involves violence – creates aspects of what Klein (1971) has called "mythic violence," the legends and stories shared by gang members about their participation in violence. The telling of these stories increases cohesiveness among gang members. Further, mythic violence enables gang members to engage in acts they may otherwise regard as irrational, risky, or both.

Padilla (1992) reports the most common initiation ritual is being beaten in or "V-ed" in, a finding similar to those of Moore (1978), Hagedorn (1988), and Vigil (1988). Gangs in St. Louis also employ this method of initiation. This form of initiation included seventy of the ninety-two gang members who offered an answer to this question. While it took many forms, in its most common version a prospective gang member walked between a line of gang members or stood in the middle of a circle of gang members who beat the initiate with their fists. Falling down, crying out, failing to fight back, or running away sounded the death knell for membership.

> I had to stand in a circle and there was about ten of them. Out of these ten there was just me standing in the circle. I had to take six to the chest by all ten of them. Or I can try to go to the weakest one and get out. If you don't get out they are going to keep beating you. I said I will take the circle. (Male #020, "Lil Thug," sixteen-year-old Gangster Disciple)

Taking "six to the chest" was commonly reported as a means of initiation, especially by gangs who use the six-pointed star as one of their symbols, such as the Disciples.

> Well it's like this, if you around us and we recommend you to G, we just make up our minds and then somebody look at they watch we'll yell it's on, we'll initiate you. Then after you initiated you on the ground we pick you up hug you and say what's up G, just showing him that it's love. It wasn't that we wanted to rush you or hurt you nothing like that. It's meant because we want you to be around us, we want you to be a part of us too. (Male #036, "NA," eighteen-year-old Compton Gangster BIC)

The initiation fulfills other purposes, such as communicating information about the gang, its rules, and activities.

> INT: So that was your initiation?
> MALE #099, "Joe L.," eighteen-year-old Insane Gangster Disciple: Yeah. And then they sat down and blessed me and told me the 16 laws and all that. But now in the new process there is a 17th and 18th law.

Other gang members reported that they had the choice of either being beaten in or going on a "mission" or a "posse." A mission required a prospective gang member to engage in an act of violence, usually against a rival gang member on rival turf. Nearly a fifth of our respondents were required to confront a rival gang member face to face.

> You have to fly your colors through enemy territory. Some step to you, you have to take care of them by yourself, you don't get no help. (Male #041, "C. K.," twenty-two-year-old Blood)

> To be a Crip you have to put your blue rag on your head and wear all blue and go in a Blood neighborhood that is the hardest of all of them and walk through the Blood neighborhood and fight Bloods. If you come out without getting killed that's the way you get initiated. (Male #084, "Rolo," fifteen-year-old Rolling 60's Crip)

The requirements of going on a mission also may include shooting someone. Often the intended victim is known to the gang before the prospective member sets out on the mission.

> Something has got to be done to somebody. You have to do it. Part of you coming in is seeing if you for real and be right on. The last person came in, we took him over to a store. That person identified somebody out of our gang members that shot somebody. We told him that in order to be in

the gang he had to shoot him. So he did. (Male #013, "Darryl," twenty-nine-year-old Blood)

INT: How was he brought in?

MALE #069, "X-Men," fourteen-year-old Inglewood Family Gangster: We asked him how he wanted to get in and he said he wanted to do a ride-by and shoot the person who killed his brother. So he did a ride-by shooting and killed him.

INT: Was his brother a gang member?

069: A Neighborhood Piru Blood.

INT: His brother was killed?

069: Yeah, that's why he wanted to be in. He wasn't gonna get in anyway but his brother got killed.

Gang members and their victims in such encounters are not always strangers, as seen in the case of a gang member who shot his brother, a member of a rival gang.

INT: What did you have to do to be accepted as a member of the Rolling 60's?

MALE #087, "Blue Jay," eighteen year-old-Rolling 60's Crip: Either kill somebody close to you or just shoot somebody, do harm to somebody close to you like family or something.

INT: Which one did you take?

087: I shot my brother. He didn't know I did it.

Others told us that shooting someone, especially a rival gang member, as part of the initiation gave them "rank," higher status, and responsibility in the gang.

Six gang members reported an alternative means of initiation. Two members told us that they got "tagged" (tattooed) with India Ink and a needle or with a white hot coat hanger as part of the initiation process. Another gang member told us he was expected to sell a certain amount of crack cocaine in order to be accepted. Three gang members told us that as relatives of influential gang members, they were able to avoid the initiation ritual that characterized entry into their gang. These examples illustrate the adaptive nature of most of the gangs we studied; after all, for the most part, they were organized and run by adolescents. As such, we would not expect to find a rigid set of procedures to govern the initiation process.

In late 1991, we received a fax from city hall, advising the public of a new form of gang initiation taking place across the country. The fax described a process by which gang members drove a car at night with their lights out and followed anyone who flashed their lights at them. It was reputed that the gang members would then kill those individuals. We were skeptical about the validity of such claims, a skepticism shared by local law enforcement officials. At scores of local and national conferences, we have been unable to verify a single instance in which this process occurred. This incident illustrates the symbolic threat represented by gang members and how effectively the process of cultural transmission of gang images can work. The creation of images such as this leads to further isolation of gang members from social institutions and interactions.

The steps by which women were initiated into the gang varied considerably from those reported by men. While one, a leader of the G Queens, reported that fighting was the primary means of being initiated, other women said female members of her gang had the option of engaging in property crimes such as burglary or shoplifting. We did hear stories, exclusively from male gang members, that prospective female gang members were required to have sex with male gang members. Two male gang members illustrate that contention.

> Yes, they with it. For them [the Crippettes] to be down they got to have sex with us. One night one little gal and her friends were out saggin, she was a fine little gal, and she said she wanted to be down with us. She had to fuck everybody but I felt sorry for the little gal. (Male #033, "Larry," eighteen-year-old Thundercat)
>
> INT: Did she have to be beat in?
> MALE #084, "Rolo," fifteen-year-old Rolling 60's Crip: No, she got to poke everybody in the crew to get in. There was about 30 or 40 of us.

Female gang members, however, disputed this notion. Not one woman indicated she chose this means of initiation; indeed none could recall a woman who had. One woman's response, when asked about being required to have sex with members of the gang to be initiated, was laughter. This discrepancy illustrates the belief systems and bravado of adolescent males about their sexuality and control over females.

Reasons to Be in a Gang. We now consider what gang members regard as the positive features or advantages of gang membership. We presented subjects with twelve features of gang life, asking them to specify whether they represented a good reason to be in their gang. The responses to this question are found in Figure 3.1, where we list, in rank order, the percent of gang members who indicated that each category was a good reason to be in their gang.

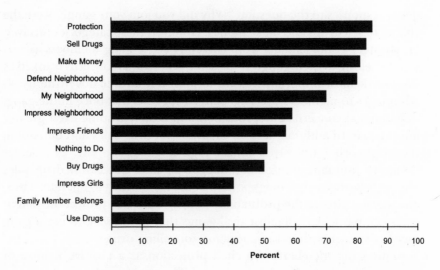

Figure 3.1 Reasons to Belong to the Gang

Protection was identified as a positive feature of gang membership by 86 percent of the subjects, more than any other category. However, selling drugs and opportunities to make money were seen as advantages of gang membership by 84 percent and 82 percent of subjects respectively. Defending the neighborhood also was viewed as an important reason to belong, as 81 percent of gang members responded in the affirmative when asked if this activity was a positive feature of gang membership. Interestingly, impressing people in the neighborhood, impressing friends, and impressing girls, all measures of status, received lower levels of support from gang members than did the categories just reviewed. In general, status concerns were endorsed as advantages to being in the gang by fewer members (thirty-eight) than were more instrumental aspects of gang life such as protection (eighty-three) or making money (seventy-nine). These responses reflect a preference for instrumental benefits of a more tangible nature than status concerns.

It is interesting to compare the responses to this series of questions to the answers gang members gave us about their reasons to join the gang. The desire for protection was the overwhelming motivation cited by gang members in their decision to join the gang. Their experiences in the gang had done little to change this. However, two notable differences can be observed between the reasons to join the gang and, once having joined, the advantages of membership. The second and third most frequent responses to the question "Why did you join your gang?" were the chance to sell drugs and make money. However, these categories received far stronger endorsements from currently active gang members as reasons to belong to their gang. At the same time, status concerns (ranked as the fourth most important reason to join) fell farther down the list as advantages to membership. This pattern suggests that once in the gang, instrumental concerns like protection and money assume even greater importance. In addition, it is no surprise that drug sales and defending the neighborhood received similar high levels of support. In a sense, these are mutually reinforcing categories, since successful drug sales require a secure turf or neighborhood base from which to operate. Thus, one way to enhance the profitability of drug sales is to protect the neighborhood, particularly against rival gangs that would seek to use a gang member's neighborhood as a location for selling drugs.

Many gang members who cited protection as a positive feature of gang membership echoed sentiments similar to those who cited this as a reason to join. There is a very utilitarian tone to these comments.

> It's like a comfortable feeling, you got someone to back you up and protect you. (Male #017, "Billy," twenty-one-year old North Side Crip)

Those who noted the importance of the gang for making money have a similarly utilitarian perspective toward drug sales.

> There's money in a gang. I want to be in it, you see a lot of money in it man. That's why I really got in the gang, money and all. (Male #033, "Larry," eighteen-year-old Thundercat)

> You live in a neighborhood that's run by a gang you just can't up and start selling drugs getting they profit. They'll tell you. You either got to be in their gang or give them half of what you make or don't sell at all. (Male #038, "G. O. D.," nineteen-year-old Compton Gangster)

Gangs can "organize" drug sales in two important ways. First, some gang members have the economic capacity to "front" drugs that would allow an individual gang member to begin selling drugs or to make more profit than they could if they were independent of the gang. Second, and more importantly, gangs have both the will and the mechanism to use violence in order to control a particular turf and keep competing drug sales from interfering with their profits. The ability to accomplish these goals contributed to the large number of gang members who responded that making money or selling drugs was a good reason to be in the gang.

Despite these instrumental concerns (protection and making
a number of members indicated that their gang fulfilled a va
more typical adolescent needs – especially companionship and s
While we maintain that violence or its threat is central to understanding
gangs, street gangs of the 1990s meet a number of the emotional needs
of adolescents that do not differ much from those of nongang adolescents.

> One thing I like about gangs it's more people to be around, more partners
> to go places with. Like certain days we do, like Saturday and Sunday we go
> up to Skate King. Like next weekend we might go out to Northwest Plaza
> (a large shopping mall) and wear all blue colors. (Male #003, "Jerry,"
> eighteen-year-old Thundercat)

> Social stuff and if somebody mess with you. You know you grow up into
> this shit. Mostly social. (Male #012, "Lance," twenty-year-old West Side
> Mob member)

Each of these quotes illustrates typical adolescent activities – hanging out
at the mall, being in the company of friends, and engaging in "social
stuff" – behaviors that resemble those of other adolescents.

Symbols. Becoming accepted into any organization is a more or less
gradual process; gangs are no different. Displaying the symbols of gang
membership (clothes, hand signs, tattoos) is a way of being enculturated
into the gang, or "learning" to be a gang member. Wearing gang clothes,
flashing gang signs, and affecting other outward signs of gang behavior
are also ways to become encapsulated in the role of gang member, especially through the perceptions of others, who, when they see the external
symbols of membership, respond as if the person was a member. In a
sense, exhibiting the external symbols of the gang is a way of "trying out"
a gang identity. When that identity is confirmed by both gang and nongang members in the community, the identity of an individual as a gang
member is solidified.

Symbolic representations of gang membership fulfill a variety of functions for gang members. First, the symbols of gang membership help to
identify both rivals and allies, providing a "perceptual shorthand" by
which the threat represented by an individual can be gauged. Many
gangs have grown too large for all the members to recognize each other
by sight, and the use of symbols allows one to quickly determine the gang
allegiance of another individual. A second function of gang symbols is to
announce the presence of a gang or gang member in a neighborhood.

This can help identify oneself to potential drug customers or serve as a recruitment tool by making the gang member and his (or her) gang highly visible to others in the neighborhood. A third function of symbols is to communicate threats to others. Individuals who exhibit the symbols of membership inform others they are in danger if they claim allegiance to a rival gang and that they should give a wide berth to the gang member, because of the ever present threat of violence. A final function of symbols is to increase cohesiveness among gang members. The process of symbolic communication (either through visual recognition or exchanging common symbols) serves to heighten the identification of individuals in the gang to each other. Through this process, bonds of membership are strengthened and gang activities attain a group context, hence a certain legitimacy.

Assuredly, the spread of gang symbols has been aided by popular culture, particularly films, and music. Within this context, it is important to underscore the role of imitation, an especially powerful force among adolescents.[3] The most common symbolic representations of gang membership included wearing specific colors (mentioned by fifty-seven subjects), giving hand signs (eight), painting graffiti (eighty-one), or being tattooed (fifteen). Most of our subjects identified one or more of these when asked to provide examples of ways in which they distinguished gang members from others.

> If they throw up signs or wear their pants sagging or got on too much of a color. (Male #045, "C-Loc," seventeen-year-old Rolling 60's Crip)

> They be throwing up signs, got they clothes sagging, top of their shirt buttoned up, what kind of shoes they got. (Male #080, "Coke Cane," thirteen-year-old Rolling 60's Crip)

The use of hand signs was particularly important as they often served as a prelude to violence. A number of the violent encounters our subjects participated in were precipitated by showing a gang sign and having it met with the sign of a rival gang.

> Then I throw up a sign and if he throw one back then he a Gangster, or if he do it different you know he in a different gang. (Male #008, "Robert," fourteen-year-old Compton Gangster)

> We could dress natural, we can dress what we want. It's basically not into the colors thing any more. It don't matter. It's about the signs you throw. If you at a party and someone throw up a sign then we know what that cat

is and we got to get that cat. (Male #092, "Derone," twenty-one-year-old Rolling 60's Crip)

A substantial fraction (27 percent) of our subjects told us that clothes were a means of identifying potential gang members.

INT: How can I tell who is a gang member?
MALE #031, "John Doe," sixteen-year-old Thundercat: Most of the time you can tell by the colors they wear. At first there wasn't a color code but now there is. Crips wear pants sagging and all blue mostly white tee shirts or something like that and you can tell a Slob from wearing red and black.

You can tell Rolling 60's because mostly we walk around in all black sometimes and a hat with an S on it. So either by how we dress or our hats. You see a hat with an S like Chicago White Sox that a Rolling 60's. (Male #050, "John," nineteen-year-old Rolling 60's Crip)

The wearing of a "rag" or bandana, either as a head band, on the upper arm or hanging out of a pant's pocket, was offered as another means of identifying gang members. Our subjects indicated that rags were generally worn for gang functions such as meetings, going on campaigns (when a large number of gang members invade rival territory for the express purpose of engaging in violence), or funerals.

Most likely he'll die and on his will[4] he will ask to have his rag on his coffin or lay it on his body or something like that. (Male #020, "Lil Thug," sixteen-year-old Gangster Disciple)

The wearing of tattoos, or getting "tagged," was another symbol of membership, especially for older members of the gang. Fifteen of our subjects showed us their tattoos, most of which were crudely applied with either a needle and India ink or a hot wire or coat hanger. Tattoos were not confined to the males in our sample, as several of the women we interviewed had tattoos. The tattoos generally reflected the set or gang a member belonged to, either by including part of the name of the gang ("60" for Rolling 60's, "19" for 19th Street Long Beach Crips) or a symbol of the gang (pitchforks for Disciples). In some gangs, tattoos have special relevance.

INT: Does it mean anything different if you have a tattoo?
MALE #083, "Winchester," fourteen-year-old Rolling 60's Crip: It's different. If you have a tattoo that means you willing to kill somebody, like if

they mess with your boys, it's like a symbol. If your boy dies then everybody, Bloods, Slobs, they got to go look for them and shoot them.

Not all gang members wanted a tattoo, however. Anticipating his future,
one gang member indicated he hadn't been tagged because "I'll probably
be going to jail too much" (#057), and being tattooed would make him
an obvious target for rival gangs and special attention from authorities.
Consistent with this observation was the response of "Lance" (male
#012, twenty-year-old West Side Mob member), "I ain't got none of them
[tattoos]. Cause that's the first thing the police ask you, 'you got any
tattoos?'"

Symbols play another important function in gangs, distinguishing
"real" members from individuals imitating gang behavior, or wanna-bes,
as they are known on the street. Because gang signs, clothes, and other
symbols have become widely diffused through American culture as a
consequence of movies, music videos, and the media, many people –
gang members and nongang members alike – are aware of the common
symbols of membership. Thus, concern over wanna-bes has grown, both
among gang members and the public. One gang member, though, offered this pragmatic assessment of wanna-bes.

> There ain't no wanna-bes to me. If you claim a gang, I believe it. A
> perpetrator [wanna-be] will shoot in a real gang bang. To me there ain't
> no perpetrators. But you can tell a perpetrator because they are always
> throwing up signs and saying what's up brother, what's up brother. But to
> me, I don't believe there are no wanna-bes, cause to me a fake one is just
> like a real one. He can pull the trigger. He can fight his way out. (Male
> #015, "Karry," fifteen-year-old Crenshaw Gangster Blood)

Who Belongs to the Gang?

Race and Gang Membership. Race is an important element of the
composition of gangs. The growth of the underclass, especially in predominantly minority neighborhoods, is clearly related to the high numbers of minority gang members (Hagedorn 1988; Jackson 1991). While
the majority of individuals we interviewed were black (96 percent), not all
gang members in St. Louis are black. However, nearly half (45 percent)
of our gang members said their gang would accept white members, and
an equal proportion told us that there were white members of their gang.
Only one-fifth of respondents said they were "dead set" against having
whites in their gang.

Gang members who told us they would have whites in their gang said that, for the most part, color doesn't matter. For a number of gangs, the proof of this assertion could be seen in the racial composition of their membership; a large number of the gangs whose members we interviewed had mixed-race membership. Typically members of such gangs informed us that the gang transcended race.

> We feel that color ain't nothing about gang banging, they can be any color. (Male #101, "Money Love," twenty-year-old Insane Gangster Disciple)

> INT: How did white guys get in?
> MALE #015, "Karry," fifteen-year-old Crenshaw Gangster Blood: The same way a black man does. They was just real cool. We don't care about they skin color as long as they was cool. There's some white guys in our group in St. Louis.

The majority of whites (3/5) who joined the gang did so as a consequence of living in the neighborhood where a black gang was operating. This underscores the importance of neighborhoods as a setting for gangs.

> INT: Any white guys?
> MALE #048, "Corkey," sixteen-year-old Rolling 60's Crip: Yeah.
> INT: Why is that?
> 048: I don't know, they in a black neighborhood and they just get hooked onto us.

> INT: How come you all let them in?
> MALE #087, "Blue Jay," eighteen-year-old Rolling 60's Crip: Cause, they grew up in the hood. They was there when I came. Ever since then they been hanging with us, they cool.

This sentiment was echoed by a white gang member who belonged to a predominantly black gang.[5]

> INT: So there are black and white members in your gang, right?
> MALE #100, "J Bone," nineteen-year-old Insane Gangster Disciple: There's only about two or three other white people in our gang, the rest are all black.
> INT: Out of the 50 to 100 members, there are only two or three white?
> 100: Yeah. I'm one of them two or three. There's about four I guess.
> INT: How did you all, if it's predominantly black, how did you all get interested?
> 100: I live in a predominantly black neighborhood and that's just where I was raised at. Most of my friends are black and all that.

Other black gang members told us that having white members provided their gang with access to either drugs or guns. In this sense, having a mixed-race gang provided instrumental advantages to the gang. These advantages were strong enough to transcend parochial concerns over race.

INT: Do you have white guys in there?

MALE #063, "Bobtimes," sixteen-year-old 6 Deuce Blood: Why not? I mean, you know, they claiming, they down for us.

INT: By having white guys do you get special connections or something?

063: Sometimes, yes.

INT: What kind of connection would that be?

063: Dope.

INT: What kind of dope do you sell?

063: Cocaine.

INT: Why do you have white people in your gang?

MALE #092, "Derone," twenty-one-year-old Rolling 60's Crip: Easier to hook up with guns. They know how to get to the guns, they know how to get to anything really.

The majority of subjects (55 percent) came from gangs with only black members. However, slightly more than half (52 percent) of this group told us that their gang was open to the possibility of having white members. A major impediment to expanding the racial diversity of gangs stemmed from the rigid racial segregation in most St. Louis neighborhoods. Underscoring this fact was the response of one black gang member who said, "How many white guys do you find in the city?" (#042). This observation is supported by the high level of racial isolation in four of the areas we recruited in.

INT: Why there no white dudes?

MALE #065, "BK Kill," nineteen-year-old North County Crip: Cause they don't live in our neighborhood.

INT: Any white people in the gang?

FEMALE #046, "Lady Tee," sixteen-year-old 74 Hoover Crip: No.

INT: Why not?

046: There's no whites who live in our neighborhood.

Twenty gang members told us they were opposed to whites joining their gang. Some of the opposition centered on what was referred to as the "Three K Posse" (the Ku Klux Klan). Others simply stated that they didn't like whites. Some of the dislike was linked to the belief that whites would readily "snake out" black members.

> We just don't like them. They snitch too much, can't be trusted. (Male #094, "John Doe," fourteen-year-old 107 Hoover Crip)

> We don't mess with no white dudes. They some snakes. (Male #068, "CK," sixteen-year-old Piru 104 Blood)

The racial composition of gangs confirms the strong neighborhood character of St. Louis gangs. Most gangs members we interviewed belonged to gangs that were exclusively black (56 percent). However, their members were drawn from the neighborhoods they lived in, neighborhoods that had experienced decades of racial segregation. While most claimed to be open to white members, few were to be found. Ethnic and racial identification was generally not strong among the members of our sample, perhaps because of the absence of interracial conflict. Gang conflicts were almost exclusively intraracial. Thus the conflicts between racial and ethnic groups likely to generate and strengthen ethnic identification were generally absent from the lives of our members.

Women. Despite notable exceptions (Bowker and Klein 1983; Campbell 1984; Taylor 1993) female gang members and female gangs have received little explicit attention. In some ways, this makes sense, because males dominate gang membership and are arrested with much higher frequency for violent offenses. On the other hand, female gang membership may be a more significant problem than their numerical representation in gangs suggests. Female membership in gangs is an important topic of study because of shifts in sex roles, particularly in poor communities where changes in family structure over the past two decades have had important consequences for the role of women. Female gang membership seems to accelerate several years after males begin to form gangs and expand membership. Thus the growth in female gang members may be a sign of the increased formalization and expansion of gangs. In addition, many reports of female gang activities indicate that they engage in considerable amounts of violence (Curry, Ball, and Fox 1994). The consequences of female gang membership also are magnified, because women in gangs often attract males to gang membership. Finally, because women tend to play the primary role in raising children in poor communities, the consequences of increased female gang membership may have profound effects for intergenerational transmission of gang membership.

We examined the involvement of women in St. Louis gangs by looking at the extent to which women: (1) were members of gangs dominated by males or (2) had their own gangs, separate from male gangs. We also asked about the activities women engaged in under each circumstance, hoping to learn whether their roles in mixed-gender gangs was different. In general, we found few differences between the roles and activities of women regardless of whether they were in an all female gang or a male-dominated gang. It is important to keep in mind that we were studying gangs in a city where they had only recently reemerged. Over the course of our study, we observed an increase in female gang members as well as in their activities.

Gang members in St. Louis reported that women were integrated into their gangs, even though those gangs were dominated by males. Indeed, 70 percent of our respondents said that the roles of women were indistinguishable from those of men. A high value was placed on being able to get the job done, and women who could be counted on to achieve this goal were held in high regard.

> INT: Are they a separate part or are they mixed in with the guys?
> MALE #001, "Mike Mike," twenty-year-old Thundercat: Mixed in with the guys. B-Dogs and C-Dogs.
> INT: Do they sell drugs too?
> 001: Yes they does.
> INT: And how about, uh, guns and stuff? Are they involved in that?
> 001: Yeah, they shoot them pistols.

> Yeah, they fight, they shoot. They do anything just like us, but I can't tell you about they meetings cause we ain't be in they meetings. (Male #013, "Darryl," twenty-nine-year-old Blood)

> INT: What role do they [women] play?
> FEMALE #078, "Tina," fifteen-year-old Treetop Blood: They like drug dealing, steal cars, do drive-bys, they act like boys.
> INT: So they basically play the same role as the boys.
> 078: Yeah.

> They do the same thing we do, shoot, hang out, party, make some money. (Male #086, "Gunn," nineteen-year-old Rolling 60's Crip)

Other accounts of the female gang members' activities placed women in a role secondary to males. This group represented one-third of the sample. From this perspective, women joined the gang because they were following their boyfriends or were just hanging around with the boys.

> Naw, they ain't really but they hang wit us, they try to hang wit us but we be like go on, ya'all better quit following us. We kick em around, somethin like that they be still tryin to follow us cause, cause most of them got a baby by each other and then when they be tryin to follow they boyfriends and stuff we be like, go on, go on, we don't want ya'all on us too cause we try to holler at some other girls you know they be blockin and stuff. (Male #002, "Eric," sixteen-year-old Thundercat)

> They basically brought in by their man friends. (Male #085, "2-Low," eighteen-year-old Rolling 60's Crip)

> INT: Are there any women in your group?
> MALE #088, "T-Loc," twenty-one-year-old Grape Street Crip: Yeah, we got a few.
> INT: How do they figure in?
> 088: Most of them go with us.
> INT: They really girlfriends?
> 088: Yeah.

These secondary roles often involved the use of women to "set up" rival gang members. Women gang members were used to attract rival gang members making them vulnerable to attacks.

> INT: Are there women in your gang?
> MALE #060, "Bullet," twenty-year-old Inglewood Family Gangster Blood: Not in the gang but there is girls that do more dirt than we do, but they not really Bloods, they just down with us and all. They wear colors, they do everything we do but they just down with us. We will have them do certain things for us like if we wanted to set up somebody we would use one of the gals to get them and get them off where we can get them at. They go pick up things back and forth for us and stuff.

The diversity of female involvement in gangs was reinforced by the comments of the female gang members we interviewed. Two women indicated that their gangs were separate from males, while the others told us they played subservient roles within male gangs. One woman reported that most female gang members were affiliated with male gangs.

> INT: Are there girl gangs that don't have boy gangs or aren't part of boy gangs?
> FEMALE #011, "Lisa," fifteen-year-old Compton Gangster: That ain't part of boys? No. Most girl gangs that I know of is with the boys.

And another woman told us that her gang was separate from boys.

> INT: Do the girls in your gang have a separate kind of group?
> FEMALE #007, "Tina," fourteen-year-old Hoover Crip: Yeah. We don't be like with the boys.
> INT: Hang out by yourselves most of the time?
> 007: Yeah.
> INT: If you got into fights would the boys support you?
> 007: If they around they would.

Another variety of female gangs was less organized than their male counterparts.

> INT: Are there some gangs in the city that are just girls other than the Switch Blade Sisters?
> FEMALE #046, "Lady Tee," sixteen-year-old 74 Hoover Crip: Yeah but they just cliques.
> INT: But they tend to be less organized and smaller?
> 046: Yeah.

Finally, one woman told us that women in her gang, while integrated into a male gang, have the same functions as males in the gang.

> INT: How many females are in the gang?
> FEMALE #078, "Tina," fifteen-year-old Treetop Blood: About ten.
> INT: What role do they play?
> 078: They like drug dealing, steal cars, do drive-bys, they act like boys.

In sum, it is difficult to categorize the role of women in gangs as such roles display considerable diversity. Some female gangs were independent from male gangs. Other women played subservient roles in male gangs. These findings were consistent across reports from men and women involved in gangs.

Conclusion

This chapter has reviewed several membership issues, including the process of joining the gang, symbols of membership, reasons to join, and the positive features of membership. In addition, we examined two of the primary dimensions of gang membership, race and sex. Reports from our subjects reveal the importance of *process* in becoming a gang member. This process has its origins in neighborhoods and has important consequences for the structure of gangs, the topic covered in the next chapter.

CHAPTER FOUR

"We Ain't No Worldwide Thing or Nothing": Gang Structure and Relationships

> To be in a gang you have friends. It's kinda good to be with some friends instead of being out cause if you aint got no friends it's really hard to get along out there. If we in trouble they help you. (Male #009, "Marrien," fifteen-year-old Compton Gangster)

> To be with the in crowd, be with the fellas. We been together so long if they doing something, I'm doing it. I do something, they doing it. (Male #030, "Kenneth," seventeen-year-old Thundercat)

THERE HAVE BEEN gangs in St. Louis since the end of the nineteenth century. Indeed, Thrasher (1927) makes numerous references to gangs in St. Louis, their influence on Chicago gangs, and the nature of their activities. Similar to other cities, St. Louis had a "gang problem" during the 1960s. However, this does not account for the presence of gangs in St. Louis in the 1990s. No member of our sample claimed that their gang was an extension or outgrowth of a St. Louis gang from an earlier era. Thus we must explain the origins of contemporary gangs and, in doing so, focus on the role of cultural transmission – the process of communicating the values, images, symbols, and behaviors common to gang members across the country.

Gang Origins

We examine two views about the origins of St. Louis gangs in the 1990s. The first view, more instrumental in nature, argues that gangs reemerged in the city from the purposive efforts of gang members in other

85

cities to bring their gang to new cities. We refer to this as the "importation" model, one that emphasizes the role of gang members in other
cities (almost exclusively from California) consciously coming to St. Louis
(among other cities) to open up new markets. The second view emphasizes the role of informal factors such as popular culture and cultural
transmission. This approach argues that gangs grow out of "normal"
features of urban life. We refer to this approach as the "imitation–
adaptation" model. This approach emphasizes conflicts between neighborhoods, fights that emerge between different groups of young people,
and popular culture in its explanation of the origin of gangs. The evidence from our research provides more support for the imitation–
adaptation perspective.

Only a minority of our sample (16 percent) provided responses consistent with the importation model. These individuals argued that a small
group of gang members had come to St. Louis from Los Angeles for the
express purpose of starting gangs.

> MALE #041, "C. K.," twenty-two-year-old Blood: Some Bloods came from
> California and they was off into selling dope then. I didn't really know
> nothing about rock cocaine and they started schooling me on how much
> is how much and how much I can get and how to cut it and break it up.
> INT: Where were they from California?
> 041: Inglewood, California. In order to really be down with them be
> around them, some of them didn't matter if you was gang banging or
> not but in order to get a connection, a steady connection, you might as
> well just go and hook up with us and that's how I went from there, I just
> hooked up with them.

> Didn't nobody from out here started the set, people from California came
> here and initiated us. (Male #092, "Derone," twenty-one-year-old Rolling
> 60's Crip)

> People say *Colors* brought the Crips but when I was at Beaumont [High
> School] they came from California. They was on our set. (Male #050,
> "John," nineteen-year-old Rolling 60's Crip)

However, even when it is claimed that gangs from California had a hand
in starting St. Louis gangs, explanations do not always follow the importation model. In many cases, gangs in St. Louis did originate due to the
efforts of Los Angeles gang members but in the normal course of life
events, such as visiting relatives. In fact, one member of our sample was
sent to Compton (in South Central Los Angeles, a notorious gang loca-

tion) by his mother so that he would stay out of trouble in St. Louis. When he returned, he had learned how to be a gang member and quickly transmitted his new-found knowledge to his friends in the neighborhood.

I'm from St. Louis but I got 10 people that stay in California. Sometimes I go up there and visit. I know my way around California like I do here. (Male #017, "Billy," twenty-one-year old North Side Crip)

Before I got into the Bloods I was down here on the West Side and a friend of mine, a Blood, he be what's up Blood and all this and that. Then I have an auntie and her and her husband stay up in L.A. So we went up there, me and my mother and my sister and all them went up there. I ran into a bunch of Bloods and that's how I became one up there. Then my grandfather passed away, my mother moved back down here to be with my grandmother. (Male #060, "Bullet," twenty-year-old Inglewood Family Gangster Blood)

More typical descriptions of the origins of St. Louis gangs emphasized the neighborhood affiliations that were influenced by popular culture. As noted earlier, St. Louis is a city with strong neighborhood divisions and allegiances. These divisions have been the source of conflict for generations and these antagonisms often produced gangs.

It started bout six or seven years ago. Somethin like that. See, the Crips, we didn't know nothin about the Crips and then there was this other neighborhood that they use to wear red all the time and we use to wear blue all the time just like to be the opposite of em or something like that. We didn't even know nothin about the Crips then till one came down there and got kilt. (Male #002, "Eric," sixteen-year-old Thundercat)

We started out, we didn't want nobody coming out and tellin us, walking through our neighborhood cause we grew up in this hood and we was going to protect it even if it did mean us fighting every day, which we done. (Male #036, "NA," eighteen-year-old Compton Gangster BIC)

Some of these antagonisms grew out of break-dancing contests often held between neighborhoods, an occurrence similar to that reported by Hagedorn (1988) in Milwaukee.

How we uh, ya know how it first got started, you know, they used to go to little dances and if the sink [an uncontested or unclaimed spot where neighborhood youths converge] at the southside get into a fight with the Vaughns one persons and then all the southside and all the Vaughns be together and then I guess they just kept on fighting, kept on fighting they say, oh man we gonna get into a gang cause the Vaughns fixin to start takin over. (Male #001, "Mike Mike," twenty-year-old Thundercat)

People who dance against each other at first. One person might move and the other person might win. That person lost because the other person won so they would get in a fight and his group would fight his group. Throughout the years it just got in deeper. (Male #031, "John Doe," sixteen-year-old Thundercat)

The powerful images of Los Angeles gangs, conveyed through movies, clothes, and music, provided a symbolic reference point for these antagonisms. In this way, popular culture provided the symbols and rhetoric of gang affiliation and activities that galvanized neighborhood rivalries. This helps to explain why the characteristics of gangs in Los Angeles, nearly two thousand miles away from St. Louis, came to dominate rather than those of Chicago gangs, only three hundred miles to the north. Indeed, Chicago gang traditions had been carried to East St. Louis, Illinois (just across the river from St. Louis) through the Illinois prison system. Unlike Los Angeles, Chicago gangs lacked the means of transmission for their beliefs and practices found in popular culture. In a sense, the symbols of gang membership served to strengthen and make more visible antagonisms that had long existed. Once these antagonisms found an attractive and efficient vehicle for transmission – through the images of popular culture – they spread the threat of gang violence. Our argument has underscored the role of the *threat* of gang violence in the spread of gangs and the growth of gang membership. Absent the symbolic aspects of gang membership – colors, rhetoric, clothes, hand signs – the long-simmering neighborhood antagonisms would likely remain just that. However, popular culture provides the mechanism or catalyst by which gangs in St. Louis come to resemble those in Los Angeles.[1]

The reason how it got started is they had the movie *Colors*, that was a gang-related movie and the action impact that had on teenagers, they liked stuff like that. They looked at it like the real reality of things in the movie *Colors*. (Male #017, "Billy," twenty-year-old North Side Crip)

All I know is when *Colors* came out that's when they started sparking up all of these gangs, Crips and Bloods and all that. (Male #045, "C-Loc," seventeen-year-old Rolling 60's Crip)

And for many gang members, the movie Colors provided an important reference point for the origins of gangs in St. Louis.

The Crips been around for a long time. People just never heard of them until the movie Colors came out then it started spreading from LA out to here. Coming down here to St. Louis. (Male #050, "John," nineteen-year-old Rolling 60's Crip)

Other symbols of Los Angeles gangs were evident in descriptions of the origins of gangs in St. Louis. Six gang members specifically identified "King David," a Crip leader, as one of the three kings of gang lore. Despite references to his name, there was little agreement about who he was, his role in the gang, or whether he was alive. Some reported that he was still an active gang member in Chicago, others claimed that he was in a California prison, another offered that he was in prison in Illinois, while others believed that he was dead. Notwithstanding the fact that nineteen of our subjects were affiliated with a gang that had the name "Hoover" in it, none knew who Larry Hoover was or his whereabouts.[2] Three of our subjects made specific references to King Piru, who originated the Bloods. These insights confirm the role of popular culture and its function in the transmission of belief systems from one city to another. The mythic status that King David and King Piru had attained was important in spreading the word about gangs, generating a mythology or belief system to support gang activities, and providing symbolic links between St. Louis gangs and gang members to those in Los Angeles.

In sum, imitation played the largest role in the spread of gangs to St. Louis and their subsequent growth. While some evidence exists to support the contention that gang members purposively came to St. Louis to expand drug markets, and used gang affiliation as a vehicle to do so, there is little basis for this as an explanation of the rapid growth in gangs and gang membership in St. Louis. Rather, long standing neighborhood antagonisms (which themselves produce threats that create the impetus for more individuals to join gangs seeking protection) coupled with the images of gangs produced through popular culture, provide a plausible explanation for the origin of gangs and their growth in the late 1980s and early 1990s.

Cities. The role played by Los Angeles gangs in the origins of St. Louis gangs has been examined in the preceding section. However, gangs in a number of cities have ongoing relationships with those in St. Louis. These relationships may be instrumental (providing guns, drugs, or support for campaigns or battles) or the relationships may be more symbolic in nature. In this section, we explore the extent to which gangs in St.

Louis have relationships with gangs in other cities and the nature of those relationships. As was the case in describing the origins of St. Louis gangs, these relationships have a more informal character; that is, they are dependent on relatives and mobility to a far greater extent than they are on the provision of "criminogenic commodities" such as guns or drugs. Often there is variation within a gang regarding the effect of gangs from other cities. Such variation is linked to individual experiences (a cousin from that city) rather than the experiences of the gang collectively.

A number of gang members (sixteen), told us that their gang had no ongoing relationship with gangs in other cities. These gangs were active in their neighborhood and had rather narrow horizons.

> We ain't no worldwide or anything like the Crips and the Bloods. There's about 30 of us, that's all. (Male #012, "Lance," twenty-year-old West Side Mob member)

Other links were more amorphous in nature, consisting primarily of the symbolic ties between groups that share the same name and some of the same symbols. A Compton Gangster from St. Louis described the relationship his gang maintained with a similar gang in East St. Louis, Illinois in the following way.

> It's not what they do for us. It's like they Insane Gangsters and we hooked up with them. When we first hit town we was the Compton Gangsters. They was the Insane Gangsters and they just made our posse bigger. If they need our help they call and if we need their's we call but we never had to call them for nothing. (Male #036, "NA," eighteen-year-old Compton Gangster BIC)

Others focused on the more symbolic aspects of their membership such as "being down" for each other.

> INT: What kind of relationship do you have with them?
> MALE #066, "Short Dog," fifteen-year-old Crenshaw Mob Gangster: They down for Bloods.
> INT: Most of these places that you all have relationships with, you all are just down for each other?
> 066: Yeah.
> INT: But it's nothing in particular that you get from them or they get from you?
> 066: No.

Gangs from Los Angeles were often used as a barometer against which the status of St. Louis gangs were gauged. In some cases, gangs in Los Angeles were romanticized.

> We related to the Crips of L.A. Some of them come back here to do something. Sometimes we hang with the big boys. (Male #032, "Skonion," seventeen-year-old Thundercat)

In other instances, Los Angeles was rejected as the standard by which St. Louis gangs could be measured.

> Some people name us wanna-bes. What is the difference? You don't die faster in L.A., you don't shoot any different, what's the difference? I just want somebody to explain it to me. (Male #042, "Leroy," seventeen-year-old Rolling 60's Crip)

A quarter of our respondents, the modal category, identified a relative in another city as the primary link between their gang and the gang in the other city. Yet even this category showed considerable variation within gangs, illustrating the diverse nature of membership. These contacts included Indianapolis, Kansas City, Chicago, Detroit, Los Angeles, East St. Louis, and several cities in Mississippi.

> INT: What is the relationship that you got with the Detroit gang?
> MALE #033, "Larry," eighteen-year-old Thundercat: When I need something, like I need a weapon. A certain kind of weapon that I want to get like an AK or something I'll call up Detroit and put the word out. I got family up there that's Crip and they like older men like in they 20s and 30s. I got connects up there.

> INT: What is your relationship with the L.A. gang?
> MALE #048, "Corkey," sixteen-year-old Rolling 60's Crip: They claiming the same thing we claim. Some of the guys we know that claim 60 got family in L.A. that claim 60.

The majority (54 percent) of subjects identified the relationship with gangs in other cities as instrumental. This was particularly true for relationships with gangs in Los Angeles and Detroit who were cited as the source of guns and drugs. When asked about relationships he had established with gangs in Los Angeles and Detroit, one gang member told us that the form of his relationship with gangs in those cities consisted primarily of "ammunition, guns, and drugs" (#072).

INT: Any relationships with national gangs?

MALE #004, "Anthony," seventeen-year-old Thundercat: Yeah, the Crips in L.A.

INT: What's the nature of that relationship?

004: They bring drugs. We'll buy them. They'll bring them down to us cheap and we will buy them cheap from them and sell them at a higher price down here.

From California they send in drugs. In Atlanta they mostly have guns, artillery. (Male #031, "John Doe," sixteen-year-old Thundercat)

Though it represents an outlier, the response of "Darryl" (the oldest member of our sample and a former Los Angeles gang member) indicates the level of organization and coordination seen by some gang members in their relationships with gangs in other cities.

INT: To what extent does your gang deal with gangs outside of the St. Louis area?

MALE #013, "Darryl," twenty-nine-year-old Blood: It's like the Coca Cola thing man. Everything we do is big. We travel to different cities and set up organizations.

INT: So is it mainly to disperse drugs?

013: Disperse drugs, robbing, and murder.

Gangs in other cities play a role in maintaining gang life in St. Louis. This role has a strong symbolic character and is often sustained by relationships with relatives in those cities. However, just over half of the gang members we interviewed identified an instrumental role played by gang members in other cities, especially in the provision of drugs and guns.

Relationships with Other Gangs in St. Louis

Every gang in St. Louis maintains relationships with other gangs in the city. These relationships show considerable diversity, and while many of them are antagonistic, a number are supportive. Many of the antagonistic relationships have their origins in the division between major gang groups (Crips versus Bloods), but others are rooted in long standing disputes between the residents of adjoining neighborhoods. Even these antagonistic relationships perform useful functions for the gang, often serving to increase cohesiveness among members, a process that occurs through fights or the threat of attack by rival gangs. Such threats recommit gang members to their own gang, uniting them against a common enemy. However, we found that almost all gangs (85 percent) had positive relationships with members of other gangs. These relationships almost exclusively occurred within the larger divisions of gangs. Crip sets from different parts of the city would do things with each other, as would Blood sets. These activities between gangs reflected the age related interests of their members, usually focusing on traditional youthful concerns such as drinking, partying, and dating members of the opposite sex.

Most of the antagonistic relationships between gangs involve Bloods and Crips who report that they fight over colors, turf, or respect. Major campaigns or wars occur between members of these two gangs. However, many of the fights between gangs reflect long standing antagonisms that have their genesis in neighborhood rivalries that precede the arrival of gangs in St. Louis.

> INT: How about the south side? Do you guys get along with the south side?
> MALE #033, "Larry," eighteen-year-old Thundercat: No. I hate them.
> INT: Any guys from the Thundercats hooked up with the south side?
> 033: The Peabody Projects, we been fighting them since before the Crips and Bloods came up. We been fighting them since 1981. Since we Crip they was claiming Slob.

Despite the fact that fights between major gang divisions (Bloods and Crips) are more common, there were frequent reports of fighting between different sets of Crips. This appears to be the case for several reasons. First, Crip sets in St. Louis outnumber Blood sets by about three to one, so sheer numbers alone make this more likely. The number of Crip sets also means that there is greater rivalry between them for dominance. Because Blood sets were fewer in number, and therefore in more danger from outside gangs (i.e., Crips), they could ill afford to fight one another. There is another reason for less violence between Blood sets; a major difference between Crips and Bloods in St. Louis is that Bloods were consistently more committed to making money. Put simply, fighting is bad for business, detracting time and effort from more lucrative pursuits. Crip gang members knew the allegiances among Crip sets very well.

> MALE #044, "Paincuzz," sixteen-year-old Rolling 60's Crip: Our set is hooked up with the Disciples, 19th Street and the ECG's.
> INT: Do Crips fight other Crips in St. Louis?
> 044: Some of them do.
> INT: How about Rolling 60's?
> 044: Yeah, they fight Hoovers and 8 Tray.

Knowing these alliances can be important for maintaining personal safety.

Most gang members (85 percent) reported that there were other gangs with whom they were allies. A number of activities took place between the members of two allied gangs, most of which followed patterns of adolescent behavior typical of males. These activities centered around fighting, drinking, and hanging out.

> We sit around and get high or go out and do some fighting. (Male #065, "BK Kill," nineteen-year-old North County Crip)

> INT: Does your group, your neighborhood gang do other things with other Crip groups in the city?
> FEMALE #006: "Yolanda," nineteen-year-old 23rd Street Hoover Crip: Yeah, go places or whatever.
> INT: Get into fights together?
> 006: Yeah, get drunk and fights together. I always get into fights.

> INT: What do you all do together with them [other gangs]?
> MALE #069: "X-Men," fourteen-year-old Inglewood Family Gangster: Help them fight together, hang out together, that's about all, or go places together.
> INT: What kind of places?
> 069: Skating, dances, that about all like that.

There is one interesting sidelight to the issue of intergang relationships. Following the Rodney King verdict, there was considerable discussion of a truce between Crip and Blood gangs in Los Angeles. Similar talk was heard in St. Louis, though there is little tangible evidence to support the view that such a truce actually took place. One of our subjects did tell us, however, that his gang (a Crip set) had established relationships with Blood gangs.

> INT: Do you all have relationships, are you all cool with some other Crips?
> MALE #094, "John Doe," fourteen-year-old 107 Hoover Crip: Yeah, some Bloods too.
> INT: You all cool with Bloods?
> 094: Yeah.
> INT: How did that work?
> 094: Since they heard about that Rodney King deal on the television, all Crips and Bloods are joinin' together.

When asked what activities Bloods and Crips did together, his response was that they "went to the arcade." We encountered only one other example of political awareness in the course of our study. In 1991, the Greater Ville, an historic neighborhood that had produced a considerable amount of African American cultural heritage in St. Louis was "leafletted" by the Ku Klux Klan. The leaflets were placed under the windshield wipers of hundreds of cars in the neighborhood and carried a simple message: the Klan thanked black residents of the city for doing their job so efficiently by killing so many young black males. This outraged neighborhood leaders, one of whom painted "Bloods and Crips will kill KKK" in alternating blue and red letters on an abandoned gas station in a prominent location. This was not the work of a gang member, and in general we found very low levels of political awareness of gang members.[3] The lack of political involvement is consistent with the description of gang members as individuals who must be concerned about threats of violence from within their own and adjoining neighborhoods. In a sense, such political concerns are foreign to the day-to-day requirements of survival. In this respect, St. Louis gangs differ little from those described by Short and Moland (1976) in Chicago between 1959 and 1962.

Heirarchy

Organizations can be defined in a number of ways. In the following sections, we examine the level of formal organization within the gangs we studied. We focus on four measures of organization: roles, rules, meetings, and the existence of junior gangs. The extent to which a gang has roles, rules, or regular meetings is an indication of their level of formalization.

Roles. Role differentiation is an important characteristic of formal organizations. The presence of different roles or levels of responsibility would be evidence of increasing formalization or organization within the gang. Though twenty-six different roles were identified, few were of a well-defined character. The most typical role identified in the interviews was that of "leader." However, not all gangs reported they had leaders; indeed, many of the gang members we interviewed (16 percent), expressed hostility toward the idea of having leaders.

INT: Does anybody got the power? Do some people have more power than others?

MALE #008, "Robert," fourteen-year-old Compton Gangster: If somebody want to run everybody we say you don't run nobody, we all together.

INT: Ok, so what is your role in the gang?

008: That nobody runs me and nobody really going to tell me what to do.

Ain't nobody be running it. It's like everybody does. (Male #009, "Marrien," fifteen-year-old Compton Gangster)

Ain't no leaders. If we put a ride on somebody, they will come to me to bring the play in. But there ain't no leader, everybody just listen to one another, ain't no leader. (Male #033, "Larry," eighteen-year-old Thundercat)

Most gangs, however, reported *some* form of leadership. The leaders of these gangs did not have *de jure* powers granted to them by all members for all situations. Rather, gang leadership had a more informal, situational character to it and often varied between subgroups in the gang. This is evident in the following responses to questions about the nature of leadership within the gang.

INT: Do you have a reason why they look up to your brother a little bit more?

MALE #051, "David," eighteen-year-old Blood: Because he the strongest one out of the group but they don't call him the leader.

Yeah, it's not like he'll tell you what to do; he just keeps it together so that we don't fall apart. So we won't fight each other. (Male #020, "Lil Thug," sixteen-year-old Gangster Disciple)

INT: Do some guys in the gang have more juice than others do?

MALE #045, "C-Loc," seventeen-year-old Rolling 60's Crip: Yeah, some of them.

INT: How do they get more juice than other folks?

045: They bigger and talk more.

Size and age were identified as the two primary criteria by which leaders assumed that role in the gang. In a social group that formed largely in response to physical threats, initiated members through violence, and engaged in frequent fights, it is no surprise that physical prowess demonstrated through fighting would emerge as a criteria for leadership.

Lance [a leader in the gang, not the subject] like the oldest one, he tough I guess. He is the toughest one. He been in more fights and in jail more than all of us. He's bigger than a motherfucker too. (Male #012, "Lance," twenty-year-old West Side Mob member)

The reason why they become leaders is because they are so powerful. They know how to handle things and they are going to get down to it. In real bad situations they always try to handle it. (Male #017, "Billy," twenty-one-year-old North Side Crip)

Age (in combination with length of time in the gang) was also noted as a major criteria that set leaders apart from other members. In particular, the old gangster, or OG, was a role identified with leadership.

When I first came down here I was already in the gang four years so they made me a old G, old gangster, cause I been in longer than most of the guys that been over there. (Male #014, "D. C.," sixteen-year-old Disciple)

Others talked about the need for the OG or leader only under special circumstances.

If we got a little trouble we think we can handle we take care of that ourselves but if we got some trouble with somebody that have cars and stuff like the Peabody's then we'll go tell him [the leader]. He got the people with the cars and he got most of the guns. (Male #090, "Rellol," fifteen-year-old 19th Street Long Beach Crip)

The significance of age as a criterion for leaders included female gangs.

I'm the leader of the girls. I'm the oldest one. I've been around more than them. (Female #006, "Yolanda," nineteen-year-old 23rd Street Hoover Crip)

Age and physical prowess were not the only criteria for leadership though. Nearly half of the gang members identified leaders as persons who could provide material advantages, thus ascribing a functional character to leadership within the gang. Since half of our sample was in their early teens, someone with the ability to procure cars, drugs, guns, or alcohol could play a valuable role in the gang. Consequently, it was no surprise to find that over half of gang members identified leaders as persons who could "deliver." Because of the situational nature of leadership, persons moved in and out of this role. This was especially true in the case of being able to provide drugs in large quantities for street sales.

INT: Does someone have more juice in the gang?
MALE #041, "C. K.," twenty-two-year-old Blood: Yeah, you always got someone that got more juice.
INT: What is the type of person who usually have more juice?
041: The one who got the connection with the drugs.

INT: Who has the most juice?

MALE #071, "B Daddy," seventeen-year-old Inglewood Family Gangster: Dude named T-Loc.

INT: Why does he have more juice than everybody else?

071: Cause he travels a lot. Gets the good stuff.

INT: What's the good stuff?

071: Like guns, cocaine, weed.

INT: What gives him the juice?

MALE #093, "Lil-P," sixteen-year-old Crenshaw Mob Gangster Blood: He has a lot of dope and stuff like that and he handle our business.

Others reported that selling drugs gave people "juice," or influence, within the gang.

If you sell dope, you get the power. If you don't sell dope, you just one of the boys. (White male #091, "Paul," eighteen-year-old 107 Hoover Crip)

The functional quality assigned to leaders within these gangs suggests that leadership is not a product of motivational skills (i.e., charismatic leaders) or organizational skills (bureaucratic skills) but rather emerges from the ability to satisfy everyday needs of the gang.

Having a leader is the first step in role differentiation for gangs. While half of our sample told us their gang had a leader, fewer told us that there were distinct roles within their gang. Often this varied within gangs, with older members more likely to identify roles (however general) than did their younger counterparts. This indicates that the structure of the gangs whose members we interviewed were more informal and less organized than has been suggested by at least one commentator (see especially Sanchez-Jankowski 1991). Little role specialization exists within these gangs beyond being able to provide drugs or guns. This is reflected in the role differentiation reported by gang members. Only two-thirds of our sample reported that their gang had identifiable roles, and there were few gradations between those roles. Indeed, most members fell into one of two categories, regular members (56 percent of that group) or those who occupied a middle status, situated between the leaders and regular members (44 percent of that group). In most cases, this "rank" was earned as a consequence of engaging in acts of violence against rival gang members.

I was a G. Most gangsters say I have more brains than a lot of people. I was a G3. When I left I was a G6. G6, that's a whole lot of rank. (Male #014, "D. C.," sixteen-year-old Disciple)

Another gang member told us, "Some of the rules are just passed on from way back" (#031).

The specific behaviors prohibited by the rules included five major categories: (1) disrespecting your colors, (2) fighting members of your own gang, (3) "snaking," or turning in a member of your own gang, (4) running from a fight, and (5) "perpetrating," or pretending to be a member of a rival gang. Just under half of the gang members mentioned rules governing what colors could be worn and how they could be displayed. However, we received the most strongly worded responses when questions about perpetrating were asked. Just over half of the gang members told us that perpetrators (or "busters" as they were also known) would hang around with rival gang members or pretend to be a member of more than one gang.

> MALE #027, "G-Loc," fifteen-year-old Gangster Disciple: The worst rule you could break would be being a perpetrator.
> INT: What do you mean by perp?
> 027: A perpetrator like say you down with the Gs and then they see you with the Bloods.

> INT: Are there any rules to you all group?
> MALE #089, "C-Note," fifteen-year-old 88 Street Mob member: Yeah. Just don't be perpetrating. If you gonna be down with us don't be down with somebody else.
> INT: What happens if somebody get caught perpetrating?
> 089: They would probably end up being shot.

In a life under threat of physical violence, it is important to know who can be counted on when actual violence is encountered. Clearly, a perpetrator cannot be depended on under such circumstances. Similarly, someone who would run from a fight is not worthy of trust, especially since the majority of gang members define the gang in terms of violent activities.

> One of them [rules] is never run away from a fight, help one another if it's a fighting thing. (Male #082, "Dough Boy," fourteen-year-old B Gangster Disciple)

> MALE #036, "NA," eighteen-year-old Compton Gangsters BIC: We made a vow when we first started. Whenever we fight, whoever we fight, if one fight we all fight.
> INT: What happens if somebody break the rules, like don't fight?
> 036: He getting his ass whupped. Like if I was fighting and one of my

> boys don't help me. If I get put in the hospital or something then the rest of them going to whup them.

The need to depend on fellow gang members is enhanced by the threat of violence common to life in the gang. Because gang members face the potential for violence moving throughout the city, as well as in their own neighborhood, the need to know who they can count on is intensified. For this reason, rules that proscribe deceiving fellow gang members take on added importance. It is not surprising that such rules were reported by a number of our subjects.

> Don't steal from me. Don't snake your partner out. And, uh, don't lie. (Male #001, "Mike-Mike," twenty-year-old Thundercat)

> There are certain individual rules like snaking and stuff like that. We don't like them to be with us and them be with somebody else. (Male #030, "Kenneth," nineteen-year-old Thundercat)

The need to respect the symbols or colors of the gang was reported as a rule by just over one-third of subjects. Such rules included the colors that could be worn, how much of a particular color could be worn, which way a hat could be turned, what letters could be used in speaking, or how the pants could be worn. Crip gangs generally wore blue clothes, turned their hats and belts to the right, and refrained from using the letter "b." Blood gang members generally wore red, turned their belts and hats to the left, and avoided using the letter "c" wherever possible. In addition, the "rag" or bandana worn hanging from the pocket was of particular importance. These symbolic representations of membership had significant consequences for being able to recognize whether a member was "safe" or in enemy territory.

> You wear red you get beat. If you wear green or brown you got to take it off. (Male #032, "Skonion," seventeen-year-old Thundercat)

> Don't throw your rag on the ground. That's it, no other rules. You put your rag on the ground and you might get killed. You don't get killed you gonna wish you would be and don't fraternize with no Crabs. (Male #041, "C. K.," twenty-two-year-old Blood)

We found no consistent source of the rules reported by the gang members we interviewed. Indeed, the most notable feature of the responses to this question was the lack of a pattern. One gang member told us that "everybody" made the rules, "Everybody does. I can't really say who made the rules" (#016), while another told us that they came from the movie *Colors* (#034). Other gang members reported more abstract sources for the rules that governed their behavior. These included such authors as the "High Priest" (#023), King David, originator of the Hoover Crips (#016, #028), King Piru, originator of the Bloods (#059), or simply the King (#097). When pressed, our subjects were unable to confirm the existence of any of these individuals.

The punishments for violating the rules reflected the centrality of violence to the gang. Some reported that a rule violation would result in a loss of rank. In most cases, however, the punishments were more severe, involving, at a minimum, a beating.

> MALE #043, "Lee Roy," sixteen-year-old Rolling 60's Crip: We would have to see what's up with them, beat them down once or twice then see if he wants out.
> INT: Give him a whupping?
> 043: Yeah.

> We'll beat them up then give them a second chance. Then if they want to get out they can get out. If they get out they might join another gang, and if they join another gang we gonna get somebody to get 'em. (Male #069, "X-Men," fourteen-year-old Inglewood Family Gangster)

Another gang member reported that when he was initiated by gang members from California, he was told that people who broke the rules would be killed. When pressed, this gang member (#005) said that he had not seen it happen. One final statement captures the underlying tone of many comments about the consequences of breaking the rules, underscoring the violence that is ever present in the lives of gang members.

> INT: What happens if somebody breaks that one rule.
> MALE #072, "Blood," seventeen-year-old Swan Park 59 Blood: Tragic things could occur. If someone was to break that rule anything could be happening.

Meetings. Another measure of the degree of formalization in organizations can be seen in whether or not the organization holds meetings. The gang members we interviewed were evenly split on this matter; about half indicated their gang held meetings and half said the gang did not meet. There is a remarkable similarity, however, in the way members of these two groups describe gatherings of gang members, suggesting that the term meeting is too formal to account for most of these engagements and that variation in responses by members of the same group were common. A frequent theme among those who denied that the gang had meetings was that they just "hung out" with each other.

> We just chill on the corner and talk to each other. (Male #093, "Lil-P," sixteen-year-old Crenshaw Mob Gangster Blood)

> We get together everyday. We decide on anything. Like today when we go home we might meet up at the park and decide. One of us might say let's go downtown to the mall. We say we down and go all the way down the line to see who's down. (Male #003, "Jerry," eighteen-year-old Thundercat)

Approximately half of the gang members who reported that they did not have meetings said there was no need to meet, as they saw each other on the street anyway. Typical of such comments were those offered by two gang members who denied that they had "meetings" but acknowledged that they did indeed "meet" with other members on a daily basis.

Even for those who claimed the gang met regularly, an air of spontaneity and informality characterized their accounts of the meetings. The most formal description of a meeting was given in explaining how to deal with problems from drug sales.

> All heads to the table. We go over to Terry house and all sit down and talk. Hey man, shit ain't going right, you fucking up the money. We have meetings like that talking what we need to do and who tripping. (Male #012, "Lance," twenty-year-old West Side Mob member)

The informal character of meetings was evident in the activities that went on at such events.

> MALE #015, "Karry," fifteen-year-old Crenshaw Gangster Blood: We hug each other, do little hand shakes, drink, smoke weed, bless a 40 [forty-ounce bottle of beer].
> INT: Bless a 40, what's that?
> 015: Bless your homies, them your family.

The informal nature of "meeting" described by gang members provides insight into the level of formalization within the gangs we have studied. One of the functions of meetings is to reinforce the cohesiveness of the gang. The absence of such formal events, however, does not mean that the frequent, informal meetings of gang members on the corner don't fulfill that purpose. Quite to the contrary, the bonds of membership are reinforced daily by the steady pattern of "hanging out" that most members engage in. When pressed, this is what the vast majority, over 90 percent, of gang members identify as meetings.

Junior Gangs. Another measure of the extent to which gangs have a formal structure concerns whether they have a separate gang for younger members. Gangs that have a formal "training ground" for younger members have a more formal structure and have taken active steps to insure their perpetuation beyond a single generation. Nearly two-thirds (65 percent) of gang members we interviewed told us that their gangs lacked such groups, and even those who claimed that their gang had a separate named group for younger members described a very loose structure. This is not to discount the imitation of older gang members by younger individuals in the neighborhood, because such patterns of imitation were indeed quite pronounced. However, we discovered few purposive efforts by older gang members to organize youngsters in the neighborhood. One third of our respondents told us that their gang maintained a junior gang. Despite this, activities in the gang remained age graded, with drug sales and weapons procurement being the province of older gang members (generally seventeen and over), and fighting, property crime, and general expressive gang behaviors being most common among younger members (usually sixteen and younger).

The imitative process is often extended to adolescents who were quite young.

> They try to stick together. I say what happen this summer. Through the summer it be so hot everybody just hang out. That little huge park where everybody hang out, bring they radios over there, little kids be trying to wear blue, doing the signs, talking about I'm down with you guys. They try to get together and do something like that. They be about seven or eight years old or something like that. (Male #003, "Jerry," eighteen-year-old Thundercat)

> Yeah, we be together and they want to be with us and then they just make their own little group and copy us. (Male #008, "Robert," fourteen-year-old Compton Gangster)

The attractiveness of the hip street life that gang members have come to represent minimizes the need for forming such groups. Young children in neighborhoods find the behavior of gang members attractive enough that gangs need not consciously organize them. However, even among those who deny the existence of junior gangs, the need to think about the future of their gang has an effect on their relationships with younger gang members.

> Mostly we put them in a situation of being used to being in a gang now running around with they little partners and stuff they age. We getting older, we feel like all of us ain't going to be around forever. Some of us might get killed, some of us might get locked behind bars or some of us might just stop and go on with our life. We still got to look back for the future so it's more like we plan on them taking care of this neighborhood too. (Male #036, "NA," eighteen-year-old Compton Gangster BIC)

More vehement denials of a training gang for younger members came from a twenty-one-year-old Crip who replied, "This ain't no community center" (#092) when asked if there was a gang for young people to graduate from.

Just over a third (35 percent) of respondents indicated that junior gangs did exist. However, even among these subjects the descriptions of the level of organization, links to the gang for older members, and activities more closely resembled those of the young people who imitated neighborhood gangs. Referred to as "young schoolers," "Pee Wees," Baby Crips, or Junior Bloods, these organizations were even more loosely organized and informal than the gangs of older members to whom they were related. Others denied that younger residents of the neighborhood were really in the gang, referring to them as "wanna-bes."

Neighborhood Gang. We have characterized gangs in St. Louis as having a strong neighborhood base. Thus there are strong pressures – another form of threat – for young people to join the gang active in their neighborhood. Most gang members told us that, while there was typically no direct coercion to join the gang, life could be pretty difficult for those who refused to do so. Most young people in a neighborhood with an active gang could expect to be "tested" to determine if they were interested in or worthy of joining the gang. Many would decide that joining the gang was their most prudent choice, especially in those neighborhoods plagued by the highest levels of violence. However, we received very few reports of physical coercion in the recruitment of new members.

The neighborhood orientation of St. Louis gangs means that most members, at least at the time the gang began, lived in the same neighborhood. However, urban mobility patterns play a role in dispersing members of the same gang throughout the city. Since most poor city residents move frequently, often from one neighborhood to another, many gang members don't remain in the neighborhood where they joined the gang. This could have two potential effects. On the one hand, by dispersing gang members throughout the city, high residential mobility could weaken ties between individuals and the gang. After all, leaving the neighborhood is one way to diminish the threat presented by one's own as well as rival gangs. On the other hand, high levels of residential mobility could spread the gang throughout the city. The effect of high levels of residential mobility in St. Louis has been compounded by the closing of several public housing projects, where gangs had operated. This had the effect of splintering one of the earliest gangs in St. Louis, the Thundercats. Rather than leaving the gang, or affiliating with other gangs, members of the Thundercats recruited new members and increased the size of their gang, despite the fact that the initial members of the gang no longer lived in close proximity to each other. Such dispersion led this gang to engage in more formal levels of organization, as it depended on meetings and leaders more than did gangs whose members were concentrated in a single neighborhood. It appears that gangs begin in specific neighborhoods and have a strong membership base from that neighborhood. Over time, though, many members leave the neighborhood, and their affiliation with the gang remains.

Most respondents indicated that at the time of its origin, all members of their gang lived in the same neighborhood. For some of the gangs, this remained true, sometimes by design, but other times because the gang was relatively new and none of the members yet had moved with their families to another neighborhood. Maintaining neighborhood affiliations for membership was viewed as important because it was a way to keep out "questionable" members, that is, those who may be "perpetrators" or not tough enough.

INT: So nobody lives outside the neighborhood and is still a member?
MALE #025, "Tony," seventeen-year-old 107 Hoover Gangster Crip: Right.
INT: How long has it been that way?
025: I don't know. We just don't trust nobody that stay outside our neighborhood cause they might bring some little boys from over where they stay to where we at. We don't know nothing about them other dudes.

INT: Do all the members live in the neighborhood?
FEMALE #046, "Lady Tee," sixteen-year-old 74 Hoover Crips: Yes.

INT: Can you live outside the neighborhood and still belong?
046: No.
INT: Why not?
046: Because you can go perpetrate. You claim 74 Hoovers and go back over on the west side and claim Bloods. You will never know.

The neighborhood orientation of gangs illustrates the need to protect against the threat of outsiders or those who may be unreliable because of their allegiance to more than one neighborhood gang. This further illustrates the role of threat in the neighborhood context of gangs. It also serves to increase the cohesiveness among members, heightening their commitment to a common symbol, and enhancing the chances that gang members will commit violence against "intruders."

Over time, however, many gang members move with their families. This is not an unexpected development, since residential mobility is high among the urban poor. This means that while the gang still is based in the same neighborhood, some of its members no longer live there. Most gangs found it necessary, even desirable, to keep these individuals in the gang. And, similarly, the individuals maintained ties to their original gang, in part because they had already been identified as a rival by other gangs. The majority of gang members reported that their gang started by having members exclusively from the neighborhood but that this had changed over time.

> When it first started they all was stayin down there together. Ya know some people moved, some people got put out [evicted] because they in too much trouble, mama was gettin' violations, peace disturbance, trippin with the security guards and all this little stuff. (Male #001, "Mike-Mike," twenty-year-old Thundercat)

In situations where gang members had left the neighborhood, their responsibilities to the gang were not diminished. They were still required to "hang" with the gang.

> You don't necessarily have to stay in the hood as long as you be over there hangin' with the boys. (Male #093, "Lil-P," sixteen-year-old Crenshaw Mob Gangster Blood)

> It's been like that for a while though but you still got to come in the hood every day and say what's up to everybody and say your GD [Gangster Disciple] prayer. (Male #084, "Rolo," fifteen-year-old Rolling 60's Crip)

While it is possible to remain in the gang once you have moved out of the neighborhood, it is essential that you lived in the neighborhood at one time and could be trusted.

> You got to know the hood real good and you got to know everybody in there. If you lived in the neighborhood before. You can't just come in from the outside. (White male #091, "Paul," eighteen-year-old 107 Hoover Crip)

Three-quarters of Laclede Town,[5] a large federal housing project in St. Louis, was closed in the late 1980s, displacing the Thundercats. Members of the gang moved to a number of different neighborhoods, though they still claimed alliance to the Thundercats, and Laclede Town was still their meeting place.

> They separated but I guess that's where everybody moved to that got kicked out of Laclede Town and stuff. It's about six different people that used to stay in Laclede Town stay in O'Fallon Place so they, they got the little O'Fallon place cats hooked up. People just come down there [Laclede Town] to hang out. They come 'bout every weekend to hang out and uh go over to one of their friends houses or something and spend the night down there. (Male #002, "Eric," sixteen-year-old Thundercat)

Thus, even when a neighborhood is rendered uninhabitable, its importance to the gang remains.

The neighborhood was the primary source for recruiting gang members. The gang members we interviewed were evenly split about whether or not individuals were coerced to join their gang, and there was some disagreement within gangs. Most of those who said there was little direct pressure brought to bear on potential members underscored the attractiveness of the gang. In these cases, there was no need to pressure people to do something they wanted to do anyway.

> No, we never did pressure people to join. It was like the cool thing to do. It was like respect, you know what I'm saying. OK, all of us go to a dance, it's a Crip dance, everybody want to start joinin'. (Male #003, "Jerry," eighteen-year-old Thundercat)

> INT: What happens to someone in the neighborhood who doesn't want to join the gang?
> MALE #005, "Antonio," nineteen-year-old 6th Street Hoover Crip: That's up to him. If he don't want to join that's up to him. Now if it's somebody out and they don't live in our neighborhood and they wear other colors we are going to ask them what side they plan to be staying on.

We just tell them to go on your way boy. We don't want nothing to do with you. (Male #008, "Robert," fourteen-year-old Compton Gangster)

Belonging to the gang does confer some advantages, most notably protection, or in some cases, the promise of retaliation against a rival gang if they were to harm an individual. The following quote also illustrates the strong identification of the gang with the neighborhood, as the terms are often used interchangeably.

Nothing actually happens to them. It's just that if they don't help the neighborhood, nobody will help them. Everybody gets in a tight spot sometimes. (Male #040, "Knowledge," twenty-one-year-old Compton Gangster)

Another gang member indicated that people in his neighborhood might as well join the gang, because they will be perceived as a gang member anyway and therefore be a target of other gangs. In this way, the threat posed by gang members in a neighborhood extends to people who live in the neighborhood, whether or not they claim membership in the gang.

It's on his choice. I'm not going to make this man be in a gang if he don't want to gang bang. That's on him. But then there is going to be times that if he hang around us that he going to be labeled as a gang banger anyway. (Male #036, "NA," eighteen-year-old Compton Gangster BIC)

A small number of individuals told us they did put direct pressure on neighborhood residents to join the gang. It was important that people in the neighborhood in the "eligible" categories (i.e., age, race, sex) be affiliated with the gang, to strengthen it in numbers as well as to prevent them from joining a rival gang or being susceptible to becoming a "snitch." The most direct statement of this position came from "Darryl," at twenty-nine, the oldest member of our sample.

If you refuse to be a Blood somebody in your family going to get killed or you are going to get killed. (Male #013, "Darryl," twenty-nine-year-old Blood)

Others told us that people who refused to join were beaten up, either in retaliation for not joining, as an inducement to join, or as a message to others.

They stupid. Most of the time they would get beat anyway or they get loked [stomped] over. (Male #031, "John Doe," sixteen-year-old Thundercat)

They get beat up every day till they join. Spray paint they house. (Male #063, "Bobtimes," sixteen-year-old 6 Deuce Blood)

INT: What happens if there is somebody in the neighborhood that you want in the gang and they refuse to join?

MALE #083, "Winchester," fourteen-year-old Rolling 60's Crip: Well, it's kind of difficult then. We ain't never ran up to nothing like that but if we do, they caught up with them and beat them up bad, I mean whip them up. You talking about somebody that's come in the hood and they say they don't want to be in the gang?

INT: Yeah.

083: He gonna have to make a choice or get his butt whipped every day.

Not all of the threats against people who refuse to join are hypothetical.

They get called stuff. Some of them get beat up. Just a couple of weeks ago someone got shot because they refused and they got killed. They was only 14. He came to basketball practice and they asked him if he was claiming and he said no so they shot him. (White male #100, "J. Bone," nineteen-year-old Insane Gangster Disciple)

The neighborhood plays a vital role in the life of most gangs in St. Louis as it is the principal recruitment ground for new members. Because most gangs emerge from existing neighborhood groups, the ties between members of the same neighborhood and the antagonisms against rivals in neighboring areas already exist. Even when gang members leave their neighborhood, they maintain some level of commitment to the place where their gang originated.

Turf. If the neighborhood defines the rough boundaries of where the gang operates, its "turf" is a specific location of importance within that neighborhood. With only two exceptions, every gang member told us of a specific location that was important to the gang. The responses to this question elicited among the strongest reactions to any issue we raised, typically underscoring the role of threats to gang turf, and the need to be vigilant in defense of that turf against threats from outsiders. Not surprisingly, there was consensus within gangs on this issue. Eighty-one percent of gang members identified the symbolic importance of their turf, either because the gang started there, they lived there, or, most importantly, it was theirs, and its defense was a matter of honor or respect. A smaller number (eleven) pointed to more instrumental reasons in defending their turf, particularly drugs sales, since successful drug sales required a secure turf.

Symbolic reasons were identified by 81 percent of gang members as a reason their turf was important to the gang. For many, because the gang got its origins in a particular area, it was imperative for the gang to protect it.

INT: Is there a particular area or turf that is important to your group?
MALE #004, "Anthony," seventeen-year-old Thundercat: Just Laclede Town.
INT: Why is Laclede Town important to the Thundercats?
004: I guess because that's where it originated.
INT: If somebody from a rival gang comes onto your turf, what does the group do?
004: Whoop them.
INT: No matter what?
004: No matter what.

For others, defending their turf was important because they lived there, and failure to defend it against rival gangs would put them in physical jeopardy or in jeopardy of being run off. This group represented twenty-three of the fifty-nine gang members who responded to this question.

We fought every day. If you walked through the neighborhood and we didn't know you or you didn't know where you was going in the neighborhood we would rush you. (Male #036, "NA," eighteen-year-old Compton Gangster BIC)

INT: Why is it [your turf] important?
MALE #085, "2-Low," eighteen-year-old Rolling 60's Crip: It's important because basically it's where I was raised at. I can't stand to see nobody come on my street and beat me up on my street.

We don't want anybody coming into our neighborhood and thinking they run it. Make sure other gangs don't come and take over your turf and run you out of your own neighborhood. (Male #008, "Robert," fourteen-year-old Compton Gangster)

Just over a third of gang members told us that a particular turf was important to them because of the simple matter of respect; it was their turf and they were not about to see others come onto it. The "trespass" of members of other gangs onto their turf was seen as an affront to the gang, presenting a direct threat of violence as well as the threat that gang members would be "run" or "told what to do" by other gangs.

INT: Is there a particular area of turf that's important to your gang?
MALE #075, "Tyrell," sixteen-year-old Bounty Hunter Blood: My old street.

INT: Why is it important?
075: It's where we used to hang out, old memories and stuff.

While symbolic reasons, like respect, provided the justification for defending their turf for the majority of gang members, a sizable fraction expressed more instrumental concerns. Almost exclusively, these concerns focused on the need to have a secure turf from which to sell drugs.

> You let them know cause you got the area so tight. This house right here we selling out of, this house across the street we selling out of, right here. If you come up in there and they still there doing some stuff, they don't get out of there, they come in but they don't come out. (Male #019, "Anthony," twenty-two-year-old Crip)

INT: Is there a turf or an area that's important to your gang?
MALE #015, "Karry," fifteen-year-old Crenshaw Gangster Blood: Dope house is the most important. That's how you make your living.
INT: If somebody from another gang tried to come into your dope house or come on the property of your dope house, what would happen to them?
015: He would get shot.

Nearly 90 percent of gang members acknowledged that they had defended their turf against rival gang members in the past year. The primary means by which the turf was defended was through fighting, and guns were used in over 95 percent of these skirmishes. When asked how they defended their turf, most gang members provided graphic responses that indicate the extent to which they were willing to insure that it was secure.

INT: If someone from another gang comes to your turf what does your gang do?
MALE #019, "Anthony," twenty-two-year-old Crip: First try to tell him to leave.
INT: If he don't leave?
019: He'll leave one way or the other, carry him out in a Hefty bag.

MALE #013, "Darryl," twenty-nine-year-old Blood: A guy came in [to our turf], he had the wrong colors on, he got to move out. He got his head split open with a sledgehammer, he got two ribs broken, he got his face torn up.
INT: Did he die from that?
013: I don't know. We dropped him off on the other side of town.
INT: In that incident, did you do anything?
013: Yes, I'm the one that split his head open.

If they Crips, if they don't come prepared then that's where they gonna lay. That's just like trespassing, if you get caught you go to jail. If they get caught on our set they going to hell. (Male #072, "Blood," seventeen-year-old Swan Park 59 Blood)

These responses illustrate the matter-of-factness associated with acts of violence used to protect turf. Almost all gang members accept it as a given that incursions on their turf will be met with violent responses, as will their trespasses onto the turf of rival gang members. Talk of the need for defending gang turf occurs on a regular basis among gang members, far more often than do actual acts of defense. In this way an atmosphere of symbolic vigilance against the threat of outside intruders draws the gang together and prepares it to use the expressive (and excessive) violence often associated with defending home territory against rival gangs. These processes again underscore the role of threat in providing explanations for the nature and level of violence which occurs between gangs. When such acts are actually carried out, they provide the basis for "legends," the mythic violence identified by Klein (1971) that serves to increase cohesiveness among gang members. In the end, then, defending gang turf is an important activity, one that generates a considerable amount of violence and discussions of violence.

Subgroups

Every gang member reported that there were subgroups within the gang that he or she hung out with most often. This is not surprising; after all, gangs in our sample averaged just over two hundred members, too large for daily associations and activities and certain to attract police scrutiny. However, the subgroups within gangs reflected more than these pragmatic concerns. Subgroups consisted of between two and ten friends and were based on friendships usually formed prior to entering the gang. Two different sorts of activities were more likely to take place in the subgroups than within the entire gang. First, members of the subgroup engaged in conventional adolescent activities together. These activities included such things as watching television, playing basketball, "chilling," drinking, shopping, and interacting with members of the opposite sex. Many of these activities were not related to the gang; indeed it is hard to think of "gang-related television watching" as a meaningful category of behavior for understanding gangs.

However, the subgroup was also the locus for a second type of behavior, one that had a more instrumental character. Drug sales, stealing, and robbery were activities far more characteristic of the subgroup than the gang as a whole. In fact, only a handful of gang members told us that income-generating crime was motivated or organized by the gang as a whole. These activities were much more likely to occur in the context of smaller subgroups. This stands in stark contrast to the activities that took place when the gang as a whole got together – campaigns, drive-by shootings, and retaliatory strikes against rival gangs. These activities have a much more expressive character, providing little of direct, instrumental gain, but reinforcing the bonds of membership and allegiance to the gang and territorial boundaries.

As observed above, subgroups within the gang were the source of "typical" adolescent activities not narrowly associated with gang membership. The activities mentioned most frequently in this context were social in nature.

> Go shopping, play basketball, hoop up, getting beer, walk ourselves around the neighborhood, find some whores. (Male #065, "BK Kill," nineteen-year-old North County Crip)

> We mostly go to the show, we go shopping. Sometimes we might even ride bikes. (Male #031, "John Doe," sixteen-year-old Thundercat)

> The Gs mostly the ones I hang out with. We just sit around playing cards, watching TV or some videotapes, go over to some gal's house, something like that. (Male #036, "NA," eighteen-year-old Compton Gangster BIC)

Girl gang members differed from their male counterparts in two primary ways: they more often indicated that they went shopping with their gang subgroup and were interested in looking for boys.

Many of our subjects explained that there was a small circle of friends they spent most of their time with.

> I say five that I hang out with: BJ, Redrum, Looney, CKR, and Blue Gauge and that's it. We just be chilling sometimes. Just chill at one of they house and watch TV or something. (Male #067, "$hortDog," fifteen-year-old Inglewood Family Blood)

These friendship subgroups were also the locus of criminal behaviors of an instrumental nature.

> We do stuff together, make our money and stuff. (Male #082, "Dough Boy," fourteen-year-old B Gangster Disciple)

Go to the movies, most of the time we go buy Nintendo cartridges and play Nintendo for awhile. Go to Children's Palace. They be going in there stealing and stuff. (Male #084, "Rolo," fifteen-year-old Rolling 60's Crip)

The whole gang only seemed to come together when under the threat of danger from a rival gang. Many respondents divulged that the gang got together as a whole only when "something" was about to happen, typically a fight.

But if something happen like a fight or something then that's when you hook up on everybody. (Male #048, "Corkey," sixteen-year-old Rolling 60's Crip)

The threat of violence from a rival gang plays the important function of a catalyst, uniting members of the gang against a common enemy. Initially, we were puzzled by the consistent reports we received from gang members that they went skating with the whole gang, not just their subgroup. This seemed inconsistent with the general explanation that informal social activities were confined to the subgroup, and expressive actions (or their threat) took place in the context of the whole gang. We learned an explanation for this puzzle from "X-Men," a member of the Ingelwood Family Gangsters.

INT: As a gang what do you all do?
MALE #069, fourteen-year-old Inglewood Family Gangster: Go skating.
INT: What else?
069: That's about all on the weekends. When the skating be open all gangs be up in there, all the Bloods be up in there.

Because the skating rink is a site where rival gangs are known to congregate in large numbers, it is important to go there with the entire gang, not to go there only in a subgroup. The skating rink serves as a staging ground for violence given the presence of large numbers of gang members from rival gangs; thus it is important to have the protection afforded by large numbers of fellow gang members.

The gangs whose members we interviewed had little in the way of formal structure or organization. Rather, St. Louis gangs were loosely confederated groups of neighborhood residents. Cultural transmission plays a central role in the spread of such gangs, and informal processes play a large part in keeping gangs together. Despite their lack of a formal structure, St. Louis gangs are involved in a variety of minor and serious criminal acts. In the next two chapters, we examine these topics.

"Where You Hanging? Let's Go Banging": What Gang Members Do

MALE #013, "Darryl," 29 year-old Blood: Yeah, we hang out together, we go to parties together. We drink together, we also go kill together.
INT: What activities do you do the most with other gang members?
013: Just fuck around.

SO SAYS THE OLDEST active member we interviewed.[1] His conjunction of harmless socializing and lethal violence is echoed in the voices of younger gang members, and their words reflect two polar opposites of the group behavior of gang members. Like most teenagers and young adults, gang members in St. Louis do a lot of "hanging" with their friends – watching television, drinking beer, sitting and talking, shooting hoops, smoking weed, cruising, looking for girls. Gang members spend their lives (and most often commit their crimes) in groups (Zimring 1981; Klein 1971) and what those groups usually do together is nothing more than "just fuck around."

But the litany above finishes with: "we also go kill together," an indication of the integral role violence plays in the lives of gang members. Nonlethal and lethal force is routinized through initiation rites involving "beating in" and shooting at enemies, in dealings with drug customers, and in "gang banging" – fighting with rival gangs, beating up interlopers or insulters, drive-by shootings, planned killings. Violence is both a defining attribute of gangs (Thrasher 1927) and an epitomizing activity that sharply differentiates the lives of gang members from their nongang peers. One sixteen-year-old male subject, a member of the 6 Deuce Bloods, pointed out the contradiction of being both "just like young people" and a violent criminal:

MALE #063, "Bobtimes": We chill out, sell dope, mess with girls just like young people.

INT: Is that all you all do? Gang banging?

063: Yeah, we gang banging, shoot, 187.

INT: 187? What's that?

063: A drive-by.

INT: You said sell drugs, chase girls, gang bang, chill out, 187s, anything else?

063: No, just act like teenagers.

Teenagers who use guns and sell drugs.

It is important to distinguish between gang and nongang activities as well as between serious and nonserious criminality of gang members. In order to identify the role of the gang in enhancing criminality, it is necessary to distinguish between those activities that take place with other gang members and those with nongang members. In addition, it is important to differentiate serious crime from more minor offenses that are commonplace among both gang and nongang members. The next two chapters describe what our subjects do as members of their gang (group activities) and what they do with other gang members (as friends) – a distinction that some subjects perceived quite acutely. In this chapter, we first discuss how gang members spend *most* of their time together – hanging out – as well as the varied noncriminal activities they engage in. Next is a discussion of "cafeteria-style" minor delinquency of gang members (Klein 1971, 125): shoplifting, thefts of services, petty thievery, public order violations (disturbing the peace, gambling in public, loitering), spraying graffiti (and other forms of vandalism), underage drinking, and drug taking. The third section discuss nongang activities of gang members – things they do with friends, peers, and/or relatives who are not in the gang.

"Me and My Partners Just Chill Out, Talk to the Females": Noncriminal Gang Activities

Gang members spend much of their time together being "normal" teenagers or young adults: hanging out at each others' homes, in parks, on street corners, at fast food joints, malls, skating rinks, bowling alleys, and youth clubs. When we asked subjects "what do you do the most with other gang members" the dominant answer was "hang out" (or one of many equivalents – "chill out," "playing," "hang," "fuck around"). Figure 5.1 displays the percentage distribution.

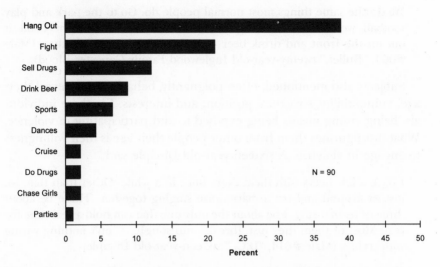

Figure 5.1 Most Common Gang Activity

About two-fifths of the subjects chose "hanging out." Nearly two-thirds of the responses involved fairly innocuous and noncriminal behaviors (drinking beer, sports, dances, cruising, chasing girls, doing drugs, parties). Other researchers have found a similar pattern of activity among gang members in a wide variety of times and places (Klein 1971; Moore 1978; Vigil 1988; Padilla 1992; Sanchez-Jankowski 1991; Short and Strodbeck 1974; Thrasher 1927). Given the importance of friendship subgroups or cliques within St. Louis gangs this dominant activity is unsurprising – it is a continuation of both pregang and nongang behaviors. In other words they "just act like teenagers" with their friends, who (not so coincidentally) are also gang members.

Hanging out includes watching television, drinking beer, smoking weed, playing sports, walking malls, cruising for girls.

> The Gs [old gangsters] mostly the ones I hang out with. We just sit around playing cards, watching TV or some videotapes, go over to some gal's house, something like that. (Male #036, "NA," eighteen-year-old Compton Gangster)

> We have our own little baseball team and stuff. We go swimming all summer long, stuff like that. Be with our girls. Like two or three of us will be at whoever's house with our girls. Go over and have fun like that. Get drunk most of the time together. (Male #039, "Kaons BIC," seventeen-year-old Compton Gangster)

We do the same things most normal people do. Go to the park and play football, we do the same thing they all do, it's just that we tight. I still sit out on the front and drink beer with them. We always together. (Male #060, "Bullet," twenty-year-old Inglewood Family Gangster Blood)

Subjects also mentioned, often poignantly, behaviors that reveal their age, vulnerability, structural position, and interests. For these individuals, being young means being exposed to and participating in violence. What distinguishes them from other people their age is their willingness to engage in violence. A sixteen-year-old Disciple said:

I have a few beers with them every once in a while. Other than that, we just sit around and try to harmonize singing together. There be about three of us that sing. I be about the only one that can hold a real tune for real. Most of them they just. [breaks into song] . . . ain't nothing wrong with trying. (Male #014, "D.C.," sixteen-year-old Disciple)

Sports are an important part of many of these adolescents' lives (although few remain involved in school-sponsored or other organized team sports after joining a gang).

We just hang around most of the time. We mostly hang around and do sporty things. (Male #009, "Marrien," fifteen-year-old Compton Gangster)

Play football against the Crips or something like that. We have it where there is no violence. (Male #020, "Lil Thug," sixteen-year-old Disciple)

But not all subjects were athletically graced:

No, don't nobody play no sports. (Male #067, "$hortDog," sixteen-year-old Inglewood Family Blood)

These behaviors are not against the law and, in fact, many of our subjects do not view themselves or their acts as criminal. Two young men interviewed together illustrated this.

Talk about each other and joke around. We be wrestling and stuff. (Male #021, "40 Ounce," sixteen-year-old 107 Hoover Crip)

We ain't what you call real bad people. We just trying to take over our set that's all. We down. It ain't like we a lynch mob hanging together. (Male #022, "8 Ball," fifteen-year-old 107 Hoover Crip)

Gang members' joint activities also reflect various constraints. Age, for example, may limit what they can do and when they can do it. Two of our youngest subjects, thirteen and fourteen years old, gave age-dependent descriptions of what they do most with their gang. One said that he "go[es] downtown. We walk or ride our bikes" (male #094, "John Doe," 107 Hoover Crip). These young gang members apparently did not steal cars (or do not hang with older members who do). The other subject, a Rolling 60's Crip, said that what he did most with the gang was "sit around, spray paint on the corners" (male #080, "Coke Cane").

Forty percent of our subjects were still in school when we interviewed them, and 17 percent had legal jobs. Although they hung out with fellow members in school (and sometimes worked with other gang members), they were mainly "down with their boys" after school or work and on weekends.

It's Friday, it's the weekend, baby. We might kick it all through the whole week. Like today we might go down to the mall later, like when it starts getting dark. That's the only time we out when it starts getting dark, terrorizing, but we ain't going looking for no trouble because we don't want to get locked up on the weekend. We might buy ten forty-ounces, just walk down there and get full, and just go down there and clown or something like that you know. We not real bad until we have to get bad you know. We not a really dangerous gang you know. (Male #003, "Jerry," eighteen-year-old Thundercat)

Postadolescent gang members are also constrained. A twenty-two-year-old Compton Gangster described a typical day for himself and his subgroup within the gang:

Well mostly what we do, we hang out. We start our day out looking for a job. We fill out applications. We stop looking for jobs about 1:00, start at 8:30 and stop at 1:00. We get a little R [reefer]. Sit in the park and get R'ed out. All us be rapping about our boys that just passed. We sit up and rap about it. We call them our dead homies. If none of our boys come with a problem, somebody rolled them or something like that, we just sit out in the park and chill. We laugh, rap, have a little moment of peace for our boys, take a swig, everybody breaks to a crib and eats and then meet back up. Then everybody go and do what they gonna do, just like that. (Male #037, "Big Money")

Being identified or known as a gang member also limits activities as members are easily recognized. Our subjects said the best way an average person could tell who was in a gang was because an individual was "wearing colors" (fifty-seven subjects), by their "clothes" (twenty-seven subjects), or by "hand signals" (eight subjects).

Cause I be going around wearing red and throwing signs up. (Male #080, "Coke Cane," thirteen-year-old, Rolling 60's Blood)

I be wearing my hat to the right and my rag hanging out of my pocket and the way I be saying things and when I be throwing up my signs and stuff, that's about it. (Male #084, "Rolo," fifteen-year-old Rolling 60's Crip)

Police surveillance or harassment of known or suspected gang members was another restraint on subjects' activities.

Sit around, chill, eat, go over to girl's house, that about all. It's me, my cousin and about two more boys, that about all, around four of us. We can't walk in Pine Lawn with more than three people. (Male #069, "X-Men," fifteen-year-old Ingelwood Family Gangster Blood)

Sometimes they [the police] just mess with you. Like a dude will be sitting on a porch and ain't bothering nobody. They come up and start checking you and stuff to see if you got any dope. Sometimes they make you pull your pants down, take your shoes off, socks off, coat, jacket, hat and all that. (Male #055, "Chris," seventeen-year-old Hoover Crip)

Neighbors are also, in general, unsympathetic to gang members and often actively hostile to their presence.

No, they think it's a bunch of hoodlums. Yeah, bunch of kids getting ready to do something bad. When they hear shooting and all that they call the police and the police is everywhere. They usually be scared for real and don't come out of they house or something. (Male #063, "Bobtimes," sixteen-year-old Six Deuce Blood)

They hated us. They asked for more security. They just really hated us, just put that. (Male #092, "Derone," twenty-one-year-old Rolling 60's Crip)

Only three subjects said that the neighborhood had positive feelings toward their gang (although thirty members said that the neighborhood liked them as individuals).

MALE #018, "Maurice," twenty-year-old 107 Hoover Crip: They think it's [the gang] silly and crazy and stupid.
INT: Do they like you?
018: Yeah, they like me but they want me to better myself cause they knew me for a little while and when they talk to me and I talk to them they say this boy got a head on his shoulder, you don't need to be in there. You got too much to live for. Look at you, you are twenty years old. Think about when you turn 65. I said that's some thought. The lady next door

to me she brought it to my attention. She say, don't you want to see your grandkids? I said yeah I want to see my grandkids. Well you better get out of that gang or you won't see them. Yeah, they feel threatened. Only reason they feel threatened is they can't even walk out of they house or they can't drive down the street without seeing somebody get killed or getting shot. Bullets passing them.

Yeah, most of the people in my neighborhood like me, they just don't like the people that I hang out with. (Male #084, "Rolo," fifteen-year-old Rolling 60's Crip)

Our subjects were evenly split in their answers to the question "Does the neighborhood feel threatened by you?" Thirty-three said no; thirty-three said yes; thirty-three gave no answer. But only twenty-six said that the neighborhood was not afraid of them (or their gang), while forty-three indicated that the neighborhood *was* afraid. And fifty-eight subjects said that residents regularly called the police about their gang. Some members said they got revenge on those neighbors who "snitched" on them (although this may have been wishful thinking).

> MALE #002, "Eric," sixteen-year-old Thundercat: Yeah. Call theyself snitchin, but they don't tell my momma nothin she don't know.
> INT: So they tell your mother?
> 002: Yeah, they call theyself tellin my mother. Then when they get they window bust out, shot out door, they gonna be wishin they never did nothin like that.
> INT: Have you actually done that?
> 002: Naw, yeah. But they didn't tell my momma, call the police or somethin like that. But I done busted some people window out for tellin my momma cause I didn't want to hurt em wit no gun so I bust out they window. But if they call the police on me yeah, I'm gonna shoot up their house door or something for a warning.

Relations with the neighborhood are not always negative. At least two members of one gang, the Compton Gangsters, argued that they were a positive force in the neighborhood.

No, we cool with all our neighbors. We protect everybody in our neighborhood. You can be a neighbor, say you are a lady, if a boy goes over there jumping on her and we see it we will jump on him. We watch out for our neighborhood, don't let nobody do no burglaries or jumping. If there is fighting around there we doing it. (Male #038, "G.O.D.," nineteen-year-old Compton Gangster)

> Our group is 66 members all trying to eliminate the gang flow and violence that flows through our community. We can't worry about somebody else's community. We just try to stop it from flowing through our community. We look out for the elderly, we cut grass for nothing, we go to the store for our old people, we do all that stuff like the Italian gangsters used to do. Throw barbecues, we throwing a barbecue today for the whole hood in the park. We went to the store yesterday and spent about six hundred dollars on meat. (Male #040, "Knowledge," twenty-one-year-old Compton Gangster)

But most gangs did not hold block parties, throw barbecues, or otherwise try to create any sort of "collective effervescence" with their neighbors. We find no evidence, however, that gangs have emerged as neighborhood vigilantes, protecting residents from street crime or the unscrupulous practices of businessmen. And the notion that gangs were actively involved in efforts to quell violence, while popular in the media, was unsubstantiated by the actions or words of our subjects.

Fear was the most commonly mentioned constraint on gang members, especially with regard to concerts and dances, although fears regarding rival gangs and the possibility of serious violence did not necessarily prevent some members from doing things. This further illustrates the role of threat, which constrains the activities of gang members while compelling them toward violence. Over time, such threats limit interactions between gang members and nongang peers and activities.

> Ok, they all be at the concerts right, the VTOs, the Crips, Thundercats and the Bloods, and one, a few, one little Bloods can just walk up to em and what's up with that dude, bam, hit em in the jaw and then it's gonna be the Bloods into a fight. That's just how it be. (Male #001, "Mike-Mike," twenty-year-old Thundercat)

> Mostly we go to concerts. It be plenty of Blood gang and that's the only time we really do some heavy fighting. You know where the Arena is? We went down in blue, stole us a couple of vans, went to the concert, packed all the guns we had. (Male #003, "Jerry," eighteen-year-old Thundercat)

> No. You can get busted at concerts. (Male #048, "Corkey," sixteen-year-old Rolling 60's Crip)

Age and danger also interact to constrain activities, as these quotes from members of the same gang illustrate. First, an older member on going to concerts:

Oh, yeah. We don't go without our boys, never know what's gonna happen down there. (Male #060 "Bullet," twenty-year-old Inglewood Family Gangster Blood)

And then his younger compatriot:

INT: Do you guys go to concerts together?
MALE #067, "$hortDog," fifteen-year-old Inglewood Family Blood: No.
INT: How come?
067: Sometimes you always find Crabs somewhere.
INT: So it's kind of dangerous?
067: Yeah.

Partying, in various guises – dances, parties, drinking, using drugs, cruising, looking for women – is also often cited as a common activity done with other gang members.

Go to dances. Just chill and drink, smoke dope. Go get a couple of beers, chill out, find a female. Me and my partners just drink beer, chill out, talk to the females, whatever. (Male #004, "Anthony," seventeen-year-old Thundercat)

Go to ball games, out to eat. We go to dances more. (Female #011, "Lisa," fifteen-year-old Compton Gangster)

Drink and go to dances. (Male #044, "Paincuzz," sixteen-year-old Rolling 60's Crip)

Three of these rather harmless activities – drinking, drugs, and driving – do involve criminality. The mean age of our subjects is seventeen, well below the legal drinking age of twenty-one, yet 9 percent of the active members said they spent the most time with the gang drinking, and almost all subjects mentioned drinking as a common group activity. Beer in forty-ounce bottles is the beverage of choice; malt liquor and wine are occasionally drunk; hard liquor is seldom mentioned. Drinking can also lead to fighting and violence and, it appears, sex (or mythologized sex).

MALE #018, "Maurice," twenty-year-old 107 Hoover Crip: Drink beer, smoke weed, sit back and laugh and joke, sell dope. Sometimes we fucked the same woman about three or four times.
INT: What kinds of things did you do the most with the gang members?
018: Mostly selling drugs and doing it with the same woman three or four times.

Yeah, we calmed down from the way it used to be. There used to be a time every Thursday was DGF, don't give a fuck. We just get drunk. Get stupid drunk and whoever we see walking we just jump on them. Fool around, selling dope. (Male #038, "G.O.D.," nineteen-year-old Compton Gangster)

Drink beer and after we get drunk we go out and get rowdy sometimes. But we like to get rowdy when we are sober too. Like in the summertime we have barbecues and shit, have ourselves not a party, but have 10 or 12 of us out there. And then somebody will say hey man, I heard them hooks out there in Golden Gardens is talking that shit again. (White male #099, "Joe L.," eighteen-year-old Disciple)

Only two subjects nominated doing drugs as the most common gang activity, although almost all subjects said that drug use (usually only marijuana smoking, according to them) was fairly common for most members.

Get high. (Female #096, "L. C.," twenty-three-year-old Inglewood Bounty Hunter)

Chill and smoke weed. (Male #042, "Leroy," seventeen-year-old Rolling 60's Crip)

Cruising – riding around in cars with "no particular place to go" – was mentioned by two subjects as the most common thing they do with their gang. Often linked with looking for women or girls, it is a very common young adult and teenage pursuit that is not, of course, illegal. But cruising by gang members often involves serious illegality. Most do not have a driver's license, insurance coverage, or, for that matter, a car. They borrow vehicles from older relatives – siblings, parents, cousins – or, more typically, steal from the gang's or a nearby neighborhood.

Yeah, mostly we does that [steal a car]. We catch up on new areas, new territory where we can sell our dope, stuff like that. (Male #018, "Maurice," twenty-year-old 107 Hoover Crip)

Everybody goes and steals them a car or whatever and we go cruising. (Male #005, "Antonio," nineteen-year-old 6th Street Crip)

Steal cars, go riding, go start some trouble with some Crabs. (Male #067, "$hortDog," fifteen-year-old Inglewood Family Gangster Blood)

Cars are also "borrowed" from drug "fiends."

No, we get all our cars from fiends. They give them to us for awhile but we don't give them back. They got to catch us, trick us. We go to the liquor store and come out and they sitting on they car like man, your time up. I want my car back. We give them the keys and say all right, drop us off here. But the next week they come back. We always keep it longer than we supposed to. Except when they got to go to work we give them the car back so they can go to work cause we know when they get off they gonna come and give it right back to us. (Male #038, "G.O.D.," nineteen-year-old Compton Gangster)

Much of what gang members do together is innocuous and not atypical for their age or social position. Nongang members from the same neighborhoods and schools hang out together, drink, use drugs, go to parties, dances, and concerts. Most of the time our subjects spend with other gang members is a continuation of pregang behaviors – things they did before they joined the gang, usually with the same group of people – and activities they would probably engage in if they were not gang members.

There is, however, a discontinuity in our subjects' descriptions of what they do together. The disjunction of harmless adolescent and young adult behaviors and varying levels of criminality is vividly emphasized by many subjects.

Chill out. Nothin, we don't do nothin. Hey man, that's about all we do together you know. We have shoot outs and stuff. (Male #002, "Eric," seventeen-year-old Thundercat)

We sell drugs together, fight together, go to dances together, hang out together, we do a lot of stuff. Smoke together, drink together. (Female #046, "Lady Tee," fifteen-year-old 74 Hoover Crip)

Do different things just like a family. Hang out together, rob, steal cars, fight other gangs like for competition. Mostly just fight against other gang members then sell drugs. (Male #017, "Billy," twenty-one-year-old North Side Crip)

These descriptions of common gang activities – with their overtones of violence, drug sales, and criminality – conform more to common stereotypes of gangs. And indeed, criminality of various kinds can be seen as a distinguishing marker both of being gang members and of the existence of a particular gang.

We found little evidence of intergang variation in our subjects' dominant behaviors. Only a few subjects (usually older ones) stressed that they did not regularly hang out with their fellow members. For most respondents, "hanging" with their gang peers was their dominant activity, and we have no evidence to think this is not true of their gang compatriots we did not speak with or observe.

But much of the criminality associated with gang members is not necessarily gang motivated or gang initiated. And here again our subjects are not probably much different from their nongang peers in St. Louis neighborhoods. Low-order illegalities engaged in by teenagers and young adults – shoplifting, petty thievery of various kinds, order violations, drug use, graffiti and other vandalism – are committed by both gang members and nongang delinquents. As we shall see in the next section, it is often hard to identify these activities as "gang" related.

"Smoking Joints, Spraying Paint, I Stole These Pants I'm Wearing": Minor Criminality Among Gang Members

Although the most common gang activities are legal and fairly harmless, the lives of members are permeated by a wide variety of criminality. Arrests provide one measure of this, albeit an imperfect one. Although nineteen of our subjects said they had never been arrested,[2] the mean number of arrests for the other eighty active members was just under ten. This criminality began at a fairly early age – sixteen subjects had been arrested before they were thirteen years old (the lowest age of first arrest was eight), and the mean age of first arrest was fourteen. Sixty-one subjects had been arrested within the year prior to our interview with them; and thirty-four within two months of our contact. Their most recent arrests ranged from homicide to disturbing the peace, with the most common crime being assault (seventeen subjects). Fifty-three subjects said they were with other members of the gang at their last arrest, only eighteen said they were alone.[3] Given the social characteristics of our subjects, the pervasiveness of illegal activities revealed by this abbreviated statistical portrait comes as no surprise.

This section discusses low-level criminality of gang members – misdemeanors and nonviolent felonies. These activities may take place as part of their membership, with other gang members but not as a gang activity, with nongang members, or as individuals. We have already discussed underage drinking, probably the most prevalent criminal behavior of gang members. We have also mentioned car theft for cruising and use of illegal drugs. Gang members also steal cars for profit – selling parts or the entire car – which we consider with other serious property crimes in the next section. Our discussion here focuses on public order crimes, small-time thefts of various sorts, and drug use.

Peace Disturbances and Painting Names. Our subjects often commit crimes or are arrested solely because they are gang members. They are easily distinguishable from other adolescents or young adults in their neighborhood (a differentiation that they sometimes violently maintain), and when they congregate their presence is often disturbing. Six subjects said their most recent arrest was for a "peace disturbance" of some kind, and two were most recently arrested for "obstructing police" – crimes that often result from a refusal to "break it up," "move along," or "get out of here."

> Yeah, a whole lot, about every other night. They call the police around 8:00 for peace disturbance and the police are just as prejudiced to me because they come by and tell us to turn the music down or whatever. We'll tell them, look, [inaudible] it's only 8:00 so why are we peace disturbing somebody. One time we had people to call the police at 12:00 in the afternoon saying peace disturbance, our radio was up too loud. (Female #096, "L. C.," twenty-three-year-old Inglewood Bounty Hunter)

One subject's most recent arrest was for gambling – shooting craps on the street with his "boys" – not exactly the heinous crime of a dangerous deviant.

> MALE #067, "$hortDog," fifteen-year-old Inglewood Family Gangster Blood: Every day. I got locked up once five times in one week shooting craps and stuff.
> INT: What was the most recent arrest for, gambling?
> 067: Yeah [shooting craps]. About a week ago.

These kinds of arrests are often used by police to control and constrain gang members' movements and to remove or break up public "hanging out" by groups.

> MALE #065, "BK Kill," nineteen-year-old North County Crip: In Pine Lawn on the corners. The police get upset and we used to fight a lot. The fine is a lot now, two-fifty.
> INT: $2.50?
> 065: No, $250.
> INT: They got illegal gambling or something?

065: They say there's a lot of drug problems in the neighborhood so they prefer us not to hang on the corner.

Another example of criminality arising from gang membership is vandalism and/or destruction of property. The young man who broke a neighbor's window because they snitched on his gang activity is a good illustration. More typical, though, is police attention as a consequence of painting graffiti.

INT: Have you been getting more heat from the police?
MALE #067, "$hortDog," fifteen-year-old Inglewood Family Blood: Yeah. For writing our names on buildings and stuff.

Eighty-one of our subjects said their gang painted graffiti, although this label was sometimes misunderstood, and a number of gang members did not recognize the term graffiti. This reveals the extent to which members of the gang subculture are enmeshed in a linguistic life apart from mainstream culture.

INT: Do you guys paint graffiti?
MALE #012, "Lance," seventeen-year-old West Side Member: No, we wrote our names on the side of buildings but we don't go nowhere where people will see us.
INT: Like West Side Mob?
012: Yeah, we got that on our elementary school building. We write on vacant houses but we don't go nowhere like.

INT: So you guys paint graffiti?
MALE #025, "Tony," seventeen-year-old 107 Hoover Gangster Crip: What?
INT: Do you know what graffiti is? It's like what you guys were doing down there on that blackboard [in a conference room while waiting for the interviewers]. Do you guys paint gang symbols up on walls?
025: Yeah.

Graffiti usually takes the form of street names, set names, and symbols. Thus, graffiti serves to identify gang territory as well as the location of the gang. The messages graffiti displays are targeted at rival gangs, neighborhood residents, and members of the gang.

The location of graffiti was also significant. While not generally concerned with the physical appearance of their own neighborhood, rival territory was often viewed as the appropriate location to spray graffiti.

Not in our neighborhood we don't. Our neighborhood clean. We got over to the Slob territory and paint there to make them mad. (Male #021, "40 Ounce," sixteen-year-old 107 Hoover Gangster Crip)

A fair number of subjects, however, saw painting graffiti as something "juniors" did, and not serious or important gang business:

They be, they be doin it sometime. I be tellin them man don't do that man, that ain't what's happening. (Male #001, "Mike-Mike," twenty-year-old Thundercat)

MALE #037, "Big Money," twenty-two-year-old Compton Gangster Blood: The little juniors was doing it but we stopped them.
INT: How come?
037: We want our neighborhood to look decent.

One subject mentioned the role of graffiti in initiation:

My partner brought him down and said he wanted me to sit down with him. I asked him was he ready to get with it. He said yeah. Well let's ride. Go on over there. Put his name up on the wall. (Male #033, "Larry," eighteen-year-old Thundercat)

Reactions to the removal of graffiti and gang symbols varied, depending on who did the painting over or defacement. Some subjects said that it did not bother them, especially when done by officials.

Police or something? We will put it back up there. If they continue to take it down I ain't going to waste my money on putting something up there if I know it coming right back down. (Male #027, "G-Loc," fifteen-year-old Gangster Disciple)

[If the city does it] we just respray paint. There's a couple of walls that we put our symbols on it. We just went and got a couple more cans and spray painted again. (Male #038, "G.O.D.," nineteen-year-old Compton Gangster)

One subject provided an economic rationale for his gang's vandalism:

INT: What if it was the parks department, that wouldn't piss you off?
MALE #029, "Randell," seventeen-year-old Thundercat: No. A lot of people keep jobs that way. If we didn't litter then a lot of janitors wouldn't have jobs.
INT: So you think you are doing a community service by painting graffiti?

Another subject pointed out that graffiti is "just paint."

> If my name is on the wall in all black and white and somebody comes
> over with red paint and spray it out I'll say something real smart. If
> he can't give me a good reason why he did it I'll just say ok cause it's
> just paint, man. (Male #040, "Knowledge," twenty-one-year-old Compton
> Gangster)

But most subjects felt that removal was disrespectful and to be responded
to forcefully.

> If we know that they removed it we go over there and fight them or shoot
> at them or whatever. (Female #006, "Yolanda," nineteen-year-old 23rd
> Street Hoover Crip)

Crossing out a name (or painting RIP – rest in peace – over or near a
member's gang name) is a sign that a rival gang intends to kill that
member.

> If you go to their neighborhood and say you crossed one of the gang
> members name out, like when you kill him and his name is still up on the
> wall you going to cross it out or when you getting ready to kill him you
> might put RIP over his name. (Male #031, "John Doe," sixteen-year-old
> Thundercat)

> It depends. A lot of them just write over our stuff. We'll go write over
> theirs. If they put an X through our name we got to find out who put the
> X on there and we got to go get them. X through you name means you
> dead, they out looking for you. I've had X put through my name a lot of
> times but I'm still here. (Male #060, "Bullet," twenty-year-old Inglewood
> Family Gangster Blood)

> Mostly when we go over there and cross out they stuff that ain't cool with
> them because we put our stuff up. If there is a person we are looking for,
> we'll put 187 up by his name or something like that, put a shotgun
> pointed to his name or something like that. (Male #084, "Rolo," fifteen-
> year-old Rolling 60's Crip)

**"I Stole these Pants I Got On, Just Put the Pants On and Walk
Out".** Sixty-seven subjects said that the gang stole things together, although only forty-three said that these joint property crimes were
planned. Most minor thefts seem to be spur-of-the-moment actions involving a group of members who just happen to be hanging out together
when someone (or many of them) decide to steal something.

FEMALE #011, "Lisa," fifteen-year-old Compton Gangster: Sometimes we have the car pulled up in the back and we will toss the sodas in there. They [the gas station] put them inside because we emptied them out.

INT: Does the gang sort of plan these things?

011: Well we spotted them and everybody just said let's go get us some sodas from Clark's.

Like at gas stations or they be walking down the street. Some of them steal out of stores and some of them steal tapes and stuff. (Male #068, "CK," sixteen-year-old Piru 104 Blood)

Gang motivated thefts do occur, both as part of initiation or to raise money for desperately wanted necessities (like beer or jackets).

Get initiated by fighting like ten people jump on them, other people have to steal something. (Female #078, "Tina," fifteen-year-old Treetop Blood)

INT: What kinds of things do you take?

MALE #092, "Derone," tewnty-one-year-old Rolling 60's Crip: Shoes, shirts, pants, jackets, hats, cars, stereos, all the necessities.

Planning of property crimes by gangs, however, appears fairly simple, more similar to the Andy Hardy refrain of "hey gang, let's put on a show, we'll go to the mall and steal something (clothes, food, liquor, tapes, CDs, etc.)" or "let's steal a car so we can go cruising (gang banging, etc.)" than the actions of a professional safe cracker.

INT: Do you guys plan those things?

MALE #042, "Leroy," sixteen-year-old Rolling 60's Crip: No, that's disastrous. You got to have a good mind to plan something like that and have it work. The spur of the moment, the only time you do that is when you know you can get away with it. That would be the best time.

Sometimes. We really don't shoplift. If we was going into a store we wouldn't call it shoplifting cause we just, everybody just grabs what they want and walk out the store with it in they hand. Somebody just say come on come on you all, let's go hit Famous [a large department store], something like that. (Male #004, "Anthony," seventeen-year-old Thundercat)

Planning for serious property crimes – car thefts for profit, robberies, burglaries, jackings – does occur, but as we shall see in the next section, even those are most often opportunistic and ill conceived.

INT: Do you all ever set a plan how to steal cars?

MALE #093, "Lil-P," sixteen-year-old Crenshaw Mob Gangster Blood:

Not really, we just walk around the neighborhood earlier. We'll just chill
around here playing basketball until 12 or 1:00 and then steal it.
INT: So you all see it, stake it out.
093: Come back and get it.
INT: And you all usually do that when you bored right?
093: Yeah bored or need some wheels to get to a party on the north side
or get some guns and bring them back over.

These gang members, and the gangs they belong to, do not strike us as
organized thieves. Forty-three subjects said that their gang planned
property crimes, twenty-three subjects answered no, and thirty-one did
not answer. Members of the same gang also gave opposite responses to
the question, testifying to the loose structure of St. Louis gangs.

Besides auto theft, shoplifting is probably the most common property
crime committed by our subjects.

MALE #030, "Kenneth," nineteen-year-old Thundercat: We rob the
stores. No we don't rob them, we steal from them.
INT: Shoplift?
030: Yeah, just take it.

INT: What do you steal?
MALE #032, "Skonion," seventeen-year-old Thundercat: We just go down
there when we want some junk food.
INT: At the convenience store, 7-11?
032: Yeah.
INT: So food, clothes?
032: We steal clothes from the mall and shoes.

Various "thefts of services" are also popular – our subjects attempt to
sneak into movies, concerts, amusement parks, skating rinks, and other
entertainment venues, much like juveniles anywhere. Minor theft and
public disturbances are part of gang culture, but not its defining feature.

**"Everybody and They Mama Smoke Weed," or "You Just Married a
Pipe:" Drug Use by Gang Members.** No other topic we discuss better
illustrates the frustration, ambiguities, and contradictions inherent in
interviewing gang members about their criminality than drug use. In
media stereotypes, after all, contemporary street gangs are well-organized
purveyors of crack cocaine – cool, steely eyed, determined businessmen
and women who would never use their debilitating wares. Or they are
fiends with hair-trigger, violent impulses and reactions. Which of these, if
either, is true?

Neither, of course, yet both of these extremes can be found in our subjects' self-reports of drug use by themselves and their fellow members. Recall that only two subjects said that the most common gang activity was "doing drugs," yet sixty of our subjects said that a "lot of members are doing drugs." Also, no subjects said that "doing drugs" was a good reason for joining their gang, although sixteen said that the opportunity to do drugs was a good reason to belong to (or stay in) a gang.

INT: [Does the gang provide an opportunity] to use drugs?
MALE #026, "Chill," fifteen-year-old 107 Hoover Gangster Crip: Smoke weed.

Thirty-three subjects, however, said that "a lot of members were *not* doing drugs." Many subjects flatly deny that anyone in their set does drugs, and seven subjects answered "never" to our question "How often do members use drugs?"

Well we don't. It's something that we know is wrong for a change. We know drugs is bad but if you want to buy it from us of course we are going to give it to you. (Male #020, "Lil Thug," sixteen-year-old Gangster Disciple)

Not really. If you going to sell drugs keep your mind clear so you can be alert. You can't be high and nodding off and tripping and the police ride up on you with rocks on you. (Male #041, "C. K.," twenty-two-year-old Blood)

Or do they? Our subjects often contradicted themselves over the course of the interview about drug use, or perhaps more commonly were not sure what we meant by "drugs."

INT: Do a lot of gang members use drugs?
MALE #014, "D. C.," sixteen-year-old Disciple: They smoke weed.

One subject, "C-Loc," a seventeen year-old Rolling Sixties Crip, (male #045), said early in the interview: "No, nobody do drugs." But later on in our questioning the following exchange took place:

INT: Are a lot of gang members involved in using drugs?
045: No, not really.
INT: What kind of drugs do the gang members use?
045: Usually rock, that's about it.
INT: They like to smoke the Primo's?
045: Yeah.

INT: And weed right?
045: Yeah.
INT: What happens if somebody in the gang uses drugs?
045: Nothing.

When we asked subjects "What kinds of drugs do members use?" we counted four mentions of cocaine, five of crack, two of heroin, one of PCP, and forty-nine of marijuana.

> FEMALE #006, "Yolanda," nineteen-year-old 23rd Street Hoover Crip: Yeah, there's a whole lot of them like about 20 or 25 of them are using drugs like coke. Not really crack. Now they're not using crack, they using it but they really on that coke and stuff.
> INT: Marijuana?
> 006: Yeah, but some of them say that ain't nothing now. Like if they mix it up with coke, then yeah, that's Primo. But weed is not really hot or nothing like that. [T]here's a whole lot of them on heroin. Majority of the men. Some of it shooting it in and some of them snorting it. Really the majority of them are shooting it in they arm.

> Rock, marijuana. Mostly on Fridays. Like before going to the show. (Male #008, "Robert," fourteen-year-old Compton Gangster)

> They might smoke some weed but that's about all. Everybody and they mamma smoke weed. (Male #060, "Bullet," twenty-year-old Inglewood Family Gangster Blood)

> For me it has been every day. I started smoking weed when I was, I was selling weed. There is so much drugs in my family, you could have anything you want. The table would be full of marijuana. In our gang now there is nothing but marijuana. That's all. (Male #034, "Lil Gene Mack," eighteen-year-old 19th Street Rolling 60's Crip)

Yet when we asked "How often do members use drugs?" seventy-one subjects could not provide an answer. Gang members in St. Louis apparently do not want to be perceived as hard-drug users, probably because of the low regard in which "fiends" are held.

> INT: What happens to people in your gang who use drugs?
> MALE #028, "Killa 4 Ren," fifteen-year-old 187 Crip: They die out. They are fools.

> INT: Those guys that smoke Primo, are they looked down on?
> MALE #033, "Larry," eighteen-year-old Thundercat: They looked down on. We don't even tell them that. Ain't no sense in hiding it man but they just try to hide it. They don't even hide it no more. They be sitting

out, like we smoking a joint out on the porch, they be out there smoking Primo out on the corner. They so sharp, clean, with jewelry, you can't tell, man. If they want to do it that's why they want to do it.

[Rocks?] That's a downer. That's a rich man's high and a poor man's dream. (Male #037, "Big Money," twenty-two-year-old Compton Gangster)

Subjects may also be differentiating between "regular" use of drugs other than marijuana (and alcohol, of course) and infrequent, experimental, or occasional use of other drugs. Others didn't regard marijuana as a drug. Some, certainly, were also lying to us! Our field-worker, for example, had subjects who told him in interviews that they never snorted coke or smoked crack and then subsequently witnessed these same subjects using these drugs.

Drug activity (use or sales) is pervasive in our subjects' lives, whatever their denials may indicate to the contrary. Eighty-five subjects indicated that their gang was involved in drug activities (either sales or use); only fourteen did not mention drug sales or use as a gang activity.

We asked subjects "What happens to members who use drugs?" hoping to find out what happens to members who get addicted or habituated to drugs other than marijuana. Again, the answers are ambiguous and somewhat contradictory. Apparently, many subjects thought we were talking about marijuana use – or did not believe that their fellow members ever could or would be that stupid. The modal category, forty-two subjects, did not provide an answer to this question. Twenty-nine subjects said that the gang does "nothing" about drug users.

INT: What happens if somebody in the group do use drugs?
MALE #051, "David," eighteen-year-old Blood: Nothing, that's they life they wasting.
INT: So if they are a Primo king it don't mean shit?
051: Yeah.

Nothing, they just get fucked up. That's it, they just get fucked up and have a good time. (Male #092, "Derone," seventeen-year-old Rolling 60's Crip)

Thirteen subjects said that the gang would separate from drug users.

MALE #040, "Knowledge," twenty-one-year-old Compton Gangster: Yeah. No cocaine smoking at all. You get caught smoking cocaine you an outcast, black sheep.
INT: Including Primos?

040: I mean no cocaine, no heroin, no PCP.

INT: How did you all get that rule?

040: Just sat down and talked about it. One day me and [another member] sat out there and said can't nobody smoke cocaine or we ain't dealing with you. Simple as that. We ain't going to jump on you or shoot at you or nothing. You got no more friends, you just married a pipe.

INT: So if they break the rules you all just through with them?

040: Yeah, we just don't deal with them anymore. We will try to talk with them. That would be the first thing. To me a person out there smoking cocaine don't care about they self.

No. I would say all right Cuz, slow down. You can talk to him and tell him. Nothing else you can do, just tell him. (Male #042, "Leroy," seventeen-year-old Rolling 60's Crip)

Five subjects said the gang would help a member quit drugs.

Weed, that's all. If somebody in the gang and we find out you smoke rocks or anything we beat you up and make you check yourself into a care unit or something cause we just hate to see one of our boys go out. We know fiends that look bad and we don't want none of our friends to go out like that. (Male #038, "G.O.D.," nineteen-year-old Compton Gangster)

Yeah, if we see its getting to be a problem and we see that he want to get some help we all chip in some money and put his ass in rehabilitation. If that don't help then there ain't shit that we can do for you. (Male #041, "C. K.," twenty-two-year-old Blood)

Violence and separation were also mentioned.

We might smoke every once in a while but no cocaine, no Primos. I know what that shit can do to you and if I catch anybody, like one of my boys, he used to sell dope, he turned into a smoker. I beat the piss out of that man. I said you in violation, you lucky you don't get capped. We don't want you around no more and the homie ain't around no more. (White male #099, "Joe L.," eighteen-year-old Insane Gangster Disciple)

For many subjects the most important reason for separating from drug users and for members refraining from using drugs was economic.

Yeah. I gave my partner some dope and he was smoking dope. He was smoking Primos, weed, and cocaine. He messed up. People that have gave me some dope, they took losses. You going to take some losses in the dope game. He telling me he lost the dope. I knew what time it was but I believed him. Tried him again, tried him again and he messed up. I said man I can't give you no more and then about two weeks later he wants a

bag. I gave him like a pound of weed and he got stupid. I gave him half
ounce of cocaine and he came back with the money and everything. Now
he got him a little car. He chilling. He still smoke it but he chilling. (Male
#033, "Larry," eighteen-year-old Thundercat)

You can't have too many doing it because I can give a man so much
amount of this stuff and I ask him to knock it off and he wind up smoking
half of it. That's not making a good profit. We have to kick them out. They
get so hooked on to it. (Male #017, "Billy Kelly," twenty-one-year-old
North Side Crip)

MALE #018: "Maurice," twenty-year-old 107 Hoover Crip: We'll tell them
    don't take no losses. You wait until you finish selling and then you can
    buy whatever you want to buy with your own money but don't fuck up
    our profits. You mess our things up we going to mess up your thing.
INT: So you will kick him out?
018: No, we will beat his motherfucking ass cause we took a loss.

Surprisingly, none of our subjects mentioned the potential causal link
of drug (and alcohol) use with violence. Although respondents regarded
drug "fiends" as tricky, untrustworthy, and violence-prone, they did not
appreciate the relevance of this last characteristic to their own drug and
alcohol use. Violence against gang members who overused drugs is mentioned, but the possibility that gang violence could be curbed by lower
consumption or that it arose from overconsumption of drugs and drinks
is strikingly absent from our interviews. This omission is perhaps due to
the accepted and commonsensical nature of the linkage – it just does not
need to be repeated. But even so, the omission – which is in part ours for
not asking it directly – is particularly striking.

This section has illustrated the pervasive low-level criminality that
characterizes the lives of gang members. Some of their minor criminal
behavior arises from the fact of their membership in gangs; order disturbances, loitering, and curfew violations are probably enforced more routinely and harshly on gang members than on other adolescents or young
adults in the same neighborhood. And the vandalism or destruction of
property arising from graffiti spraying is a direct function of gang membership, sometimes as a requirement of initiation, sometimes as a "stand-
up" or "macho" necessity.

Petty theft – shoplifting, thefts of services, stealing from open cars –
although sometimes gang motivated or "planned," is more likely to be an
incidental or coincidental, spur-of-the-moment action. Drug use is not,
of course, a requirement for joining a gang or continuing in good stand-

ing (quite the contrary, in fact), but the ease with which members can obtain drugs probably increases the amounts and rates of use. Nevertheless, many subjects vehemently denied any drug use by themselves or their fellow gang members.

There is some internal differentiation in these activities. Younger members, under sixteen, were more likely to mention petty criminality – shoplifting, sidewalk gambling, graffiti, thefts of services. To some extent this may be a matter of economics, younger members may not have as much ready cash to purchase some of the items stolen. They are too young to hold jobs and are not yet sufficiently trusted, experienced, or established to sell drugs as regularly or lucratively as older members. Old gangsters are also likely to be more cautious and thoughtful and more experienced in assessing the payback of minor criminality.

We found little evidence of intergang variability in the commission of petty crimes. This is due, in part, to our sampling technique and the uneven representation of particular gangs. Only a few subjects seemed to indicate that their gang did not have any members who engaged in minor criminality. There also may be differences between cliques within gangs, although this is probably age related, since such friendship cliques and subgroups seem to be age graded and predate, in many cases, gang membership.

As we also observed in the last section, these activities and behaviors do not sharply differentiate gang members from other young adults and adolescents in the same neighborhoods. Nor do they reflect the behavior of a well-organized gang in pursuit of common goals. A life filled with petty criminality – order disturbances, vandalism, petty theft, drug use – is common in poor, black St. Louis neighborhoods.

But all three of these kinds of criminality are linked to much more serious criminal behaviors that help mark gangs and gang members as different kinds of people from their nongang peers. Petty theft through shoplifting and thefts of services becomes strong-armed robbery when large groups of gang members invade a store and dare the employees to stop them.

> We'll just walk in, it be so many of us they can't grab one of us. They grab one of us, he going to get beat so they just let us walk out. (Male #004, "Anthony," seventeen-year-old Thundercat)

Vandalism in the form of graffiti can have violent and even deadly consequences; crossing out a rival's name, having your name crossed out, catching someone painting over your set's name. And while peace/order disturbances are probably most often a controlling device used by police, they perhaps are just as often reduced charges from more serious crimes – assaultive violence, brandishing weapons.

While we would not argue that alcohol and marijuana consumption inevitably leads to a lifelong addiction to those or harder drugs, the easy availability of drugs and the need to acquire purchase money may lead to more serious crime – thefts, robberies, burglaries, drug sales, the concern of Chapter 6.

"We Do What We Do Together": Activities With Nonmembers

In this section we discuss what little our subjects do with outsiders, nongang peers and friends. If framed as a question, the answer would be "almost nothing." Gangs and gang life have a fatal attraction for our subjects (literally so in eleven cases), an attraction that, over time, constricts and diminishes their involvement in activities and events not involving the friendship group of the gang. Nearly two-thirds of our subjects, for example, did not supply an answer to the question "What activities do you do when you're not with the gang?" This may not be surprising, given the adolescent modality of our subjects, and the friendship clique underpinning of St. Louis gangs. A nearly identical statistic might occur if any group of teenagers in the metropolitan area were asked "What activities do you do when you're not with your friends?"

> INT: Do you do things without gang members?
> MALE #026, "Chill," fifteen-year-old 107 Hoover Gangster Crip: Like what? I hang out with my cousins [also gang members].
> INT: So basically other than sleeping or eating you are with the gang?
> 026: "Chill:" I wash dishes and stuff.

Sometimes, though, hanging out with nongang members was no different than hanging with gang members.

> MALE #052, "Jonathan," fifteen-year-old 107 Hoovers: Dudes that don't want to be in a gang.
> INT: What do you all do together when you with them?
> 052: The same thing.
> INT: What, drink beer?
> 052: Yes.
> INT: Do they fight too?
> 052: Yes.

Yet gangs have a strongly chilling effect on our subjects' participation in outside activities, especially institutionalized or organized groups. Eighty subjects indicated they had belonged to one or more legal groups (of a social, religious, or recreational sort) before joining the gang, while only nineteen denied any previous involvement in such activities.[4] In a stunning illustration of the near exclusivity of gang activities, only *twenty* subjects said they currently belonged to any group besides their gang, while seventy-nine subjects were affiliated only with the gang. Thus three-quarters of those involved in legal groups dropped out after joining the gang.

> INT: You were an honor student and a good athlete, what made you decide to start living on the streets again?
> MALE #035, "Edward," twenty-year-old Hoover Gangster Crip: I don't know. Just got tired of being smart. I couldn't tell you.

> INT: What other groups do you belong to besides the gang?
> MALE #083, "Winchester," fourteen-year-old Rolling 60's Crip: I belong with them, no other.
> INT: What things do you do that you don't do with gang members?
> 083: I don't know.

The withdrawal from nongang activities also extends to other social arenas. As our discussion of labor force participation in Chapter 7 shows, only sixteen subjects were employed when we interviewed them. Eighteen subjects said they had children (and five males said that their girlfriends were pregnant), yet none of our subjects were married and only seven had their children living with them. Although seventy-three subjects said they would choose their natural family over the gang if they had to make such a choice, only twenty-four subjects said that they spent "about the same amount of time or less time" with the gang as compared to with their family.

The gang has become the primary reference and peer group for our subjects. Many, if not most, of the friends and relatives they would normally interact with are in the gang, or in a gang. Their involvement in institutional activities – church, school, employment market, clubs – is constricted, with, of course, the major exception of the criminal justice system. For most of our subjects then, their primary interpersonal interactions and activities are with other gang members (and/or hangers-on). Once a member, former ties diminish and sometimes disappear completely, as members become more and more enmeshed in a world of serious crime. As many observers have noted (Esbensen and Huizinga

1993; Thornberry et al. 1991; Sampson and Laub 1993) involvement in crime, such as that produced by the gang, heightens criminal activity. Our observations offer a mechanism to explain this. Over time, gang membership reduces involvement in conventional activities and contacts with individuals whose involvement in criminal activities is low. Thus, individuals and institutions with the ability to restrain criminality lose their socializing power. When this occurs in conjunction with heightened involvement with criminal peers the result is increased criminality. Thus, the conjunction of isolation from legitimate activities and individuals, coupled with an increased involvement among gang peers produces a context in which constraints against crime are diminished and support for criminal involvement is ever present. These forces, working together in opposite directions, help to account for the increased criminality of gang members, whether those crimes are committed as part of the gang or outside of it.

"I Love To Bang": Serious Crime by Gang Members

Bang, drive-by and shoot shit up. It just feels good. Like [unclear] says, damn it feels good to be a gangster. I love to do it. I love to bang, I love to shoot shit up, we all do it together. (White male #099, "Joe L.," eighteen-year-old Insane Gangster Disciple)

POPULAR STEREOTYPES of gangs and gang members – reflected in news and entertainment media, in public opinions, in officials' statements, and in some scholarly works – consider them to be organized, violent predators on society. In this vision, gangs – guided by older leaders – plan burglaries and boostings, commit armed robberies, terrorize neighborhoods, run crack houses, distribute and sell a wide variety of drugs on the street, and revel in assaultive and lethal violence against each other, innocent bystanders, and any who thwart them. Some of this may be true, as the statement by "Joe L." implies. What is not true, at least from talking with our subjects, is the intensity of this stereotype, the well-organized nature of their group activities, and the delight in violence shown above (a more common attitude towards violence was fatalism – "you gotta do what you gotta do"; "we don't go looking for trouble"; "we use violence when it comes to us"). Serious crimes – both nonviolent and violent – are a defining feature of gangs, but gang crimes seem neither as purposive, organized, or frequent as the popular (and official) mind imagines. Often, violence is a response to the threat of violence from the presence of other gangs. This chapter discusses three kinds of serious crime by gang members: felony property crimes (burglary, armed robbery, auto theft for profit, truck jacking, boosting), sales of illegal drugs, and assaultive violence.

"I Was Robbing and Steal and This, That, and The Other": Felony Property Crime

St. Louis gangs and individual members routinely steal things, both together and on their own. Sixty-seven subjects, for example, said that their gang steals things together. Although much of this theft may be no more harmful than minor shoplifting – sodas, candy, beer, cigarettes – gangs still are involved in a lot of serious property crime. Our subjects' self-reports of their most recent arrests, for example, included two for possession of stolen property, two for burglary, four for robbery, and eight for possession of a stolen vehicle. Property crimes also occur frequently: fourteen subjects said that the gang stole things together every day, seven said that they stole weekly, and eight said monthly.

> They beat up people and take their stuff. About every now and then . . . Five times [in a month]. (Male #010, "Jason C.," fifteen-year-old Compton Gangster)

> Some of them do and some of them don't. They do it mostly everyday. (Male #052, "Jonathan," fifteen-year-old 107 Hoover Crip)

> Almost every weekend. (Male #029, "Derone," twenty-one-year-old Rolling 60's Crip)

Forty-three subjects said that the gang planned property crimes, although very few could or would elaborate on such assertions. Two examples of somewhat rational planning include:

> Well, first we won't do no robbery, we do a burglary to get some quick money. We might creep around the neighborhood, we don't do it in our neighborhood, not downtown we go somewhere like across the street you know and see a open house you know, we go in there and hit it, boom, you know come on out with a VCR, nineteen-inch TV, jewelry. We go over there on the lane, the guy selling drugs he buy all this kind of stuff. (Male #003, "Jerry," eighteen-year-old Thundercat)

> They plan them. They observe. They stake out the house, see what time they leave for like a week or so. For a whole week so you know which day they off, whatever. So one day they just go in and do the job when they ain't there. (Male #005, "Antonio," nineteen-year-old 6th Street Hoover Crip)

But other subjects pointed out that much "planning" was remarkably spontaneous and haphazard.

MALE #010, "Jason C.," fifteen-year-old Compton Gangster: They plan it.

INT: What do they say?

010: They say, see that dude over there, we are going to gang bang him. Take his stuff and run.

INT: How often do you do [robberies]?

MALE #035, "Edward," twenty-year-old Hoover Gangster Crip: Whenever we get drunk and somebody mention it. People walking downtown. They be drunk as a skunk.

INT: So you do it mainly at night when people are walking around drunk?

035: Yeah.

No, we really don't set them up. It's just if our boy work at a place he keep it open for us and we just go in there and just start jacking. It's just whatever's whatever, they know what they gonna do. (Male #092, "Derone," twenty-one-year-old Rolling 60's Crip)

The relative absence of planned, organized, and gang-motivated property crimes is also apparent in the division and use of criminal proceeds. Although forty-seven subjects said that illegally obtained profits (chiefly from drug sales) went for gang-related acts or needs, the actual percentages and items were usually inconsequential.

We'll rob somebody and everybody will go buy some drinks or something. (Male #087, "Blue Jay," eighteen-year-old Rolling 60's Crip)

Sometimes they might go out and buy ski masks or stuff that will get us in some more trouble. (Male #031, "John Doe," sixteen-year-old Thundercat)

MALE #083, "Winchester," fourteen-year-old Rolling 60's Crip: Yeah, we have to give it [money to the gang].

INT: Half the money go to the gang? If you got a burglary where you got $100, how much would go to the gang?

083: About $5.00.

Thirty-four subjects said that illegally obtained money did not go to the gang, and one subject stated quite emphatically:

MALE #092, "Derone," twenty-one-year-old Rolling 60's Crip: You mean the crimes that we do are they for the gang? No sometimes we just do it for fun, jack cars, take a nigger's shit because we don't like him, we just do it, take it to the pawn shop and pawn it or stick it in our ride and tear off the serial numbers.

INT: Have you ever committed crimes to get money for the gang?
092: No, I commit crimes to get money for myself.

Many subjects denied that they, or other gang members, currently engaged in property crimes; they were bringing in more money selling drugs.

> I don't steal no more, I got whatever I need. I don't steal no more. If I ever catch anybody in my group stealing, I'm going to get down on them cause they know they can come to me and ask anybody in the posse you know what I'm saying, that they want this or they want that. They know they will get it. Ain't no sense in stealing it. What you steal it for? (Male #033, "Larry," eighteen-year-old Thundercat)

> We don't take nothing. We pay for ours. We make money. (Male #037, "Big Money," twenty-two-year-old Compton Gangster)

"All The Necessities." Although cars were the most frequently mentioned target of theft, gang members steal a wide variety of items. Figure 6.1 shows the distribution of the first thing that gang members told us they stole when asked "What do you take?" Clothes, electronic appliances, jewelry, and cash were frequently noted.

> Jewelry, coats, shoes, money, rings, cars. (Male #010, "Jason C.," fifteen-year-old Compton Gangster)

> No, mainly like appliances like TVs, VCRs, stereos, car phones, CDs, anything that's of value that's what we get. (Male #017, "Billy," twenty-one-year-old North Side Crip)

> Shoes, shirts, pants, jackets, hats, cars, stereos, all the necessities. (Male #092, "Derone," twenty-one-year-old Rolling 60's Crip)

Drugs were also a popular target. This is not surprising, since gang members are very familiar with how much drug money is available, how it is kept, and the most opportune times to burglarize a dope house. These crimes often had the added benefit of being directed against a rival gang.

> We did a couple of burglaries. We just did it because we knew some drugs was up in there. (Male #039, "Kaons BIC," seventeen-year-old Compton Gangster)

> If we can find a dope house we take their stuff. (Male #027, "G-Loc," fifteen-year-old Gangster Disciple)

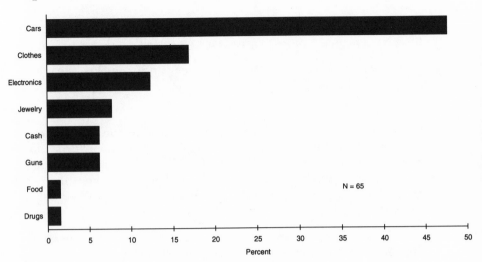

Figure 6.1 Types of Items Stolen

Guns, according to our first subject, were not the only target of burglaries.

> They don't really, they don't really do burglaries too much unless they, they be uh lookin for guns. (Male #001, "Mike-Mike," twenty-year-old Thundercat)

As Figure 6.1 illustrates, cars are the modal item stolen by gang members. Cars are stolen for joyriding or for transportation to parties, concerts, and so on. But stolen cars are also used in drive-bys and are stripped or broken down for the sale of parts or delivered to chop shops.

> No, what we do is when we steal a car then take it somewhere and strip it and get all the parts and just sell it. We take the money and buy dope for it and boom, bam, that's it. He got his money, I get my cut. (Male #017, "Billy," twenty-one-year-old North Side Crip)

> WHITE MALE #099, "Joe L.," eighteen-year-old Insane Gangster Disciple: There is a gas station right there by the car dealer place. We go up in there and just get out of the car and it's real dark, it's a Ford dealer. Go up in there with some wire cutting pliers that cut through sheet metal and shit. You have your pliers right down in here, your 2-pound sledge over here and go around like that dressed up in your black dickey fits. After you cut that lock box up, bam, bam, bust it open, start the car, put the rag top down, you bust the window out of a back car and get you one of those sticker things for a brand new car. What do they call that?
> INT: Temporary plates.

099: Yeah, you stick that up in the window of the stolen car, go get you some gas, drive it around of awhile. Then you go ahead and call the dude up that wants the car at the chop shop. Tell me when to bring it down. Bring it down tomorrow morning, drive down there, here's your money motherfucker. See ya next week.

INT: Same deal.

099: But we used to steal cars like, we would never steal people's cars. We did that a couple of times. Then one of my boys got busted on a felony.

Car jacking (or a "jack move") is also mentioned by at least three subjects:

We jack people sometimes. He pulled in front of this dude and then this dude couldn't go nowhere. Only did it about three times. (Male #064, "Pump," fourteen-year-old 6 Deuce Blood)

INT: What do you all usually do on the weekends?

MALE #031, "John Doe," sixteen-year-old Thundercat: Usually go out or jack move with somebody.

INT: Jack move is fucking with somebody?

031: Robbing somebody like somebody getting out of they car and you might want to drive they car so it's more like an armed robbery.

While thirty-two subjects said that they "protected" stores in their neighborhood, this was usually a rather hit or miss activity (only eleven subjects said that stores ever paid the gang to protect them).

MALE #001, "Mike-Mike," twenty-year-old Thundercat: They be havin some of those gang members sittin down, you know what I'm sayin, then they feed em, then they have bout fifteen of em they be feedin em, then they have their head turned to the back like just lookin ya know.

INT: Keep their eye on shoplifters?

001: Yea, I had a few of my gang members to kill some people in a restaurant and just bang em up and burn em cause somebody was trying to rob they store.

INT: Does the gang ever get money from store owners or merchants for protection? Do they ever go around and say we want some, give us a hundred bucks?

001: They be askin them so they won't do nothin to em. Hey man, I don't want ya'll to rob me, I'll give ya'll a hundred dollars, you know, just to watch the store for me, man, cause uh, I know ya'll bad and everything, we don't want nothin to happen to us.

MALE #038, "G.O.D.," nineteen-year-old Compton Gangster: Yeah. We can go in there loud and drunk and we see somebody fighting, no dudes, can't fight here. This is our neighborhood, you don't fight in our neighborhood, we do all the fighting. We throw drunks out, fucking bums. Cause the guard be scared, they punks.

INT: Do stores ever pay you money to do this, to protect them?

038: No, we just do it because they mostly our neighbors working in these places so we just do it to help them out.

Only seven subjects said that they ever extorted protection money from stores, in fact, some members were not sure what the term meant.

INT: Did you ever extort money from any stores?

MALE #042, "Leroy," seventeen-year-old Rolling 60's Crip: What?

INT: Extortion, where you go in there and say you guys either pay me $100 a week otherwise I'm going to come in here. . . .

042: No. That's what you call a cat doing stuff like that. We could do it a couple of times but you ain't going to get enough money. You can only do that so many times. You can only do it so many times.

INT: Do you ever tell store owners if you don't give us some money we'll shoot you up? That sort of thing?

MALE #002, "Eric," sixteen-year-old Thundercat: Naw, hey man we got some sense man, we don't do all that crazy stuff. Hey man, we do a little crazy stuff but what ya'll think we really doin, man, we don't be doin that.

Burglaries, after automobile theft, are probably the most common form of felony theft our subjects discussed. Gang members seem to prefer to burglarize houses, although some subjects mentioned other targets:

INT: Do you guys plan burglaries or what?

MALE #012, "Lance," twenty-year-old West Side Mob member: Yeah, sometimes we do when we broke.

INT: Steal out of stores?

012: No, we don't steal shit out of stores, we break into a house or something though.

INT: Safer?

012: Yeah, it's safer. Well, I don't know really.

INT: Do you ever do burglaries when somebody is home?

012: No, I ain't never been caught in nobody's house. If we in the house we might take some jewelry and they don't know it until later.

Big things, basically we like to hit safes. Not that petty shit, fuck that. Usually got one or two people that know about this. (Male #041, "C. K.," twenty-two-year-old Blood)

Robbery, both armed and strong-armed is another popular pastime, especially with one gang, the Laclede Town Thundercats. Their location near the Central Business District and its numerous stores, restaurants, and customers provided ample targets.

> We had went and got drunk, everybody got drunk, we went down to this faggot bar. We used to go down there and beat on them all the time, take they money and stuff. (Male #030, "Kenneth," nineteen-year-old Thundercat)

Robbery was also frequently mentioned as part of the initiation, an alternative or supplement to beating in or drive-by shootings.

> His name was C-Loc and he was about 14. He was down. He was from the hood, he was hanging out so he wanted to get in. He wanted to get initiated so someone gave him a mission, told him to do a robbery. He did the robbery and he shot the dude. (Male #088, "T-Loc," twenty-one-year-old Grape Street Crip)

> MALE #090, "Rellol," fifteen-year-old 19th Street Long Beach Crip: Somebody had a .38 and a .32 when they was downtown and they walked up to somebody and made him get out of their corner. They just went down there and whupped some ass.
> INT: So you're saying he started from a robbery or something?
> 090: Yeah.

And once it was pointed out to one of our interviewers that he was a prime target for a robbery in many neighborhoods.

> MALE #042, "Leroy," seventeen-year-old Rolling 60's Crip: Yeah, we gank people.
> INT: Robbery?
> 042: Yeah.
> INT: Ever commit armed robbery?
> 042: Yeah, that's what I was going to tell you about. No offense but if you were to come on College [Avenue] to try to use the pay phone or anything, I say you got some money Cuz, let's get him.
> INT: If you checked my wallet you would think twice about that; there's nothing in there.

Each of these property crimes provides cash or commodities of immediate use to gang members. Their concerns were for their immediate future – the next party, the next beer, the next shootout. Such concerns reflected their constrained status and orientation toward dealing with short-term goals. This orientation is consistent with a life under threat of violence from rival gangs.

We found few differences between gangs with regard to their commission of serious property crimes. Members of one gang, the Laclede Town Thundercats, mentioned that they regularly committed robberies (and indeed seemed to have grown out of organized rolling of the patrons of a particular gay bar), though not all members engaged in that crime. There were few other mentions of armed robbery, leading us to believe that it is an incidental, spontaneous act by gang members, subject to the serendipitous availability of a target and an immediate need for cash, clothes, or other items. None of the gangs in our study constituted burglary rings, although cliques and individuals in almost all groups said they regularly committed burglaries. But most burglaries were spontaneous, involve little planning, and are probably a continuation of previous criminal activities. Our subjects also made few (if any) mentions of fences, or disposing of stolen property (except as consumers), arguing further that they were not well-tied into that criminal sphere. Although at least two subjects mentioned car theft for profit (stealing cars for resale or parts or delivery to chop shops), most gang members are not involved in any major way in auto-theft rings or networks. We theorize that gang members in St. Louis (especially younger ones) do not have access to the social networks and contacts that would allow their participation in this form of crime.

Robberies, larcenies, burglaries, and car thefts are not exclusively committed by gang members in the greater St. Louis area. Other individuals and ad hoc or friendship groups in gang (and nongang) neighborhoods also engage in these crimes. Nor are these typical or defining activities for the gangs we have described. These serious property crimes are instrumental – robberies provide money and goods, as do burglaries. Car thefts provide transportation, cash, and perhaps spare parts. But most gang members agree that these activities are dangerous, risky, usually spontaneous exercises. Real money, important money, is gotten by other means, by selling drugs.

"I'm In This For Myself": Drug Sales

Gang involvement in illegal drug sales is a major concern of the public, media, and law enforcement agencies. Many observers have drawn a causal link between the rise and growth of street gang involvement in drug sales as well organized at both local and national levels (National

Institute of Justice 1993; Skolnick et al. 1988; Sanchez-Jankowski 1991). But St. Louis gangs contradict these stereotypical notions in many ways. Although every gang in our sample had some members who sold drugs (crack cocaine, in the main), gang involvement was generally poorly organized, episodic, nonmonopolistic, carried out by individuals or cliques on their own, and was not a rational for the gang's existence and continuance.

This section discusses gang and member involvement in drug sales, taking up, in order, questions of why drugs are important to St. Louis gangs, how much is earned, what is done with the money, internal gang organization, external organization and sources of supplies (including the role of drug houses), and the kinds of and relations with drug customers.

Why Drugs and Gangs. Our subjects sell illegal drugs because it is a source of money, provides prestige within the gang and the neighborhood, and, less importantly, is a source of sexual or other favors from customers. The opportunity to sell drugs, however, is *not* an important reason for *joining* a gang. Only six subjects said that they joined because of a "desire for material goods" (which most often involves the profits from drug sales).

> Girls and having a little money, things like that. Selling dope like everybody. When you selling dope you got lots of money and for protection. (Male #015, "Karry," fifteen-year-old Crenshaw Gangster Blood)

> My interest was in getting paid man, strictly getting paid. I had a job at 13. I sold dope, cocaine, but it wasn't a career thing; it was like for extra money. (Male #040, "Knowledge," twenty-one-year-old Compton Gangster)

Nevertheless, once a member, making money through drug sales assumes greater importance. This is not surprising. In addition to the money, drug sales provide opportunities for increased interaction with older, more respected gang members. Seventy-nine subjects, for example, said that "to make money" was a good reason to belong to their gang, while forty-six said that "the gang provided an opportunity to buy drugs,"[1] and seventy-seven said that "the gang provided an opportunity to sell drugs." When we asked "what is the most important reason to stay in the gang?" The two categories most often chosen were "opportunity to make money" and "opportunity to sell drugs" (virtually the same thing).

Figure 6.2 displays this graphically. The opportunities gangs provide

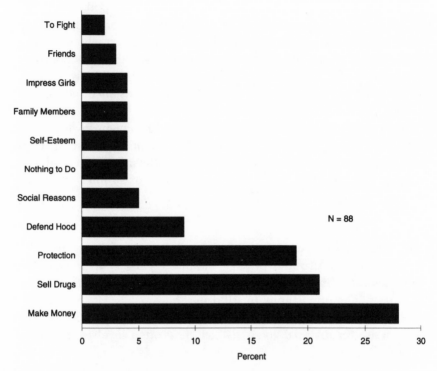

Figure 6.2 Reasons for Staying in the Gang

for selling drugs, then, are the most important reason for belonging for half of our subjects. But gangs do not control the retail drug market in St. Louis. Nor, as far as we can tell, are gangs the major wholesale source of drugs. While gang membership is not a prerequisite for selling drugs, neither is drug selling a prerequisite for gang membership. It is probable, in fact, that the majority of drug sellers in the St. Louis area are not gang members. One subject pointed this out when asked if his brother had prompted him to join the gang.

> Naw. My brother was always dope dealer, just he didn't really like gangs, you know, he just sell dope and stuff like that, I mean he party wit us, into shootin and all that you know, but he didn't really, really run wit a gang, he was his own self. (Male #002, "Eric," sixteen-year-old Thundercat)

> You can make money without them. Anybody can start selling drugs if they have the right amount of money and know what they are doing. (Male #005, "Antonio," nineteen-year-old 6th Street Hoover Crip)

Another indication that gangs do not dominate drug sales is that many (if not most) of the existing drug houses in gang neighborhoods are not operated by gang members. A third line of evidence is the extent of member involvement in drug sales. Several subjects denied ever selling drugs.

> Only about me and this other girl who don't sell it. (Female #078, "Tina," fifteen-year-old Treetop Blood)

Other subjects said that they had quit selling drugs, often because of an arrest.

> I stopped doing it though. I did it once in a while. (Male #008, "Robert," fourteen-year-old Compton Gangster)

> I quit selling dope cause the police at my house ready to kick in the door. I don't want to bring that shit to my family. That's why I got to get a job. (Male #065, "BK Kill," nineteen-year-old North County Crips)

Eighteen subjects said that less than half of their fellow members were involved in drug sales, two subjects said that none of their fellow members were selling drugs, and only twenty-four subjects said that every member sold drugs. Furthermore, only eighteen subjects said that every member of their gang had to meet a sales quota.

"I Got Me Two Golds" Because drug money is such an important reason for belonging to a gang, we might have expected subjects to wax eloquent about their earnings and expenditures. But many subjects seemed reluctant, hesitant, or confused about their income from drug sales, as this almost comic discussion illustrates:

> INT: About how much do you make per week selling drugs?
> MALE #092, "Derone," twenty-one-year-old Rolling 60's Crip: About $15,000 to $20,000.
> INT: The whole gang entirely?
> 092: No, just the people where I'm at, they make about $15,000 to $20,000. So I would say all around, you could probably make about $150,000 a week if you go through all the sets where all the niggers be at. Some in Trailwoods, some in Seven Hills like that.
> INT: About how much do you make per week?
> 092: How much do I make per week?
> INT: Yeah.
> 092: Just my check plus like if I need some money for something, on my own I can go over there and hook up with $500.
> INT: So you make about $500 a week selling drugs?
> 092: If I want to.

Twenty-six subjects could not (or did not) provide an answer to the question "How much money do you make every week from selling drugs?" Fifty-five subjects could not say how much money they made compared to other members; and twenty-nine subjects did not say how they spent money from drug sales. Aside from those members who denied selling drugs, this paucity of answers reflects the episodic and part-time nature of involvement in the drug market. Most of our subjects do not engage in steady, continuing drug sales – nor are they very reflective and attentive about the rewards of their activity, although one subject pointed out the falsity of popular views about gangs and drug sales.

> MALE #029, "Randell," seventeen-year-old Thundercat: It ain't like on TV where they stereotype us from like L.A. and all that, people got Mercedes Benz and all that. They make about $100 a day, $200 at the most so it ain't no luxury money.
> INT: We've had guys come up here and tell us that they drive convertible BMWs and stuff.
> 029: I'm talking about us. I'm not talking about if you are on a booming set like most likely they are or if they are Bloods.

Reported weekly compensation from drug sales ranges from the ridiculous of zero to the absurd of $15,000. The median and modal category was $500, with eleven subjects reporting that amount. Interestingly, this is approximately the figure reported by Peter Reuter and his associates in their study of the earning of street drug dealers (1990). But we suspect an enormous amount of braggadocio and income inflation in these answers.

> INT: Well, how much do they make a week?
> MALE #005, "Antonio," nineteen-year-old Sixth Street Hoover Crips: I estimate about $2,000 a week. As long as they have money for they car they'll spend the rest of they money. They'll like spend $1,500 and take the other $1,500 and spent that up partying or buying clothes and all that.

> About $3,000 or $4,000 in my pocket. (Male #014, "D. C.," sixteen-year-old Disciple)

> In about a week, $15,000. (Male #019, "Anthony," twenty-two-year-old Crip)

Certainly the appearance and demeanor of the vast majority of our subjects do not reflect a yearly income of $26,000 or more, especially since the most popular way to spend drug money was buying clothes, as shown in Figure 6.3.

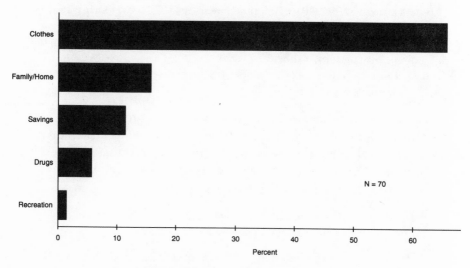

Figure 6.3 Spending Drug Money

Of the seventy subjects who answered this question, nearly two-thirds (forty-six) said that their major use of drug money was to buy clothes. Eleven subjects indicated they used the money for their family or home, three spent it on their kids, three gave it to family members, four were buying or had bought cars, and one used his drug takes for furniture.

> Clothes, gold tooth in my mouth, buying my kids stuff. I wasn't working and the police took my two cars and that led to me pawning all my jewelry. Clothes, they got too little. Gave them to my little cousin. Buying shoes, going to the movies every day, getting drunk. When I'm selling drugs we all get my mom something. She don't ask, just like here mom, here's a fifty, go buy something nice. Or give it to our little sisters, like I want to go to the show, here are a couple of $20s, buy you something. (Male #038, "G.O.D.," nineteen-year-old Compton Gangster)

> I don't spend it. I pay lawyers so if I ever get caught I have enough money to get me out. (Male #072, "Blood," fifteen-year-old Swan Park 59 Blood)

Eight subjects said they saved their drug profits, although only one used an institutional deposit; the rest kept their money at home.

> I ain't spent no money yet. I'm trying to get a job so I can tell my mamma I got a job. I put it [money from drug sales] in a shoe box in my closet. (Male #032, "Skonion," seventeen-year-old Thundercat)

INT: How do you spend the money that you make?

WHITE MALE #091, "Paul," eighteen-year-old 107 Hoover Crips: I save it, I'm buying a house.

INT: You the first one I ever heard say something smart. Most of them talk about buying tennis shoes.

091: I want a house specially made. It's gonna be a round house and it's gonna have a pool on the side.

Four subjects said they used drug money to buy more drugs (to recop) and thus continue their marketing efforts, and one member (perhaps the most honest of those who answered the question) said that he "spent it on women." Other subjects mentioned, as secondary uses, buying gold teeth, partying, or going to the movies and concerts.

> I got me two golds [teeth] and I got me some clothes. (Male #067, "$hortDog," fifteen-year-old Inglewood Family Blood)

> Going crazy buying Nintendos and toys and VCRs and clothes. (Male #015, "Karry," fifteen-year-old Crenshaw Gangster Blood)

Our sense is that much of the money earned from drug sales was used to "keep the party going," especially since drug selling was often engaged in when gang members were low on money for necessary purchases such as beer (Wright and Decker 1994).

> INT: Does the money they make go back into the gang or just into their own pockets?
> 010 MALE: "Jason C.," fifteen-year-old Compton Gangster: Some of it goes to the gang.
> INT: What do you use the money for?
> 010: Beer.

Although forty-seven subjects said that some of the money made from selling drugs went for the use of the gang as a whole; such collective or organizational uses were decidedly secondary. Subjects mentioned using drug profits to purchase weapons for the group, to buy more drugs for resale or use, and to buy "party supplies."

> INT: What do you buy together?
> MALE #017, "Billy," twenty-one-year-old North Side Crip: Mostly equipment like TV, got to keep up on the news, see what's going on, on a different turf, stuff like that.
> INT: Weapons?
> 017: Every so often. We got enough artillery that we need but it don't be used until every once in a while when we have to use it.

> Yeah, like you buy guns and cars. We need cars to get around. (Male #030, "Kenneth," nineteen-year-old Thundercat)

Instead of collective uses, the money made from drugs was usually kept by individual sellers, reflecting the fact that gang members rarely sell drugs in groups larger than pairs or trios as well as the fact that gangs in St. Louis exist primarily for noneconomic reasons. Members of the gangs we interviewed generally lacked the skills or commitment to organize for a long-range profit-making venture.

Who Sells and How They Sell. Drug sales are pervasive in our subjects' experiences, in the gang as well as in the places they stay and hang out. Only seven subjects said that there were no street drug sales in their neighborhood. Nevertheless, despite the invasive presence of the drug market and its importance to gangs, not all of our subjects sell drugs – twenty-one interviewees said that they were not involved at the time of our interview, often because of an arrest.[2]

> About 80–20. Eighty percent do and twenty percent maybe on probation and have to get jobs. (Male #031, "John Doe," sixteen-year-old Thundercat)

> Mostly all of us. At first everybody does but if they get caught they can't sell no more. (Male #082, "Dough Boy," fourteen-year-old B Gangster Disciple)

Even though not all of our subjects sell drugs (or at least were not at the time of our interview), the lure of money and prestige from drug sales is very powerful. Over three-fourths of our subjects estimated that half or more of the members of their gang were involved in the drug trade, as shown in Figure 6.4.

Twelve subjects did not answer this question (possibly because of their marginal or fringe status) and two said that no members of their gang were involved in the drug trades (an assertion denied, in one case, by the eight other Compton Gangsters we interviewed). Yet 70 percent of those who answered this question said that "most or "all" of their members were involved in drug trafficking, although subjects from the same gang gave widely different answers.

While most of the gang members we interviewed sell drugs, there is little indication that much pressure was put on members to sell. Only eighteen subjects said that everyone was expected to meet a sales quota, although these results are somewhat suspect, since we received contra-

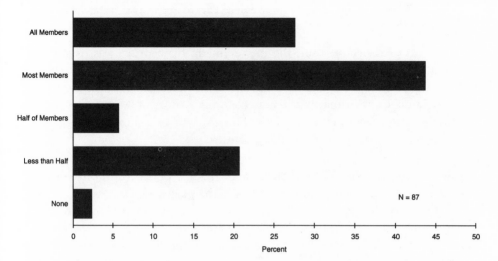

Figure 6.4 Number of Members Selling Drugs

dictory responses from members of the same gang. One Compton Gangster, for example, said that each member was expected to meet a quota, yet five indicated that was not true; four 107 Hoover Crips answered no to that question, while two answered yes; seven Inglewood Family Gangster Bloods answered no, and only one answered yes. This underscores the observation that there is considerable variation within gangs, often due to age differences.

Our subjects' confusion about how much money they make selling drugs, what they do with it, how many members sell, and whether members are expected to sell a certain amount is a reflection of the generally disorganized nature of these gangs' involvement and sporadic character of individual involvement in drug traffic. It is likely the case that one gang member is unaware of the involvement in drug sales of another member, a consequence of the lack of formal structure and organization within the gang. Perhaps nowhere is this more apparent than in the structure of selling and the allotment of sales turfs. Some members sketched out a division of labor in drug sales, with individuals assigned as rock-up men, runners, sellers, stash keepers, gun holders, and lookouts.

> Somebody sell, somebody looking out, somebody standing by a gun, everybody be on the corner watching for the police. Some on this side, some on that side watching different directions and shit. (Male #036, "NA," eighteen-year-old Compton Gangster BIC)

Somebody will hold the money, somebody will hold the drugs, somebody will hold the gun and look out, some persons will watch the street and look out for the police. (Male #030, "Kenneth," nineteen-year-old Thundercat)

One person will run and give the person the dope and he'll run back. The other person will go and get the money and run back. Some people go get the dope and say come talk to him and he'll give you $20, you give him the rock and go. (Male #015, "Karry," fifteen-year-old Crenshaw Gangster Blood)

Two subjects described how much their drug sales resembled a business:

Records, salesmen, muscles, same as a legal business. (Male #019, "Anthony," twenty-two-year-old Crip)

MALE #041: "C. K.," twenty-two-year-old Blood: You got enforcers, you got people that are like the treasurer, we have certain person just to hold the money because we might fuck up on the money.
INT: He count the money?
041: Yeah, he count the money and keep it. Then we got the person that deals with the hook up with the big person. You got the people that go get the guns.
INT: You got people that actually sell it too, right?
041: Sell what, guns?
INT: No, the dope.
041: Yeah. Everybody sell the dope.
INT: Any more: enforcer, treasurer, connections.
041: That's basically about it.

And a final subject described a well-thought-out delivery method.

Yeah, it's like my uncle used to work at Union Station and he was a valet parker. People that come there he ask them do they want some of this and they say yeah and then he will come to Laclede Town to get some from me and take it back, stuff like that. It be in their car when they come back from Union Station. (Male #004, "Anthony," seventeen-year-old Thundercat)

But most subjects could not or would not delineate a division of labor in drug sales. Only forty-three subjects could identify different jobs in selling drugs, and their level of specificity was, to say the least, less than detailed. Twenty-seven specified a "seller," eleven mentioned "lookouts," and four said "runner" in answer to our questions. Many seemed confused by the notion that there could be different jobs when selling drugs.

INT: What are the different jobs in selling drugs?

FEMALE #078: "Tina," fifteen-year-old Hoover Crip: What you mean? What else can you do besides that?

INT: What are the different jobs in selling drugs?

MALE #092: "Derone," twenty-one-year-old Rolling 60's Crips: Different jobs? Sell it to whoever you want to.

INT: I mean how many people do you need to sell drugs? Do you need like three people to sell drugs?

092: No, it don't matter, that's just money, it don't matter because you can get one seller and still make as much.

INT: So you don't need runners or watch out for anybody?

092: No. Police don't know what the fuck they're doing. You can go in the backyard and sell it out there.

One subject reacted with scorn to the thoughtless behavior of his fellow members who sold drugs.

No, everybody just out to make their money. They run out there like idiots instead of having a plan. (Male #005, "Antonio," nineteen-year-old 6th Street Hoover Crip)

In general, drug sales seem to be fairly disorganized as to time and sales structures. Many subjects said that they sold drugs when they wanted to make money, not at any fixed time. Subjects also indicated that selling on the street was fairly chaotic, with lots of individuals involved and with little coherence to the tasks involved in such sales.

Another way gang drug sales are disorganized is the lack of central direction. Although a third of our subjects said that their main suppliers were also leaders in the gang, forty-three subjects said that was not true.

INT: The guy who supplies you with the drugs, is he a leader in the group?

MALE #028: "Killa 4 Ren," fifteen-year-old 187 Crip: No, he ain't even a Crip, he ain't nothing. He just sells dope.

Again, members of the same gang contradicted each other over this point. Ten members of the Rolling 60's Crips, for example, said that their main suppliers were not leaders in the gang, while five said they were. Five 107 Hoover Crips said that their main suppliers were leaders, while one said they were not; and similarly, six Inglewood Family Gangster Bloods identified their main suppliers as leaders, while two denied their leadership role. In addition, while fifty-one subjects said that selling drugs increased a member's influence and prestige in the gang, thirty-four subjects denied that it did. Our sense is that gang members who sell large amounts of drugs or who can control distribution are influential because of the money they can spend or the help they can provide to other members but that it is not the only characteristic that leads to increased influence and importance in a gang. As with any organization, however loose its structure, those who can deliver the goods gain a number of important advantages.

Drug Turfs. Although one subject said that "anyone who wants to can sell drugs on our turf," most gang members aver that their set maintains fairly exclusive drug-selling turfs.

> INT: Do you allow other people to sell drugs on the street?
> MALE #032: "Skonion," seventeen-year-old Laclede Town Thundercat: Not in Laclede Town.

> INT: Is there a particular area of turf that's important to your gang?
> MALE #041: "C. K.," twenty-two-year-old Blood: Yeah.
> INT: What spot is that? What is it for?
> 041: Drug traffic. Not nothing but drugs.
> INT: So the drug areas you ain't going to give up and they got to be run right?
> 041: Yeah.
> INT: No bullshit in between on this deal.
> 041: No bullshit.

Encroachment on another set's drug turf is, in fact, a major cause of gang fights. Almost all subjects who discussed drug turf mentioned the use of violence (or threats) as the main method of dealing with interlopers.

> MALE #017: "Billy," twenty-one-year-old North Side Crip: Yeah, we have to push them out of our area. As long as they're not in our area and they on their turf doing their thing, that's cool.
> INT: You told me about a fight about a year ago. Was that somebody trying to sell drugs?
> 017: Yeah, trying to sell drugs. It was a stranger. That's what we don't care about, he can take his business somewhere else. Come on our turf then you messing up our thing.

> INT: What if somebody from another gang comes on you all set, what happens?
> MALE #061: "K-Red," fifteen-year-old Inglewood Family Gangster Blood: They get shot at, get jumped on.

Some favored (or infamous) locations for drug sales are shared – with more than one set of allied gangs selling drugs – and such locations may also change hands.

> INT: Have you all had to defend you all turf in the last year?
> FEMALE #096: "L. C.," twenty-three-year-old Inglewood Bounty Hunter: No. Well, yes we have.
> INT: What did you all have to do?
> 096: We had to defend our turf out selling the drugs cause we had people comin' in and try to take over.

One infamous site in St. Louis is a place called the Horseshoe. In the fall of 1991 that area was controlled by Blood gangs, as "Lil-B Dog" explains:

> INT: Do you guys have a particular turf that's important to you?
> MALE #070: "Lil-B Dog," fifteen-year-old Inglewood Family Gangster: Yeah. It's on Jennings Station Road and over in the Horseshoe.
> INT: Are you guys the only Blood set over in the Horseshoe?
> 070: No. There's a lot more. 62 Brims over there, a lot more.
> INT: Why is it important to you guys?
> 070: Cause everybody come over there and we sell our dope over there.

But within the gang, there is usually no fixed or permanent location within the larger area. Individuals or small groups select their own sales site:

> INT: How do you divide the area up amongst the gang members? You can't all be selling on the same street corner.
> MALE #050: "John," nineteen-year-old Rolling 60's Crip: No. You make your own set and I make my own set.

External Sources, Suppliers, and Drug Houses. Discussions of vertical distribution and higher-level drug trafficking were usually avoided by our subjects, most probably because they lacked the relevant knowledge (less probably is that they were too scared to discuss the topic with us). While a third of our subjects said that gang leaders were the main suppliers of drugs, forty-three subjects said that gang leaders were not their supply source, and twenty-three subjects did not know whether the main suppliers of drugs were leaders in their own gangs.

> The people who's not in the gang, they the ones with the best connections. (Male #005, "Antonio," nineteen-year-old 6th Street Hoover Crip)

The main suppliers are in our group but not leaders. (Male #040, "Knowledge," twenty-one-year-old Compton Gangster)

Higher-level drug dealers were often mentioned, but little solid information was provided about them.

INT: The guy who supplies you with the drugs, is he a leader in the group?
MALE #028: "Killa 4 Ren," fifteen-year-old 187 Crip: No, he ain't even a Crip, he ain't nothing. He just sells dope.

INT: Where do those guys get those drugs? Who supplies them?
MALE #029: "Randell," seventeen-year-old Thundercat: White man out in the county.
INT: How do they get them? Does the white man come around with a bunch of rocks?
029: Yeah. Pounds, rock it up yourself.
INT: Your gang rocks it up?
029: The people who sell it.

Drug houses exist in most gang neighborhoods, but only a few gang members are involved in either selling out of houses, protecting those in their neighborhood, or competing with drug houses. Seventy-one subjects said there were drug houses in their neighborhood (and twenty-one said there were not). Some subjects boasted about the number of drug houses their gang had.

Yeah, we got about nine rock houses, nine. (Male #001, "Mike-Mike," twenty-year-old Thundercat)

Yeah, a couple of different ones. There be about three rock houses. (Male #012, "Lance," twenty-year-old West Side Mob member)

And some seemed confused about our question:

No. We have like vacant buildings we sit up in, get us a long table, everybody just go scatter around the corner watching them. (Male #003, "Jerry," eighteen-year-old Thundercat)

When gangs do run houses, they protect them as if they were drug turfs.

MALE #015: "Karry," fifteen-year-old Crenshaw Gangster Blood: Dope house is the most important. That's how you make your living.
INT: If somebody from another gang tried to come into your dope house or come on the property of your dope house, what would happen to them?
015: He would get shot.

The general lack of involvement in drug houses on the part of gang members reflects the disorganized, sporadic nature of drug sales on their part. Maintaining a drug house requires a commitment of time and purpose inconsistent with the life the majority of our subjects chose to live.

What's Sold and To Whom. The most frequently mentioned drug being sold on the streets is crack cocaine. Ninety-four subjects mentioned this as a drug sold by themselves or in their neighborhood as shown in Figure 6.5. Thirty-six subjects also mentioned cocaine.

Marijuana (or weed) was mentioned fifty-eight times, although some subjects were rather confused about what weed actually is.

> INT: What drugs are being sold?
> FEMALE #078: "Tina," fifteen-year-old Treetop Blood: Coke, crack, marijuana.
> INT: Anything else?
> 078: Weed, that's all.
> INT: Weed is marijuana?
> 078: No.
> INT: What is marijuana then?
> 078: I don't know.
> INT: What is weed?
> 078: Stuff you smoke.

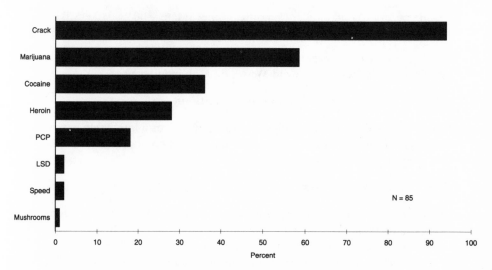

Figure 6.5 Type of Drugs Being Sold

And one subject averred that weed was no longer sold seriously by any-one.

INT: Does the gang sell more drugs since you joined?

MALE #012: "Lance," twenty-year-old West Side Mob member: Yeah man. I'm talking about hard drugs. Ain't nobody sell marijuana no more, hard drugs.

Heroin was mentioned twenty-nine times, although it appears that few, if any, of our subjects sell heroin and many are unfamiliar with the drug. One mention, for example, was made of "capsules" (not the form in which the drug is sold) of black tar being sold on the street. PCP was mentioned eighteen times – it seems most frequently to have been sold mixed with cocaine or weed.

MALE #004: "Anthony," seventeen-year-old Thundercat: Heroin, co-caine, marijuana, and Dips.

INT: What's a Dip?

004: It's like dipped in . . .

INT: Wack?

004: Yeah.

INT: Like a wack bomb, PCP.

No, we really don't fuck with that [PCP] no more. We used to sell that shit, that shit make you go crazy, man. I won't go around that shit no more man. (Male #012, "Lance," twenty-year-old West Side Mob member)

Only two mentions were made of speed or amphetamines being sold in St. Louis. Two mentions were also made of LSD (and one of mush-rooms), although the subject who did so viewed those as "county" drugs, items being sold to white kids in more affluent neighborhoods.

As far as the quantities being sold on the street, the modal category was $20 to $25 rocks of cocaine, mentioned by forty-two subjects. Two subjects said that larger quantities, fifties, were being sold, and nine subjects said that the normal amounts were smaller, sixteenths, or as they are known on the street, teenagers. Overall, these results are consistent with a number of indicators of drug use in St. Louis, including those from the Drug Use Forecasting program and the Drug Abuse Warning Network.

Figure 6.6 displays our subjects' perception of the race of drug cus-tomers. Both black and white customers are reported, although three times as many subjects said their customers were mostly or all black than said customers were mostly all white.

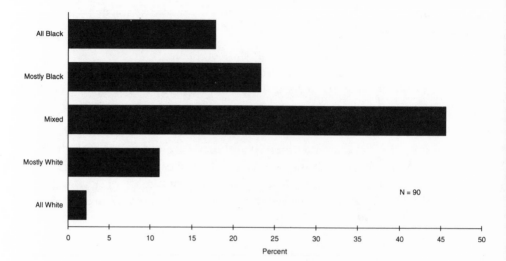

Figure 6.6 Race of Drug Customers

While this finding is consistent with what we perceive the local, neighborhood nature of St. Louis drug sales to be, subjects' statements often portrayed a more diverse customer base.

> Naw, it's people from everywhere. I got some, I got lawyers and doctors and nurses, everybody be buying coke from me. (Male #001, "Mike-Mike," twenty-year-old Thundercat)

> Some people sell to fiends, some people sell to old men, mammas, family members. (Male #068, "CK," sixteen-year-old Piru 104 Blood)

As we have mentioned, drug customers, especially crack fiends, are not held in high regard by our subjects. Although half of our subjects said there was competition for customers, this does not seem to be because buyers are a valued, long-term resource, whose favor and custom should be curried. Instead, most competition seemed to be episodic and spur of the moment (e.g., cutting out another gang member from a sale) and also reflective of the disorganized and chaotic state of the market.

> MALE #018: "Maurice," twenty-year-old 107 Hoover Crip: Fiends. You can tell a fiend a mile away. Somebody who looks like they lost a lot of weight, got on some raggedy clothes, they really don't care about theyself. They dirty all the time.
> INT: Is it mostly blacks?

> 018: All blacks. Half of the black city of St. Louis smoke coke. You got some whites but basically you got all blacks.

Drug customers are generally treated poorly by our subjects, who spoke of committing serious violence against them.

> That's why, with me, you know, I let em know right now ya'll ain't gonna take no stuff off nobody. When people come down here like this lady yesterday, she wanted to buy some rocks. And she, she played like she had a pistol, boy they whipped her. I say man don't do that lady like that. But she had a gun for real, tried to rob one of my little partners. I told 'em to kill her. (Male #001, "Mike-Mike," twenty-year-old Thundercat)

> INT: Do the rock stars sometimes try to pull off without paying?
> MALE #051: "David," eighteen-year-old Blood: Oh yeah, they try to do that a lot.
> INT: How do you all stop that from happening?
> 051: Shoot them.

Subjects also described how they stole from customers, borrowed their cars, demanded sexual favors in return for drugs.

> MALE #028: "Killa 4 Ren," fifteen-year-old 187 Crip: Yeah, they'll do anything. One lady do it with the dog.
> INT: Just for a rock?
> 028: Yeah.
> INT: You ever seen that?
> 028: Yeah. She took off all her clothes and was kissing him.
> INT: How old was she?
> 028: About 22. She was young.

> Yeah, straight up smokers. If they good looking we probably mess around with them for a minute. (Male #037, "Big Money," twenty-two-year-old Compton Gangster)

We have little evidence about whether some gangs in our sample are more involved in drug sales than others, although it is probably true that some are. There is a wide-spread perception, held by at least one-quarter of our subjects (from both Blood and Crip gangs) that gangs affiliated with Bloods are more involved in drug sales and more focused on making money than are Crip groups. This may be true in St. Louis, but it is more likely just an item of folklore about Los Angeles gangs. No single gang exhibits a monolithic drug sales organization or much more formal structure than any other gang we have information about.

Within gangs there is much variation, as discussed above, in the amount, time, and organization of drug sales. All of the gangs in our sample contain particular cliques and individuals who are more heavily involved in drug trafficking, both as sellers and suppliers. To some extent this is age dependent, as well as dependent on length of membership. Older members, and those who have been associated longer, are more involved in drug sales. They possess the necessary social capital – experience, motivation, social ties within and without the gang – that allow greater involvement. This form of social capital is crucial for successful (or even intermittently regular) retail sales, since ties to a social network are necessary for connecting with a supplier.

As we have discussed, gangs do not control the drug market in the St. Louis area. They do not have a retail monopoly, they are not the major suppliers (and in most cases are not even intermediate suppliers), and are essentially at the lowest level of retail distribution. Residential drug houses (such as the crack houses of New York) are rarely kept by our subjects. Although several members boasted of the number of drug houses their gang ran, the typical situation was the temporary or intermittent use of vacant premises, and almost all subjects who discussed the subject said that sales out of their own residence was a stupid and dangerous way to do business.

Most gang drug sales occur on the street, or as we shall see in Chapter 7, in school. Street corners, cul-de-sacs, protected locations with good avenues of escape are favored. Gang members typically sell by themselves or in pairs or trios within their own neighborhood. Guns (and drugs) are normally stashed separately and not on the sellers' person. But there is usually little organization of how sales are handled. Only four or five gangs seemed to have any rational, formal role differentiation; and that is probably applicable only to particular cliques within the gang.

Profits from drug sales do not go to any kind of common fund or gang treasury. A member's earnings accrue only to the seller and are spent on the typical purchases of teenagers (clothes, entertainment, jewelry, impressing others) or to buy more drugs for sale but seldom saved or invested for capital formation. Gang members may exist in a capitalist economy, but their behaviors are those of consumers, not entrepreneurs.

Gang members in St. Louis are, obviously, involved in crack and other drug sales in a major way. Although few of our subjects said they were attracted to the gang by the opportunity to sell drugs, once in, this opportunity to make money assumed much greater importance. But, as with many other aspects of their lives and their activities as gang members, their participation in drug sales is episodic, loosely organized, and subject to dramatic swings of interest and attention. This reflects the loose organizational structure of the gang and independence of its members. Apparently, drugs are a major source of money, though not in the amounts popular stereotypes would have us believe (nor, probably, in the amounts reported by gang members). Drug sales also figure prominently as causes of gang violence – roughing up customers, chasing off competitors, and defending turf – the topic of the next section.

"Piling on Crabs and Shooting Slobs": Violence and Gangs

> Beating Crabs. If it wasn't for beating Crabs I don't think that I would be in a gang right now. (Male #057, "Smith & Wesson," fifteen-year-old Neighborhood Posse Blood)

> [Our] group is the Rolling 60's. Basically we're just a fighting crew. What we do is to fight and make money. We rough ourselves up. Get ourselves tougher cause we feel we better than all the rest. So like if a Hoover comes up and he talks shit then we have to whup his ass because Hoovers think they crazier than us but we the craziest but we know what we doing. We like Al Capone back in his days, suited up and know what he doing. We just normally kick ass. (Male #092, "Derone," twenty-one-year-old Rolling 60's Crip)

Violence and violent crime is a central part of our subjects' lives in manifold ways. The "violence of everyday life,"[3] for example, is excessively high in their neighborhoods and families. City rates of child abuse, forcible theft, rape, assaults, and homicide are well above those for the St. Louis metropolitan area and the nation. Although we did not systematically explore the level of family and neighborhood violence in our interviews, enough background information allows us to infer its existence at high levels. Eight of our subjects mentioned having a relative who died from gunshot wounds or some other form of homicide; *more than half knew another gang member who had been shot.* Eleven of our subjects are now dead. Further evidence is apparent, as discussed in Chapters 2 and 3, by the importance of threat and the need for protection in generating gangs and membership.

A second arena in which violence and conflict are central is in the nature and characteristics of gangs and gang membership. Frederic Thrasher, writing nearly seventy years ago, observed that what boys receive from membership in gangs is the thrill and zest of participation in common interest, more especially in corporate action, in hunting, capture, conflict, flight and escape. *Conflict with other gangs and the world about them* furnishes the occasion for many of their exciting group activities. (1927, 37, emphasis added).

This finding is just as true today and, in fact, it is echoed in our subjects' own words. Conflict, especially the use of lethal violence, not only differentiates these gangs and their members from other delinquent groups (and nondelinquent groups), it also epitomizes both the nature of St. Louis youth gangs and their appeal for our subjects.

> That's what it originated from, a clique. Say we all together one day walking down the street and someone says such and such jumped me one day. Let's go find him. They came back with a whole bunch of people and got to fighting each other. Eventually those two sides decided they didn't like each other. [Our gang] originated when a person got killed out there. Before that we was just all friends hanging out. One night everybody drinking and a car rolled back and some Slobs got out and started shooting. The person who got shot is dead. When he got killed, that's when it all originated. From that one incident. (Female #046, "Lady Tee," sixteen-year-old 74 Hoover Crip)

> Because we get together and everybody drinks and then we want to holler at some girls. Some girls don't want to talk so we disrespect them or call them a name. After that they go get they brothers or whatever and they be the opposite from us and they hurt one of us and we go hurt one of them. (Male #056, "Tony," seventeen-year-old 19th Street Hoover Crip)[4]

The observation by Thrasher that conflict with other groups often was combined with the pursuit of "thrills" is echoed in the following quote.

> Somebody was playing around in the car but we knew them. They cut they lights off and started driving down. We started shooting at they car and then they came out. We seen them duck down and then they got back up and we knew them and they was just playing around. (Male #074, "Shon," sixteen-year-old Crenshaw Mob Gangster)

Every act of violence by gang members embodies a salient characteristic of St. Louis gangs – protection from real and apparent threats of physical violence and revenge or retaliation for real or perceived injuries and insults. "Jumping in" an initiate not only replicates a real event often committed against gang members; it also experientially shows the new member what he will be protected from and what he will be revenged for. This ritual also reassures old members that the initiate has the courage and ability to defend or revenge them if it is ever necessary. Other violent acts by gang members – drive-bys, drug turf protection, beating up welshing customers – serve as deterrents and warnings. These acts advertise to all that the gang intends to protect its own and how far its members will go in standing up for each other.

Finally, violence is endemic in a third arena, their individual status and role behaviors as gang members. Members are expected to always be ready to commit violence, to participate in violent acts, and to have engaged in some sort of violence in their initiation. Several measures support this assertion. Fewer than five subjects (all female) had never been in a gang-related fight of some sort. Thirteen subjects, at the time of our interviews, volunteered that they had been shot.[5] Three subjects, in fact, had each been shot twice in their lives to that point. Even more startling, eleven of the ninety-nine active members we interviewed are no longer alive – victims of homicide. Eleven dead out of ninety-nine yields a homicide rate of more than 11,000 homicides per 100,000 population – a rate more than *1,000* times greater than the U.S. rate. Even annualizing that rate over the five years since we started interviewing (2,222 per 100,000), this is a startling statistic. By comparison, the 1992 uniform Crime Reports show a national homicide rate of 9.3 per 100,000, a rate of 15.7 for the St. Louis Metropolitan area, and a rate of 57 per 100,000 for St. Louis City. The most relevant comparison group would be the national population of gang members, unavailable for obvious reasons. The best available comparison to our subjects is young black males of similar ages. In 1990 the homicide rate for black males aged fifteen to nineteen was 116 per 100,000 and for black males aged twenty to twenty-four it was 162 per 100,000. The rate of violent death for our subjects is thus thirteen times greater than the rate for twenty to twenty-four year-old black males if we annualize, and *sixty-eight times higher* as an annual rate. A grim statistic indeed.

In the remainder of this chapter we discuss the violence and violent criminality engaged in by our subjects. We start with a statistical overview of what interviews tell us about the kinds and frequency of violence and the possession and use of weapons. We then provide a qualitative discussion of kinds, causes and circumstances of violent acts committed by our subjects followed by an examination of levels and frequency. We conclude with our subjects' views on violence, responses that convey a sense of fear, fatalism, and enjoyment.

"We Just Grew Up Fightin." Violence is an ordinary part of most of our subjects lives, although it obviously intensifies once they joined a gang and become more involved in gang activities. One subject described why he joined the gang in this way.

> We just grew up like that. We grew up fightin, if, I don't know, we just grew up fightin and everybody hangin around so they decided to call they self somethin since we hung around like that went out doin things and stuff. (Male #002, "Eric," sixteen-year-old Thundercat)

Violence in and by the gang starts early for our subjects: seventy subjects said they were "jumped in" for their initiation.

> Well, first we talk to them about what we do all that type of stuff. The next day he's gotta wear all blue and stand in a circle and everybody just rush him all at one time and then back off of him and see if he still standing. If he drop he got to get back up and take it again. That's how you initiate a man. I say about nine people around and just rush him with heads and if he fall he's got to get back up. If he want out he want out, let go of the circle and walk out. (Male #003, "Jerry," eighteen-year-old Thundercat)

> A group of niggers, you in the middle of a circle, then all the sudden they rush you and you have to fight back. They have to beat you until you bleed. If you survive, you win. Then they give you hugs and stuff and call you Cuz. (Male #044, "Paincuzz," sixteen-year-old Rolling 60's Crip)

"Beating in" has different levels of intensity and often may only be the start of internal gang violence.

> No, see we got older people. They tied them down to a telephone pole and beat the hell out of them. Fuck that. Yeah, tied to a telephone pole. There be about six niggers, sometimes more than six. The younger ones just take a little beat down, not like what they go through. At least we didn't get tied down. [To become a full fledged member] you got to get a tattoo on your arm and then you got to get your Blood name carved in your left arm. Sometimes they get the end of a hangar, the hook, and they put it up under the fire for real long time and then they carve that shit in your arm. Yeah, I got one. (Male #068, "CK," sixteen-year-old Piru 104 Blood)

Eight subjects said they had to shoot someone for their initiation.

> I met these Bloods and they said do you want to get in? I had to get these Crabs and that type of stuff. I ran and got my .38, I ran by, I'm a Blood so I said what's up Fuz and they said no Cuz, I started shooting, pow, pow and we drove off. And that's how I became one. I don't know if I hit them or not. (Male #057, "Smith & Wesson," fifteen-year-old Neighborhood Posse Blood)

His name was Eliminator. He was 13. We asked him how he wanted to get in and he said he wanted to do a ride-by and shoot the person who killed his brother. So he did a ride-by shooting and killed him. (Male #069, "X-Men," fourteen-year-old Inglewood Family Gangster)

Pop somebody. Not no ride-bys, you walk up to them and you pop them. You got to do it, just get it over with no hesitation. (Male #086, "Gunn," nineteen-year-old Rolling 60's Crip)

And several subjects mentioned other kinds of violence involved in joining a gang.

To be a Crip you have to put your blue rag on your head and wear all blue and go in a Blood neighborhood that is the hardest of all of them and walk through the Blood neighborhood and fight Bloods. If you come out without getting killed that's the way you get initiated. Another set say you got to swim across some river or something like that. If you make it back you in there or you got to smoke somebody in your family or something like that. (Male #084, "Rolo," fifteen-year-old Rolling 60's Crip)

These acts at initiation serve to legitimate and normalize violence within the gang.

Not every gang member we interviewed was excessively violent.

I had to rob somebody but I didn't do it. I just told them a lie. (Male #052, "Jonathan," fifteen-year-old 107 Hoover Crip)

Well first somebody had to pick a fight and get in trouble with a teacher but I didn't get in trouble with the teacher because it was a sub and they don't do nothing to us really. Just picking a fight with somebody and getting in trouble with a teacher and stuff. (Female #078, "Tina," fifteen-year-old Treetop Blood)

Eighty-four subjects mentioned "fighting" as "something they did with their gang," while nineteen said it was what they did the most with their fellow members. Seventy-six subjects said that a good reason to belong was to "defend their neighborhood," and eighty-four said that they belonged for "protection." And if their neighborhoods are unsafe and in need of protection, the supervised confines of educational establishments were not much better. Seventy-eight subjects said there were gang fights at their schools, eighty-three said that weapons (usually guns) were brought to school, and thirty-eight said that weapons were used at school.

Gun possession and use is another window into our subjects' violent propensities and opportunities. Guns were the overwhelming weapon of choice for gang-motivated and gang-related violence. Eighty subjects said they owned guns (two subjects reported they owned over one hundred guns), and the mean number of guns reported was four and a half (the mode was one). Only 192 guns were specifically identified by our subjects, and 75 percent of those were handguns of one sort or another. Subjects also mentioned owning other kinds of weapons besides firearms.

> Hand grenades? I got about fifty of them. (Male #001, "Mike-Mike," twenty-year-old Thundercat)

Sixty-six subjects said they had used their guns at least once. When we asked what caused them to use their gun most recently, forty-seven gave no answer. Of the fifty-two subjects who answered, three gave the relatively innocuous answer of "celebrating the New Year." Twenty-six subjects had last used their guns in a gang fight, four in a drive-by shooting; four because a drug customer tried to rob them; four because they were attacked by a stranger; and eleven subjects gave a variety of miscellaneous answers (e.g., robberies, shooting at gang rivals who were passing by, etc.).

Other weapons besides guns were mentioned, though infrequently. Eighty-eight subjects (97 percent of those who answered this question) said that gang violence involved weapons, and the same number said that "guns" were the weapons used in violence (only two subjects mentioned knives, and one mentioned bats or sticks). Nevertheless, one subject mentioned rather unusual weapons involved in gang conflicts:

> Guns, knives, we even had a boy that had arrows. I ain't bullshiting you. He come up there with motherfuckin' arrows, thought he was Rambo. Sat in a motherfuckin' tree started shooting at us. Hit one of my boys dead in his leg, went right through it. The last fight that broke out was the time that cat was sitting up in the tree. He was sittin' in a distant tree. He had a three-string bow, real powerful. He sat up there and had a scope on it and everything. I don't know who he was tryin' to tag. The first time we heard it I said I could have sworn I heard something. It missed us. The second time it hit my boy dead in his leg and went right through it. It was like the end with the feathers was sittin' right at the top and the rest was sticking way out. He ran and he broke it then he fell. I said damn, somebody's shootin' arrows at our ass. So then my boy got up and he started looking around, looking everywhere, looked up in the tree and saw him shooting arrows. He climbed in the tree, swung that nigger down and beat him with his own bow and shit. (Male #092, "Derone," twenty-one-year-old Rolling 60's Crip)

The only time that we have killed this one boy named Kevin. He was a Treetop and he was runnin' through the woods and my boy had a machete and he hit him, he cut him all up in his rear. (Male #092, "Derone," twenty-one-year-old Rolling 60's Crip)

Our subjects most recent arrests also show how commonplace violence is: Seventeen were for assault, six for peace disturbances, three for weapons violations, two for obstructing police, and one was for homicide. Nine subjects had an assault conviction; six had weapons violations convictions; one had a manslaughter conviction. Ten subjects had done time for assault, four for weapons violations, and one for manslaughter.

"We Be Fighting All The Time": Causes and Kinds of Violence. While we would like to report that our subjects sharply differentiate their use of lethal versus nonlethal violence according to targets, too many subjects' descriptions invalidate the distinction. It is our impression that violence that lacks a gang motive or is unrelated to the gang is less likely to be lethal.

Yeah. I, uh close as I shot somebody was on the forty-one Lee, cause an old man got on the bus, no the man wasn't old, but he was drunk, and he kept on playing wit me, and I told 'em he better get away from me, then he kept on hittin on me, I say hey man, you better go on man, and I kept tellin' the bus driver and the bus driver wouldn't do nothin, and then so he grabbed me like this but he was standing up and I was sittin down and he grabbed me and had me in a hold, and I pulled out the gun, a .32 and popped him in his stomach. Naw. I jumped off the bus. The bus driver wouldn't let me off the bus, so I said you don't let me off the bus you gonna get shot, so he opened up the bus. (Male #002, "Eric," sixteen-year-old Thundercat)

We were at the White Castle one day and one of my partners stepped on this guy's foot. He said excuse me and he had his friend with him and my partner said I said excuse me, I'm sorry just like that. He punched my partner in the face and we just got to fighting. I didn't know my partner had this pistol in his pocket and shot him in his leg, paralyzed him. (Male #040, "Knowledge," twenty-one-year-old Compton Gangsters)

Violence by and towards gang members seems to lurk around every corner. Sometimes it is a sudden unexpected eruption, sometimes the result of long simmering feuds or disagreements that are not seemingly gang motivated or related.

I was down in the projects, Vaughn, this girl was [performing oral sex]. She was doing this to everybody. The next day my brother came and got me and we went on the south side. She was there. I got out of the car, I asked her could I have it. She got to swinging on me. I hit her a couple of times, my brother hit her a couple of times. I got tired of whupping her. I got tired of hitting her so I shot her. I didn't kill her though. She still live around the corner. [I shot her] in the side. (Male #034, "Lil Gene Mack," eighteen-year-old 19th Street Rolling 60's Crip)

[The last fist fight] that was yesterday at the community center. It was just talk about one of the guys in the neighborhood. The crazy thing about it was it was amongst us. One of the guys said that he had fucked this guy's sister and he heard it and they got to fighting. It was harmless. He was just defending his sister's name. He can't keep her pants up. (Male #040, "Knowledge," twenty-one-year-old Compton Gangster)

Just hanging around with gang members can lead to violence:

> INT: How old were you when you first started hanging out with them?
> MALE #053, "Jimmy," eighteen-year-old 107 Hoover Crip: About 14.
> INT: How old were you when you first became a member?
> 053: Not too long ago, when I turned 18.
> INT: They let you escape that long without really joining up?
> 053: Yeah. When I used to hang with them about four years ago some dude threw some gasoline on me and set me on fire.
> INT: That's how you started hanging out with them?
> 053: Yeah, been shot twice.
> INT: So they threw gasoline on you and shot you a couple of times and that's one of the reasons you started hanging out with the 107s?
> 053: Yeah.

Gang membership – claiming or perpetrating – increases the potential and actuality of violence. Initiations are violent. Colors make a person a target, a victim, and a victimizer.

> MALE #050, "John," nineteen-year-old Rolling 60's Crip: One day I was on the Kingshighway bus and I was going to go get my Social Security card. I was walking down Kingshighway. I wasn't into no gang and these dudes walked up to me. They was Bloods, we call them Slobs. They walked up to me like what's up Blood. You in the wrong hustle. I ain't with that gang stuff Cuz. So they was gonna fight me. So I say fuck that. Went back on the north side, got drunk and then got up with the Crips. Just like that.
> INT: Because the Bloods wanted to beat you up?
> 050: Yeah. I wear blue so I'm going to get beat up anyways so I say I just deal with the Crips.

Even going out to meet interviewers can be dangerous.

I got shot by a guy two weeks ago. I was walking out the door to meet Dietrich on the corner and I got shot. I was out front of the door and some of my boys was behind me. I don't know who it was. It had to be somebody outside of the neighborhood. Over in the city, the city is about three blocks from us, no North Side Bloods. It must have been somebody from over there. We was meeting Dietrich on the corner, we was walking out the door. I heard a gun shot and I got hit and I knew it. I had walked back in the house like I forgot something and raised my shirt up and it was bloody and I said I got shot. So my brother called an ambulance and I went back on outside and put my head down. I thought I was going to faint. [I got shot] at the bottom of my heart. It went through my liver and my stomach and my diaphragm. Someone from the city. I figure whoever walked out the door first was going to be shot. There's Bloods in the city, it had to be Bloods. (Male #024, "Hamilton," sixteen-year-old 107 Hoover Gangster Crip)

Disrespect has to be corrected and answered – physically. And drug turfs are defended; customers who cheat you are violently punished.

A guy came in, he had the wrong colors on, he got to move out. He got his head split open with a sledgehammer, he got two ribs broken, he got his face torn up. We dropped him off on the other side of town. If he did die, it was on the other side of town. (Male #013, "Darryl," twenty-nine-year-old Blood)

I had to pistol whip a guy, I shot him in the knee. Since then he never came back. (Male #017, "Billy," twenty-one-year-old North Side Crip)

If a member becomes a victim, revenge is necessary. And this revenge is schismogenic, resulting in an increasing cycle of retaliation and revenge.

INT: What happened yesterday?
MALE #039, "Kaons BIC," seventeen-year-old Compton Gangster: This dude had beat up one of our friends. He was cool with one of my friends but he had beat up another one of my friends before. They came back and busted one of my friend's head. We was going to get him.

I was standing on Sarah somewhere and three Bloods walked up to me. I knew I was on Blood territory but that's the route I have to go to get to my aunt's house. I was standing outside and on the corner and then they approached me. They didn't say not one word. They just hit me. I went back like this and then they ran. I just went pow, pow and shot it three times. I hit one of them in the leg. He fell down so I just ran on up to my auntie's house and called the fellas. Then they came on down and had it out. (Male #020, "Lil Thug," sixteen-year-old Gangster Disciple)

About two weeks ago some group called _____ but they Crips too, they had it out with one of our boys and stuff. We had a little argument and they came and got us. There was about ten of us walking around seeing what was up. We got to shooting at them and stuff. Some of them got to fighting and stuff and threw my friend down. He got shot in the chest twice. My boy got shot yesterday, TJ, he got shot yesterday. Some dudes drove up on him. (Male #053, "Jimmy," eighteen-year-old 107 Hoover Crip)

Getting out of this violent cycle is not easy. One subject told this story of how his brother left a gang.

My big brother. He was in the 38s. They say to get out of the 38s you got to kill your parents, kill one of your parents. My brother was making good grades, got him a scholarship and everything and he was like I'm leaving this alone. They tried to make him kill my mother. He was like, you must be crazy and I was on his side. So the leader, _____, big husky dude, him and my brother got into it. They was fighting and he pulled a gun out so I stabbed him in the back. I thought he was going to shoot my brother, which he was so, I stabbed him in the back. He paralyzed now. (Male #037, "Big Money," twenty-two-year-old Compton Gangster)

Cowardice is highly disapproved, since standing up for your friends and fellow members is almost a sacred duty (and a raison d'etre for being in a gang).

One time I had a fight, this dude was supposed to be down with me, dude named Steve. We went around the corner on Becker, that's the next street up from Genivieve. I was up there, I had beat up four Bloods up there on Lillian and everybody seen it. So the next day I went around the corner. I was standing right there and a Blood came and I said what's up man. Me and him got to banging and stuff and after that he ran and brought a whole bunch of dudes with him. The dude that was supposed to be with me, Steve, I said you down with me man? He said yeah man. So I'm up there fighting and I turned around looking for him and he was gone. Then I was fighting all by myself. I was messed up. I had six stitches right here, my two ribs is broken right here, I got cracked in the face with a 40-ounce bottle. There's still a piece of glass in my eye right, it's just stuck up in there. When I seen him [Steve] I beat him down. Male #053 "Jimmy," eighteen-year-old 107 Hoover Crip)

Gang members also get involved in gang violence through serendipity (or stupidity) as this story of the death of Hit Man T – a Blood leader – illustrates:

Somebody disagrees and then they wind up fighting each other. That's how Hit Man T got killed. It was a disagreement with the Crips. They was gonna fight and Hit Man T came between them. It was two sets, Rolling Sixties and 19th. A 60 came to a party and a 19 was on this side of St. Louis Avenue. Our side had all the pistols, they ain't have none and Hit Man T drove up to the light and he had on all red, his boys in the back seat had on red, they had they hats turned to the left. A dude shot the car up. Hit Man T pulled off to the side, why you all shooting, man? They got to hitting on him. The police came and couple of young dudes shot him in his face. Everybody was out there fighting and the police was coming up to them and dudes was popping and the police was ducking by they cars and had they thing out telling everybody freeze. Everybody run. They couldn't shoot the crowd. Him and his boy got shot but his boy never did make it to the hospital. He went and they say he had his old lady take the bullet out. Hit Man T was still alive, he got shot with a .380 in his face. He was still alive and telling the police to fuck his leg. The police was telling him he had to wait till the paramedics came cause he got shot in the leg first but he was fighting back. He shouldn't have did what he did . . . If somebody shot you car up and you ain't got no weapon it's no sense in getting out for real. He was in his car, the car was running, the light was green and there was about 100 people on that side and about 300 people on our side, gang people and people that wasn't in no gang. People on phones, getting gas, just walking around cause it's hot outside. He should have kept going. (Male #056, "Tony," seventeen-year-old 19th Street Hoover Crip)

Another similar example of misdirected behavior illustrates further stupidities.

There was some cats from Illinois. Vice Lords. They came to us, what's up, you all some Bloods? Fuck no, I ain't no Slob. What you all Crips? No, I ain't no Crips. You all Disciples? No. Then they pulled out they little .22s and shot at us. So we went and got guns and rolled down on them. We seen them at the bus stop so we went and parked in the alley. Come out and shot them, whupped they ass. All of them got shot. That was dumb what they done. They went and tried to catch the bus. They just shot at us and then go catch the bus right down the street from where we hang out. (Male #036, "NA," eighteen-year-old Compton Gangster BIC)

Unfortunately, gang members are not the only victims of gang-related violence. Several subjects mentioned having their houses shot up.

My bedroom window, man, they shot through the wall. I was up there with one of my little gals, my baby's mamma. My son was up in there. I said get down and pushed her on the bed and rolled him out of the bed. I reached under the bed. I was so mad, my son was up there. I reached under my mattress, dude, I was so mad I went on the south side and smoked like three niggers up in the projects. You can jack with me, mess with me I don't care what you do to me, don't mess with my kid. (Male #033, "Larry," eighteen-year-old Thundercat)

Others mentioned fights and/or killings with police and security guards, and with guns around there are bound to be accidents.

I had a uh little cousin got shot in the chest. Everybody was in the house playin wit a gun and uh my cousin Kenny had shot her in the uh chest. Hey man she was thirteen, yeah uh, pulled the gun back but he didn't know it was no bullet or nothing when he shot her, shot her in her chest. We was all cryin and stuff but she didn't have no funeral or nothin and then we all went to jail but they knew it was an accident so they just let em go and stuff. (Male #002, "Eric," sixteen-year-old Thundercat)

"We Don't Go Looking for It; If It Happens, It Happens": Attitudes Towards Violence. Although we began this chapter with a statement reflecting a "love" of violence, most of our subjects do not revel in confrontation to quite the degree that subject boasted of (to be fair, he was probably bragging and exaggerating both his love of violence and his involvement in it). The most common attitude toward the possibility of violence and actually initiating it was more fatalistic and commonplace.

INT: When do members of your gang use violence?
MALE #092, "Derone," twenty-one-year-old Rolling 60's Crip: Only when violence is necessary. Like at a confrontation or somebody talk crap or if somebody throw up the wrong sign then we fuck they ass up.

If a Blood would shoot me and I happen to get hit, I get hit. Then I be dead. (Male #025, "Tony," seventeen-year-old Hoover Gangster Crip)

There is, in fact, something of "a man's gotta do what a man's gotta do" about our subjects' responses to violence, perhaps because it is a normal and expected part of their lives. At times there was also a rather chilling, matter-of-fact attitude in our subjects' descriptions of violence and killing.

Oh man, you shoot somebody and they don't die they shoot you and you be feuding until one of you all dead. A dude named Scotty and Kevin. Every time they see each other. They done shot a pregnant girl at Saints a few months ago. Kevin was trying to hit him. They will go on with it. (Male #012, "Lance," twenty-year-old West Side Mob member)

INT: What's good about being in your gang?

MALE #028, "Killa 4 Ren," fifteen-year-old 187 Crip: People are killed, that's good.

INT: People are actually dead now?

028: Yeah. Paralyzed one dude two weeks ago.

INT: Tell me about the last drive-by shooting. That was two weeks ago right?

028: Yeah. We shot that guy.

INT: When was the last time that somebody was killed?

028: Last month. I tore that dude up, had to shoot him.

INT: What was it about?

028: He was a Blood so we shot him. No that wasn't last month, that was on a Sunday.

INT: So he was a Blood and that was the reason he got shot. He was killed right?

028: His brother was in the paper talking about how we killed him.

INT: He's dead though right?

028: Yeah, he dead. Yeah. The only reason we shot him was cause he threatened him in Union Station. Called him a little Crab and stuff like that. Had to shoot him. They was talking about who going to shoot him. I said I'll do it.

Other subjects seem also bored with violence, or talking about violence, and some gave the impression of being tired with that whole scene.

MALE #034, "Lil Gene Mack," eighteen-year-old 19th Street Rolling 60's Crip: We haven't had any problems for awhile now but it's been hot. It's going to come. There's going to be a lot of deaths.

INT: How come?

034: Colors.

INT: What kinds of things have you done to defend your turf?

034: I did a lot. I have did a lot. I shot people, I've been shot, I've gang banged. It's getting old, man, it's getting old. You do it so much it don't faze you no more. Every time I go out now I'm killing me somebody. It don't hurt, it don't faze me no more.

Several subjects also tried to point out that what they do is not all that terrible and that there are, after all, far worse gangs in the world (Los Angeles gangs are especially favored in this regard).

We never killed nobody that I know of. We have put people in a coma, paralyzed them stuff like that but we ain't never killed nobody. Gave them brain damage. (Male #036, "NA," eighteen-year-old Compton Gangster BIC)

INT: How are gangs on the east side different from over here?

MALE #044, "Paincuzz," sixteen-year-old Rolling 60's Crip: Worser.

INT: Worse in what ways?

044: Over here we kill Bloods and Crips but over there they will kill your mother, your father, and your little baby sister.

And a sufficient number of subjects mentioned fear or the psychological effects of being on the receiving or giving end of violence.

I've had dreams about it. It scares me sometimes. I used to walk by myself all sagging and all blue on. My girlfriend say aren't you scared some Bloods gonna drive past and start shooting? I didn't trip off of it, just walked. (Male #050, "John," nineteen-year-old Rolling 60's Crip)

When, when you shoot a person it seem like everybody watching you. I always thought somebody was after me. Everytime I'd hear a police car I'd jump. Every time my mother call me I say WHAT! cause the cops was bothering me but it was an accident. I shot him though. (Male #003, "Jerry," eighteen-year-old Thundercat)

This evidence leads to an important question, "Why is the level of violence so high among gang members, higher even than their race/age/sex cohort?" Three answers have been proposed. On the one hand, it can be argued that gangs are organized for violence. Like the military, they provide the training, weaponry, ideology, motive, discipline, and leadership for engaging in violence. From this perspective, gang violence can be viewed as the outcome of a group whose formal purpose is to organize violence for instrumental purposes. An alternative perspective argues that gangs amplify violence; that is, gangs provide a collective process that weakens ties to social institutions and increases interactions with and attachments to individuals already involved in crime.

A third explanation is that gang membership is selected for violence. Individuals who are already prone to violent behaviors, and who have such a history, select each other as compatriots, and since violence is the initial bond of their relationship, they continue these behaviors as their group coalesces and grows. Although we did not systematically probe for information on pregang levels of violence, we assume that it was at very high levels for our subjects. The neighborhood rates of assaultive violence discussed in this chapter and Chapter 2 are just the tip of the iceberg and point to an endemic culture of violence in our subjects' neighborhoods. Many of them had witnessed or been affected by lethal assaultive violence (not to mention that all had probably been witnesses to or been involved in nonlethal violence) by their early teens. By the time they joined the gang, most of our subjects were veterans of playground and street fights – which did not usually involve weapons or lethal consequences. But we assume that individuals with violent proclivities select themselves (and are selected by others) for gang membership. They both create and attract threats within their social circle and neighborhood and thus are more likely to be in need of protection. They both seek out like-inclined individuals (existing gang members and other violence-prone adolescents) and are sought out by the same.

The last two views (contagion and selection) are far more consistent with the data reviewed here, data that shows gangs lack ideology, discipline, and formal structure, and that gang violence is primarily expressive and retaliatory (or situationally spontaneous), hardly the product of a formal organization employing rational means–ends chains.

"It Don't Hurt, It Don't Faze Me No More." Not all subjects, of course, are as blase as "Lil Gene Mack" tried to be in our interview. Eight subjects, after all, could not say when their gang used violence and eleven subjects said that violence did not involve the use of weapons. Nevertheless, violence is the force that creates and holds St. Louis gangs together. Starting with threats inside and outside the neighborhood creating the need for protection and culminating in endless repetitions of revenge and retaliation, violence permeates the lives of our subjects. And it appears to be getting worse. Our subjects recognize the pervasiveness of violence in a variety of ways. Fifty-eight subjects said that the gang scene had become more violent in the year prior to their interview, and seven said there was more use of guns (only twelve said that the gang scene was less violent).

Violence comes in many forms for these gang members and their neighbors and friends. Some of what gang members do serves "functional purposes" – protection of home turf and favored hangouts, protection of drug turfs and disciplining customers, defending members and neighbors from "outsiders." But much of the violence we have recorded in our interviews seems "expressive." Gang members proving their manhood, their toughness, their hardness through initiations, trespassing on rival territories, and beating or shooting the opposition's colors. Though it contains elements of self-protection, the expressive character is evident in efforts to establish dominance or identity. Viewed in this light, violence that erupts over what appear to be petty acts – disrespecting a color, stepping in front of another person, flashing hand signs, driving through a rival neighborhood – takes on a deeper and more serious meaning. These "petty" acts represent symbolic threats to the existence of the gang and its members, as they challenge its prime values.

Some of this violence also arises from the routine interactions of our subjects as they carry out their daily activities. The inevitable frictions of daily life, especially when individuals are pursuing criminal careers, can quickly get out of hand and lead to escalating confrontations. And since our subjects are often armed, violently prone, and structurally less powerful than many of their interlocutors, their reactions are just as likely to be violent and potentially deadly (Tedeschi and Felson 1994). Fundamental personal identity is also involved. Most of the gang members portrayed in our study are proud, insecure, tough teenagers and young adults whose self-esteem, self-worth, and identity appear to be constantly at risk. Toughness, manliness, not backing down, are important values of their world and their psyches – to be upheld even at the cost of their own or others' lives.

Whatever the "purpose" of violence, it often leads to retaliation and revenge creating feedback loops where each killing requires a new killing. And too often the targets of such attacks are not even the perpetrators of the previous action – just some generalized Slob or Crab or an innocent bystander. In 1993, for example, the Fairgrounds Park neighborhood, in the middle of our subject recruitment area, had a population of 3,026. From 1991 through 1993, the Fairgrounds neighborhood averaged just under 9 homicides per year, or an annual rate of 286 per 100,000 citizens, four times higher than the city rate and thirty times the national homicide rate. Rates for serious assault in this neighborhood are also astronomical; for the same three year period, Fairgrounds Park averaged nearly 6,000 assaults per 100,000 residents, five times higher than the city of St. Louis and thirteen times higher than that for the United States.

Gangs do not really resemble the stereotype presented at the beginning of the chapter. Most of our subjects do not revel in assaultive and lethal violence against each other, innocent bystanders, and any who attempt to thwart them. Nor is gang violence as common as the public may think. Yet it is far too common and far too lethal to be dismissed easily or waved away. Eleven homicides out of ninety-nine interview subjects represents a high level of mortality, both for social science research and in the lives of most Americans.

But gang members live in a culture apart from most of us, a world in which violence is endemic and ever present. Gang members are radically separated from both public and private institutions of society, as we discuss in the next two chapters on public institutions and the family. Nevertheless, because of their involvement in criminality and violence, gang members still remain intimately connected to one American institution – the criminal justice system.

CHAPTER SEVEN

"Doing Time" in School and Elsewhere: Gang Members and Social Institutions

I used to be a nerd. Read, honor roll student. But that stuff was getting boring. I was looking for something good to do. (Male #021, "40 Ounce," sixteen-year-old 107 Hoover Gangster Crip)

HANGING OUT, DRINKING BEER, looking for excitement, committing crimes – these activities increasingly become the focus of our subjects' lives once they join a gang. As we reported in Chapter 5, involvement in legitimate social institutions or with nongang peers and relatives drops dramatically following gang initiation.[1] In most cases, gang life has an obsessively deadly attraction for our subjects, one which constricts and diminishes their life to the friendship group of the gang. Indeed, nearly two-thirds of our subjects could not or did not identify any activities they participated in outside of the gang.

This chapter focuses on our subjects' involvement with four social institutions: schools, the criminal justice system, the job market, and community groups (including church, recreational, and neighborhood organizations). Eighty of our subjects said that prior to joining a gang, they belonged to one or more legal groups (of a social, religious, or recreational sort), while only nineteen denied any previous involvement in such groups.[2] But a startling reversal occurs after joining the gang, only twenty subjects said they currently belonged to any group besides their gang, while seventy-nine subjects were affiliated only with the gang. Put differently, three-quarters of those involved in legal groups dropped out after joining the gang.

INT: You were an honor student and a good athlete, what made you decide to start living on the streets again?

MALE #035, "Edward," twenty-year-old Hoover Gangster Crip: I don't know. Just got tired of being smart. I couldn't tell you.

In Figure 7.1, we display the most prominent legal group that gang member's participated at the time of our interviews. Sports is the most popular activity, with seven mentions. However, even this involvement is precarious, since at least two subjects involved in school sports said they were not going to participate in future years. Religious activities were mentioned six times, although at least three of these mentions were for church choir groups.

The immersion of our subjects in gang activities, to the virtual exclusion of all else, extends to other social arenas. Only sixteen subjects, for example, were employed at the time of their interview. The gang has thus become the primary reference and peer group for our subjects, replacing social institutions. Many, if not most, of the friends and relatives they normally would interact with are in their gang or in a gang. Thus gang members' involvement in legitimate social institutions – church, school, employment market, clubs – is severely reduced. The

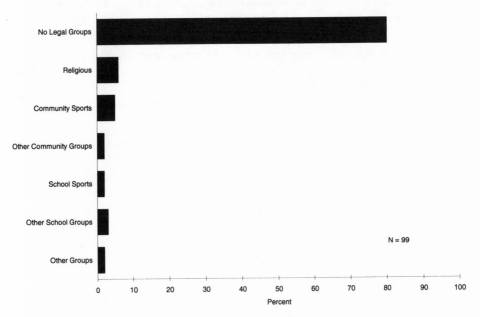

Figure 7.1 Active Members' Participation in Legal Groups

majority of interpersonal interactions and activities are with other gang members (or hangers-on). Upon becoming a member, former ties diminish and sometimes disappear completely, as members become more enmeshed in a world defined by threat, violence, and serious crime.

There are, however, two major exceptions to this prevailing pattern of noninvolvement – school and the criminal justice system. School participation, measured by current enrollment or successful completion of high school, occurred for sixty percent of our sample. Thirty-nine of our subjects were still in school when they were interviewed, eighteen had completed twelfth grade, and three had received GEDs.

Our subjects have an even higher participation rate in the criminal justice system. Eighty percent had been arrested at least once; 39 percent had been convicted and done time of some sort (including overnight juvenile detention). More than half of the gang members we talked with had daily contacts with the police, and only two said they "never came into contact with cops."

There are good reasons for these higher participation rates in educational and legal institutions, as there are for low levels of involvement in other institutional arenas. Thirty-four of our subjects were under sixteen, the legal school-leaving age in Missouri and thus were obligated to be enrolled in and attending school. The explanation for criminal justice system contacts and involvement is more complicated. Obviously, participation and membership in gangs increases the criminality of young people, their visibility to police, and the likelihood of police contact. But over a quarter of our subjects were first arrested before they were fourteen and thus probably before they had joined a gang. And, as we discussed previously, gang criminality is typically an extension of previous criminal activities, one that intensifies prior involvement in crime.

Underclass theory and the prevailing market segmentation in St. Louis also help to account for the high levels of criminality, low employment, and low involvement with legal institutions of our subjects. As we discussed in Chapter 2, the neighborhoods in which our subjects predominantly reside are characterized by high rates of unemployment, assaultive violence, poverty, racial segregation, and single-parent households. Both collectively and individually, there are exceedingly low levels of social capital in these areas, and very few means to produce and accumulate more. Entry-level manufacturing and service jobs have rapidly declined in north and central St. Louis and are not being replaced. Middle-class flight has not only diminished voluntary organizations in these communities – churches, neighborhood groups, youth clubs – but also contributed to the decline of small businesses and services that might have provided part-time or entry-level work for teenagers and young adults.

Withdrawal from legal institutions can be linked to the pervasive influence of gang peers and the attraction and demands of gang activities. It is also likely that the parents and families of gang members are not heavily involved in community and social institutions and that these are fewer and less well organized in members' neighborhoods. Nevertheless, 80 percent of our subjects were involved in some kind of group prior to gang membership, a finding that supports the contention that gang membership increases isolation from legitimate social institutions.

"Reading, 'Riting, and 'Rithmetic" or Drugs, Guns, and Fights: Gang Members in School

The gang members we interviewed are more involved with the educational system (at least in terms of enrollment and cursory attendance) than with any other social institution we gathered information about. One-fifth of them had high school diplomas and two-fifths were still in school when we interviewed them, though it would appear that the chances are high that many of the latter will not finish high school.

However, attending school, being on time, paying attention to teachers and other staff, getting passing grades – the daily routines and opportunities of our educational system – are not high priorities for most gang members. Truancy, tardiness, skipping classes, leaving school before the end of the day all appear to be popular responses to school discipline and rules. When asked what they did in school, few respondents identified classroom activities.

> We skip classes, roam the halls. Look for girls. (Male #010, "Jason C.," fifteen-year-old Compton Gangster)

> We just hung out and skipped most of the time. (Male #012, "Lance," twenty-year-old West Side Mob member)

Other descriptions of what they normally do in school also reflect our subjects' lack of involvement in school activities:

> We walked around, go in the bathroom and smoke weed, get high and everything, drink a beer or something. We stuck together. (Male #005, "Antonio," nineteen-year-old 6th Street Hoover Crip)

> [My grades were] Fs. Too busy going after girls. (Male #015, "Karry," fifteen-year-old Crenshaw Gangster Blood)

Chill out, talk, do a little Crab shooting, watching each other's back. Yeah, we get high and shit, get drunk, gamble in the bathrooms and shit. (Male #058, "Roach," fifteen-year-old Blood)

Participation in extracurricular activities at school also is limited. Only five subjects said they currently were involved in school activities (two in sports, three in other programs), whereas fifty-five subjects said they had been involved in school sports before gang membership, and twelve had been involved in other school activities.

Our subjects' grades, however, suggest that they may not be atypical students in all respects. Twenty-five percent of our subjects (out of ninety-two who answered) said they were "doing well," or had received "mostly Bs," or "mostly As."[3] Only 27 percent said their grades were mostly below average or that they had done poorly in school. Fifty-three percent said they had gotten "mostly C's." Several subjects, in fact, asserted that they were or had been exemplary students

If I keep making As and Bs in school I think I'll do pretty good. If I do go change my mind and go to college I want to be an obstetrician. (Female #046, "Lady Tee," sixteen-year-old 74 Hoover Crip)

At least sixteen of these gang members had participated in or were enrolled in the St. Louis City/County voluntary desegregation program, whereby students from predominantly black St. Louis City public schools attend predominantly white St. Louis County public schools. This program relocates some of the best students in city schools from that system. Participation is voluntary, requires passing achievement tests, and can be terminated for disciplinary problems. Students in the desegregation program had some rather interesting comments about their experiences. In some cases, they are outnumbered and thus gang activities are somewhat restricted.

INT: Ever have gang fights or anything like that at school?
FEMALE #047, "Baby", fifteen-year-old Rolling 60's Crip: No, not at school. I go to school out in white people land, excuse me.

In other cases, their "backgrounds" convey a set of expectations to suburban students.

Like you just be up at the school and the people that stay out in the county they are like, since he stay in the city he might be selling drugs so they'll come to you saying do you got this, do you got that. I say yeah and then I'll bring tto school the next dayy. That's how it usually works. Cocaine, weed, marijuana, LSD. (Male #004, "Anthony," seventeen-year-old Thundercat)

But the majority of our subjects attended predominantly black schools in the St. Louis City school district or in neighboring suburban districts, and their experiences are probably more typical of gang members in the metropolitan area.

"Our Gang" at School: Where They Go, Recruiting, and Staff Reactions. But what do gangs do in school? Although our subjects descriptions of their daily routines seems fairly typical for nonengaged students – sporadically attending classes and study halls, smoking in the bathroom, food fights in the cafeteria – popular stereotypes suggest a radically opposite regime. Gangs often are described as "running" schools, terrorizing the staff and nonmembers, selling drugs in the open with complete impunity, bringing firearms to school and using them to enforce their dominance over other students, teachers, and administrators. According to our subjects' statements, however, the reality of gang activity in St. Louis schools is more complex and problematic for teachers, administrators, and other students. We asked our subjects several questions about the activities of gangs and gang members in school, but their answers did not reveal a pattern. This suggests that any public stereotype that trumpets "gang control" of schools (or the total absence of a gang problem) is alarmist and unfounded.

If gangs really controlled schools, for example, we might expect that on-campus recruitment would be high – but only 44 percent of our subjects said that their gang recruited members at school. And about 40 percent of our subjects said that members of several different gangs or sets (including rival sets of Bloods and Crips) co-existed both overtly and covertly (if not harmoniously) at the same school.

I don't trip at my school, too many Slobs up there. I just keep a low profile at my school. (Male #022, "8 Ball," fifteen-year-old 107 Hoover Gangster Crip)

These responses are congruent both with the strong neighborhood context of St. Louis gangs as well as with the high levels of school busing in the metropolitan area. Twenty subjects, for example, said that all of the members in their gang (or set) attended the same school. Only twenty-eight subjects provided an answer to the question "What school do most of the members of your gang attend?" attesting to the diversity of schools gang members attended.[4] Where our students went to school also shows wide variation. Thirty-three different junior and senior high schools were elicited in response to asking "What school are you going to now or was the last school you went to?" Normandy District secondary schools (within whose boundaries our university is located) was attended by twenty subjects, but the district with the largest number of our subjects was St. Louis City public schools. (Fifteen city schools were mentioned by thirty-seven subjects.) Two gang members attended two different Illinois public schools, and two had last gone to school in correctional settings in St. Louis County. Sixteen students were going to or had gone to eleven different county schools under the voluntary desegregation program.

If gangs controlled schools, or were highly active and visible, we would also expect school staff to know whether individuals were gang members and to actively attempt to prohibit or limit their activities and membership. In this respect, the public stereotype of gangs and schools is on more solid ground. Seventy percent of our subjects said that adults at their school knew they were in a gang. This figure is really not surprising, given the rather overdetermined signaling of gang membership, such as clothing styles, hand signs, verbal greetings, exclusively hanging out with fellow members, although it might conceivably have been higher.[5]

> I'm sure they do cause the principal used to tell us to turn our hat back around or whatever. Got your hat turned to the right you a Crip, left you a Slob. We have our hats like this and we be all together and we be talking and he'll say our names or pull one of us out. He says to that person turn your hat around and go tell the boys to turn their hats around. (Male #043, "Lee Roy," eighteen-year-old Rolling 60's Crip)

> They was scared of us. They wouldn't never say nothing to me but they had the police right there with us. They wouldn't say nothing to me unless the police was around. (Male #060, "Bullet," twenty-year-old Inglewood Family Gangster Blood)

Some members also flaunt their participation in gang activities.

> Yeah, you throw your little rag up on their desk and they be acting with you then. You are going to be smart and tell them what you need. Everybody can hear what you are saying. That's the only way they find out. (Male #005, "Antonio," nineteen-year-old 6th Street Hoover Crip)

The extent of knowledge within the school staff about individual's gang membership also was variable. Several subjects opined that only some school staff knew they were in a gang.

My 8th grade principal, he found out. He called a lot of us to his office to find out different signs and different writing and who belonged to what and what color they wear. We told him the wrong answers though. (Male #074, "Shon," sixteen-year-old Crenshaw Mob Gangster)

Yeah, some of them do. They just tell us don't bring this stuff to school. Wait till you get away from the school then you can do all that stuff. (Male #082, "Dough Boy," fourteen-year-old B Gangster Disciple)

Some members also pointed out that school staff and teachers ought to know that they were in a gang, and probably did know of their gang membership, but had never done anything about it.

They treat you in a different way though, like you some kind of trash. (Male #079, "Hell Bone," fourteen-year-old, Rolling 60's Crip)

They tell us stop wearing all our colors and trying to make trouble. They don't really trip off our colors but they didn't want us to fight at the school or threaten teachers. (Male #069, "X-Men," fourteen-year-old Inglewood Family Gangster)

Surprisingly enough, however, given the fairly high rate of knowledge among school staff about gang membership, less than half of our subjects said the school tried to do something about it. School staff reactions varied from the extremes of expulsion and suspension . . .

Yes, put me out. But that didn't keep me from coming to the school to take care of business. (Male #013, "Darryl," twenty-nine-year-old Blood)

If the principals start asking if you in a gang and you say yeah they will put you out. Then you can't go to school until next year. (Male #024, "Hamilton," sixteen-year-old 107 Hoover Gangster Crip)

When I got shot at Vashon [outside of school at the bus stop] they found out and they put me out of school. (Male #036, "NA," eighteen-year-old Compton Gangster)

to outright complicity in gang-related criminal activities . . .

MALE #001, "Mike-Mike," twenty-year-old Thundercat: Yep. Weed. I brought weed to school. I use to always keep two pistols.
INT: At school? Like in your locker, or on you?
001: On me. I was so cool with the guard at the door, he was smokin that coke I give em bout three rocks, big ol rocks here, and he'll check me, gone. But them pistols be right there on the side.
INT: So he knew.
001: He knew.

INT: But you were buying him off with some rocks. This was the security guard.
001: Smokin that cane.

Sometimes teachers be coming in the bathroom buying $20 dollar rocks from us. (Male #018, "Maurice," twenty-year-old 107 Hoover Crip)

Yeah, we were giving them money, teachers, the guards, and everything else. Say like if you was going to make a sale and a guard pull and messing with you like lock you up. So you give them a certain amount of money to just don't say anything. (Male #030, "Kenneth," nineteen-year-old Thundercat)

More common were threats, rules about gang-related clothing, and preaching by or discussions with counselors and administrators:

Our counselor got a source that tells who in a gang and what they claim. Someone told her that I was banging and she talked to me for a whole day. What's the point of being in a gang and all that stuff. I was a good student and all that stuff. I had to give her a progress report every Friday to make sure that my grades don't slip and stuff like that. (Male #021, "40 Ounce," sixteen-year-old 107 Hoover Gangster Crip)

Numerous times they asked us not to throw up signs, not to talk to Bloods, conversation is cool, not to mix that up with trying to learn. (Male #072, "Blood," sixteen-year-old Swan Park 59 Blood)

We made no organized attempt to assess the impact of in-school gang intervention programs on our subjects, but we can report that the gang members we interviewed did not communicate high levels of antigang intervention in their schools. We know that such programs existed during our study period, yet they do not seem to have had an impact on our subjects.

Smoking, Selling, and Shooting: Crimes and Misdemeanors in School. There is little evidence that school-based interventions had any great effect on how members of our sample viewed school or gang membership. However, this does not mean that gangs are not a particularly troublesome presence in their schools. Much of what gang members do in school is fairly innocuous; attending classes, hanging out, skipping school. A majority of our subjects, however, also said that their school was a site for a variety of serious criminal activities, including drug use and sales, gang-related or precipitated fights, and firearms possession and use. While several subjects mentioned using drugs in school, fifty-seven said that drugs were sold in their schools (which contrasts with the ninety-two subjects who said drugs were sold in their neighborhood).

> Daily. At that time it was mainly weed. That [primos] and rocks, whatever you need. Like going to a drug store. (Male #019, "Anthony," twenty-two-year-old Crip)

One subject said that school was the best venue for drug sales:

> Yeah. That's the main place to sell them. Cause there's more people around the school. People like to be high at school. Some people feel they have to be high to get through the day. (Male #030, "Kenneth," nineteen-year-old Thundercat)

Yet some subjects vehemently denied that drugs were sold at school.

> Not at school. No one sells drugs at school. (Male #039, "Kaons BIC," seventeen-year-old Compton Gangster)

Subjects refrained from selling drugs in school for a variety of reasons, ranging from "ethical" sensibilities . . .

> INT: Did the gang sell drugs at school?
> MALE #005, "Antonio," nineteen-year-old 6th Street Hoover Crip: No. I wouldn't stoop that low.

. . . to the lack of a market and police surveillance.

> Cause it was like in grade school, I wasn't into much selling kids drugs, no way. Then in high school there was the police there. When you came through the door you had to show your ID. There was one that ride in the elevator and one on the main floor. You could go in the bathroom and sell it but it wasn't no big deal to me. There was some drug users there but I didn't kick into it. (Male #020 "Lil Thug," sixteen-year-old Gangster Disciple)

> No, we don't do that. Some dudes sells it in our hood but not at school. Too many 5-0s [police] at school, police. (Male #083, "Winchester," fourteen-year-old Rolling 60's Crip)

A number of subjects said that while the gang sold drugs in school, they personally did not.

> I don't [sell drugs] but they do. Cocaine, crack, marijuana, speed, water, all that. (Female #078, "Tina," fifteen-year-old Treetop Blood)

But it is likely that drugs were sold more frequently and widely than our subjects' general answer would indicate, especially since (as with street drug sales), there was variation within gangs about drug sales in school.

INT: Were drugs ever sold at school?
MALE #085, "2-Low," eighteen-year-old Rolling 60's Crip: Not at school.

INT: Were drugs sold at school?
MALE #086, "Gunn," nineteen-year-old Rolling 60's Crip: Yeah. Sold drugs every day.

"8 Ball," for example, said:

I didn't do that [sell drugs]. Not at a junior high school. (Male #022, fifteen-year-old 107 Hoover Gangster Crip)

But his friend "40 Ounce," interviewed at the same time and in the same room, described his adventures in drug selling.

I used to sell for my brother. My brother would give me 20 bags to go to school and sell them. He gave me eight dollars out of every twenty I sell. Then the eight dollars wasn't good enough so I buy my own. I make my own profit plus the profit he gives me. So that's how I used to get my money. (Male #021, sixteen-year-old 107 Hoover Gangster Crip)

The school drug market also differed from the street market in other ways: weed, and not crack cocaine, was the main product distributed in school.

Every day. Everyday I would bring like 50 or 60 joints to school. Sell them for like $2.00 a joint and they was all gone by the 5th period. They go in the bathroom or sit outside a couple of hours, sat out there for about 30 or 40 minutes. By the time you come in everybodys' eyes closing. Everybody laughing and joking. (Male #033, "Larry," eighteen-year-old Thundercat)

Yeah, we do. We find the ones that smoke weed cause there be some white boys up there [Normandy High School] and a lot of white boys smoke weed. (Male #068, "CK," sixteen-year-old Piru 104 Blood)

We also obtained few inklings that particular gangs or sets controlled school drug turfs (whether of a whole campus or portions thereof), and sales seemed to be more circumspect and hidden.

Only upon request. I would go to school on Monday and somebody needed something so I would bring it in the next day. Weed top of the list, speed, hash. (Male #040, "Knowledge," twenty-one-year-old Compton Gangster)

Almost every day. Cut 'em up, put 'em in orange. Whatever so much they want, put it in an orange. We cut up stuff and give it to 'em, act like we giving each other shoes or just switch book bags. It's just common sense, the smart way. (Male #092, "Derone," twenty-one-year-old 6 Deuce Rolling 60's Crip)

Some of the differences between drug sales on the street and in school are related to the lower ages and discretionary income of the potential customers at school.

Not by none of mine. . . . That's time [prison time] right there. It's money but you don't need it that bad. Plus there really ain't no money in the schools, no way. (Male #037, "Big Money," twenty-two-year-old Compton Gangster).

As well, there is the greater presence of surveillance by authorities (school guards, ID badges, and closed campuses, for example, are regular features at city schools and are not uncommon in suburban districts).[6]

"We Said We Was Banging, We Never Said We Was Stupid." Despite this disclaimer by one subject, gang members too often bring their ill-conceived proclivities for violence and revenge into the school yard. According to our subjects, fights, carrying weapons, and occasionally using them are the most common serious crimes committed by gang members in school. Seventy-eight subjects (of ninety-six who answered) said that gang-related violence occurred in their schools:

They fight at school. Disciples and Vice Lords, they fight. All the time on Fridays. In the cafeteria at 12:30. (Male #032, "Skonion," seventeen-year-old Thundercat)

At Parkway [a suburban school] there was some fights. Slobs from the city or people that weren't in a gang last year back from summer. (Male #065, "BK Kill," nineteen-year-old North County Crip)

Much school violence, of course, is not necessarily gang motivated or related but a continuations of other long-standing rivalries or spontaneous eruptions of ill temper.

We got into it wit each other from Clinton School. They sent Laclede Town [a St. Louis Housing Project, mostly abandoned] to Clinton Middle. Clinton is on the southside and when I told the principal, hey principal all them southside cats are out there, could you do somethin about it, he say, the dude was white, the dude say, uh well, you're gonna have to work that out on your own. I say, well o.k., I went and got that 12-gauge right out my locker, o.k. The principal looked, all those cats was gone, I told you, you didn't do nothin about it, they say go for help first, and I went for it and you wouldn't go for help. (Male #002, "Eric," sixteen-year-old Thundercat)

The school down the street from us we don't like each other so they meet us half way and we fight. (Male #008, "Robert," fourteen-year-old Compton Gangster)

We was sitting in the lunch room, they come up in there. We say what's up. One of my partners he was sitting at another table. He just stood up and came running and kicked this dude in the face. One of the dudes I think he got his arm broke in about ten places. My friend got his nose broke cause he ran across the table and kicked him in the face, broke his nose. After that they didn't come back to our school. (Male #014, "D. C.," sixteen-year-old Disciple Crip)

Violence in school ranged from low-level fisticuffs and "food fights" . . .

We do several things. We skip school together, skip classes, talk to gals. If we see a whole bunch of gals walking down the street . . . we have food fights. (Male #068, "CK," sixteen-year-old Piru 104 Blood)

. . . to near-lethal violence involving weapons (including clubs, knives, and guns).

Bout two months ago when I was at school they shot a guy though he had got away too. Caught him from the back at lunch time and just hit him and moved out and left the school and put the gun up and came back to school and was looking for him. (Male #003, "Jerry," eighteen-year-old Thundercat)

We had one at Vashon and Sumner [city high schools]. Busload of Bloods. I was on the football team. At Vashon we was having a party and some niggers was throwing my cousin. Somebody got shot. They shot my brother and then we got in a fight with them. (Male #038, "G.O.D," nineteen-year-old Compton Gangster)

Any kind of fights, chairs, anything you can reach to fight with. They take guns to school. Not too many of them use them but they take them just to have. (Male #072 "Blood," fifteen-year-old Swan Park 59 Blood)

The presence of gangs in school appears to escalate both the frequency and the seriousness of such altercations. Fights usually occur between rival gangs (Bloods versus Crips, for example) or rival sets within these blocks.

Some dudes at school from different sets and stuff. Say if I went to school
a 60 and they claiming like different sets like 19th Street, Snoovers and
different people you never seen before. Sometimes you have a fight up
there at school. Snoovers and Folk, we hurt them real bad. (Male #083,
"Winchester," fourteen-year-old Rolling 60's Crip)

INT: If you all Crips, who you all fighting then?
MALE #089, "C-Note," fifteen-year-old 88 Street Mob: We be fighting
   Slobs that come up or they go there. We had some there before but they
   don't go there no more. Six Deuce.

These fights often start as altercations or provocations between individuals.

I was fightin this dude one day in the gym. I beat em at some basketball we
was playin for 100 dollars. He push in my face and all. I, I just looked
around and I seen all my little partners, all of em and they just start
whuppin' em. I say man don't do nothin to 'em. Then I started stoppin
em. I say don't, leave em alone ya'll, leave em alone, and I say man and I
just started stoppin em. They almost kilt that dude. I told em to chill.
When that principal walked down, they was fixin to kill em. (Male #001,
"Mike-Mike," twenty-year-old Thundercat)

I can remember a couple of events that we had up at our school. Some
Slobs came up there. As soon as they walked in the door they dropped. He
went home to U City and brung his partners up to school and they just got
rushed. (Male #043, "Lee Roy," eighteen-year-old Rolling 60's Crip)

But such fights can quickly escalate to larger encounters between groups,
which sometimes extend over several days, weeks, or months.

MALE #002, "Eric," sixteen-year-old Thundercat: I use to uh, fight a
   bigger uh some dude from L.A., he was a Blood. He use to go to my
   school and everybody was scared of em except me. And then he
   thought I was scared of em. I had on a blue rag and he say what's up
   cuz, what's up blood and I say uh, what's up cuz just like that and then
   me and him got to arguin and everything and teachers would stop it
   and then me and him met up one day when nobody was round we got
   to fightin, naw, cause I told Ron, my cousin, my cousin and em came up
   to the school and beat em up. And then the next day when he seen me,
   he gonna ask me where my cousin and em at. I say I don't need my
   cousin and em for you. They just came up there cause they heard you
   was a Blood. And they whooped em. Then me and him had a fight the
   next day, yea. And then I had to fight some other dudes that was his
   friends and I beat em up, then he brought some boys up to the school

and they uh, pulled out a gun on me and I ran up in the school. And
then I brought my boys up next day and we beat on em. And then I got
kicked out of that school.

INT: They kicked you out of school? I wonder why?

002: Cause he had ten stitches in one eye and he had an iron plate in the
other eye cause I hit 'em like here and then where the stitches was at
and then he fell up against the door and the iron plate was right there.

Meeting real threats, or potential ones, plays a major role in the onset
of violence and in its escalation into weapon carrying and use.

INT: How about you, did you ever bring a gun to school?

MALE #022, "8 Ball," fifteen-year-old 107 Hoover Gangster Crip: Yeah.
The Slobs was talking and I said, you keep on talking and I'm going to
shoot your ass. I told them, just keep tripping with me. I was on the bus
one day and I was with some Crips and this big old dude he poked me
on the bus. Him and his boys was riding this bus. He got in my face and
said, I saw you with some Crabs. I said I'm a Crip. Him and his boys
bigger than me. I told him, you trip me. I was going to get him in a
couple of days. Everybody told him I was looking for him and he didn't
ride the bus no more.

Race is implicated in very few school gang fights, as is true of most
gang violence we received information about. We did, however, hear
mention of two racially motivated gang fights in school settings, both of
which occurred in county schools.

There are some whites that are Crips or whatever. They really don't have
their own little gang. Unless they are like the skinheads or something like
that at school. One day there was a whole lot of fights out there [Lind-
bergh High School] cause of the skinheads. There was about 40 or 50 of
them. We were having a school fight. (Female #006, "Yolanda," nineteen-
year-old 23rd Street Hoover Crip)

[We get in fights with] Crips. White Crips. We go to school with them.
(Male #070, "Lil-B-Dog," fifteen-year-old Inglewood Family Gangster)

While seventy-eight subjects said that fights occurred at school, a
frightening eighty-three said that weapons were brought to school (and
they did not mean Swiss army knives). The fifteen subjects who answered
no to this question are probably deluded or deceptive – especially given
the reported frequency of "carrying guns and owning guns" reported in
earlier chapters. Figure 7.2 shows that thirty-three subjects were unsure
how often guns were brought to school. But one-fifth of our subjects said
that they or fellow gang members brought guns to school every day.

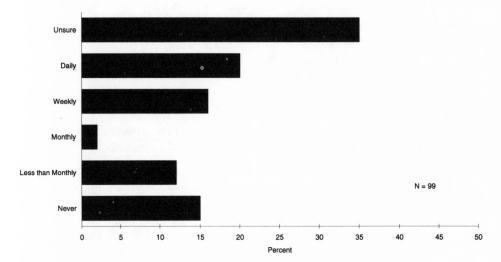

Figure 7.2 How Often Weapons Were Brought to School

We brought weapons, we brought pistols, we brought shotguns, we brought bombs and everything else. Shotguns and everything, it didn't make no difference. Everyday. (Male #013, "Darryl," twenty-nine-year-old Blood)

One time, that's why I don't see that Crab no more, he started talking stuff so I brought a .38 and I don't see him no more. So I kept it quiet. (Male #057, "Smith & Wesson," fifteen-year-old Neighborhood Posse Blood)

Our sense is that weapons were brought to school in response to both real and imagined threats.

If their group bring them one day then our group gonna bring one. Cause they don't know when we have one and we don't know when they have one. Cause some of the boys in our group don't tell us when they have they guns. They just bring it with them. (Male #069, "X-Men," fourteen-year-old Inglewood Family Gangster Blood)

We bring guns to school. Sometimes, not all the times. Like if they gonna jump us or somebody come up there looking for us. (Male #082, "Dough Boy," fourteen-year-old Gangster Disciple)

At least two subjects were offended (for different reasons) at the notion of bringing guns to school. One said:

INT: Do you ever bring a gun or knife to school?
MALE #021, "40 Ounce," sixteen-year-old 107 Hoover Gangster Crip: No, I don't want to get put out.

INT: Why not?

021: Cause. We said we was banging, we never said we was stupid.

An older gang member, "Big Money," self-righteously observed that a junior member of his gang had stupidly taken a gun to school.

> Well we had one bring a gun to school. He was tripping. He endangered the lives not only of himself but endangered the lives of hundred of other students. Taking the gun up there for one person. It wasn't no problem about the gun it was a problem by taking the gun in the school, in a public place. (Male #037, twenty-two-year-old Compton Gangster)

However, he elaborated a rather chilling rationale for why bringing guns to school was a problem.

> I said wait until after school. Catch him walking by himself down the street and hide in some bushes and do what you got to do. Don't let everybody see you. You don't want no witnesses around if you still want to walk the street. (Male #037, "Big Money," twenty-two-year-old Compton Gangster)

Schools appear to be an extension of the street for gang members in other ways. Weapons at schools means guns for most subjects, although we did elicit a few mentions of knives, one of which was rather disparaging of whites and "country" people.

> We don't be usin no knife. We might use a bat or a stick but we don't be usin no knife. Country seem like. I don't know why nobody use knives. Seem like for white people, you know, white people use knives, we use guns, sticks and things. (Male #002, "Eric," sixteen-year-old Thundercat)

MALE #012, "Lance," twenty-year-old West Side Mob member: We was strapped every day with them, a knife or a .22 or a .25 automatic.

INT: A knife wouldn't do you much good if somebody else got a 25 though.

012: No, they don't. But shit, if you ain't got no pistol you carry a knife.

Guns, however much they may be carried to school, are not used as much as they are on the street. None of our subjects mentioned personally "firing" weapons at school, even though thirty-eight said that guns were used at school.[7] Some subjects mentioned "brandishing" weapons – but our sense is that the usual function of guns at school is deterrence and reassurance. After all, as "X-Men" said, "they don't know when we have one and we don't know when they have one" – a situation that encourages a rather circumspect, if constant, "strapping on" of handguns in school.

Guns may also not be used as much at school as on the street because at least some school control and intervention procedures are partially effective, as several subjects pointed out.

> At first [we did bring guns to school] but now they check you. (Male #050, "John," nineteen-year-old Rolling 60's Crip)

> That's why I'm not in school now. I took a sawed off shotgun. Carried it in my pocket under my coat. So they kicked me out. (Male #034, "Lil Gene Mack," eighteen-year-old 19th Street Rolling 60's Crip)

> Almost every day. That was the first time I got kicked out of school – for bringing guns. (Male #039, "Kaons BIC," seventeen-year-old Compton Gangster)

We would not deny that drug sales, gang fights, and gun carrying are serious problems in the schools our subjects attended. But, these schools are not controlled by omnipotent gangs who hold the student and adult populations in terror. Neither are these schools totally safe havens from the violent world of the neighborhood and the streets. School staffs are correct in emphasizing the danger and lure of gangs in their schools. However, since we found little evidence that these gangs and gang members were actively recruiting at schools and were not selling drugs, fighting, or using weapons as readily as they do on the street, we conclude that gangs are probably much more dangerous on the street (or, more troubling for school officials, just off school property) than in school.

There are a number of reasons for the lessened dangerousness of gangs in schools. The adult presence, the disciplinary procedures, the scheduling of public schools all restrict gang members' tendency exclusively to relate to fellow gang members. There also are many more non-gang peers to associate with, activities to be engaged in, and (for the males, especially) a much greater presence of the opposite gender to impress and socialize with.[8] Many of our subjects, in fact, reported that they felt safer in school than in their "hood." School appears to be the one area where positive institutional experiences (i.e., not jail or police) penetrate their lives, and may be a fruitful arena for effective and innovative gang intervention and prevention efforts.

"I Hate the Motherfuckers": Gang Members, Gangs, and the Criminal Justice System

Unlike the majority of youths in the St. Louis region, our subjects have extremely high levels of involvement with the criminal justice system, experiences that are pivotal in their life course. Although gang members may not have as much contact with the law as the public and media would like, our subjects were frequently and seriously involved with legal institutions and had, on the whole, both a negative attitude toward legal institutions and their officials (as the quote above indicates) and a rather fatalistic and pessimistic outlook on their chances of further and more serious engagement. This section explores our subjects relations with the criminal justice system by examining their interactions with the police, their arrests, convictions, time spent in jail or prison, and their attitudes towards the officials and processes they have encountered.

"When You Gang Banging, They Looking for You Every Day" or "They Don't Like Us. We Don't Like Them Either." Gangs and the Police. Social scientists often ask dumb questions – sometimes inadvertently, sometimes purposefully – and we were was no exception to this generalization. In our subjects' eyes our most glaringly stupid question, especially when asked with some purposeful naiveté, was "How does your gang get along with the police?" We earned many disbelieving stares, starts, and wrinkled brows in concert with the following answers.

> You should know that one. They don't get along with the police. (Male #005, "Antonio," nineteen-year-old 6th Street Hoover Crip)

> I hate the motherfuckers. They be fucking with us, shaking us down all the time and shit. (Male #012, "Lance," twenty-year-old West Side Mob member)

> The police hate us with a passion. (Male #029, "Randell," seventeen-year-old Thundercat)

Surprisingly enough, however, twelve subjects said that their gang had a "good relationship" with the police.

> As long as we know we cool with them, they be cool with us, that's how it is. We don't give them no trouble they won't give us no trouble, that's how it is over there. As long as they don't sweat us, we don't sweat them. Like I say we don't go around doing things for the police to come looking for us, we don't do that. (Male #003, "Jerry," eighteen-year-old Thundercat)

> Even the police aren't bad people but once you get to know them, it might happen say if you are new out there they are going to hassle you in a minute. They just doing they job. (Male #014, "D. C.," sixteen-year-old Disciple)

> I'm cool with most of the police. I just cooperate with them. They ask me
> stuff about Crips and Bloods. I just tell them. (Male #015, "Karry,"
> fifteen-year-old Crenshaw Gangster Blood)

But it appears that a "good relationship" is one in which the police do not
hassle that particular set, at that particular time, because the gang is not
currently engaged in criminal activity.

Seven subjects did not answer this question. Six said that it depended
on a number of factors (e.g., why the police were talking with them,
individual personalities of officers and gang members, where the gang
was when the police were talking with them, etc.).

> Some police know us, some police don't know us. Some police want to kick
> our motherfucking ass and some police just want to get some of the
> money we got. There's all kinds. The police get in contact with us. Some-
> times they come in they squad car and they ask us what you got? I ain't got
> nothing, if they find some rocks on you they say, I'm going to take this.
> (Male #018, "Maurice," twenty-year-old 107 Hoover Crip)

Twelve subjects denied having any relationship with the police – imply-
ing that they seldom, if ever, had any involvement with street-level legal
officials. We have little reason to disbelieve these subjects. It is possible,
after all, that gang members could avoid the police, since not all of them
regularly engage in criminal activities.[9] In support of this, see for example Wright and Decker (1994), where a surprisingly large proportion of
the residential burglars they interviewed had never been arrested for
that crime.

Unsurprisingly, sixty-two subjects said that they and their gang had a
"bad relationship" with the police. Typical reasons for disliking the police
included violence by the police, harassment of gang members, planting
criminal evidence on gang members, and racial animosities.

> Everytime the police see me they be wantin to beat me up. Yeah, what's
> your name? Mike-Mike. You the one out here runnin all this stuff ain't
> you? I don't know nothin, I don't do nothin, I go to church, man, I'm a
> church, man. Watch out! I say, yeah ok, you'll get yours. The police be
> saying, I'm gonna get you, you fuckin nigger. Cause the police will put
> somethin on you. (Male #001, "Mike-Mike," twenty-year-old Thundercat)

A major reason for gang members' antipathy toward the police is
"brutality" or physical abuse by police officers. Most of the stories we
collected are not very clear as to the details of these incidents, but many
subjects felt that police contacts contained the potential for violence.

Police been slapping you upside your head, tell me where the dope is or they just plant some on you and take you down for nothing. Police is carrying these 9MM. Sometimes they hit you upside your head with them or they shoot you for no reason. Sometimes there be a reason, cause you ran. So what I ran, I'm trying to get away from you so you won't kill me. What's a scared person supposed to do; if he ain't got no way to fight back, he'll run. (Male #018, "Maurice," twenty-year-old 107 Hoover Crip)

They don't come down there [Laclede Town] much but if they see you somewhere else they will beat you up. (Male #032, "Skonion," seventeen-year-old Thundercat)

Everyday. Smack us and shit. They dirty. (Male #058, "Roach," fifteen-year-old Pine Lawn Organization Blood)

Certain police departments, units, or individuals had reputations of violence.

I don't wear my rag because Jennings [a suburb of St. Louis] is touchy. You can get locked up for having a rag. Cops will lock you up just for having a rag in your pocket. Then they take you down there and put it on you and say you was gang banging. (Male #021, "40 Ounce," sixteen-year-old 107 Hoover Gangster Crip)

Except I don't get along with the Jennings police cause when the Jennings police see us there's always trouble. (Male #089, "C-Note," fifteen-year-old 88th Street Mob Crip)

But not all violence by the police goes unanswered. Two subjects discussed their recent arrests for "assaulting a police officer," and another mentioned shooting at police.

I've been arrested about four or five times for assault on the police. Two times was fact but the other last three they was going to slam me on the ground and do everything to try to make it look real. Last year, November, the one policeman told me to go and pushed me and I pushed him back. Then a little tussle started. He grabbed me by my arm and tried to throw me down. I threw him down and all that. A lot of them came and rushed me, hit me and handcuffed me. They pulled they guns out, you know I deceased then. I looked up at them, oh ok, go lock me up. (Male #005, "Antonio," nineteen-year-old Sixth Street Hoover Crip)

I knocked four of them out. They tried [to kill me] but everybody was out there. They busted my head and fractured my shoulder and next time they broke my knee. (Male #039, "Kaons BIC," seventeen-year-old Compton Gangster)

They [my fellow gang members] like me so much because I be shooting back at the police when they come. They ride down my street and I run down the alley and then start shooting and they don't know who be shooting. (Male #053, "Jimmy," eighteen-year-old 107 Hoover Crip)

Many subjects reported intermittent harassment by the police.

One time they stopped us and just wanted to take a picture. (Female #047, "Baby," fifteen-year-old Rolling 60's Crip)

Others said that the police, or particular police, routinely planted drugs on gang members.

Beatings, planting drugs on you, giving you more time in jail. (Male #034, "Lil Gene Mack," eighteen-year-old 19th Street Rolling 60's Crip)

He always checks us for drugs. Sometimes if you don't have no drugs on you he will put some on you. (Male #049, "Chris," seventeen-year-old Rolling 60's Crip)

Still others averred that some police were on the take and being paid off by drug dealers or were forcing gang members to pay them.

It's certain police that try to make us pay them. They know what we do. They know that we sell drugs and everything and they try to make us pay them. (Male #037, "Big Money," twenty-two-year-old Compton Gangster)

I think the drug dealers is paying them off or something, I'm serious. I've known them for too long. Some of the police come up to us, what's up Cuz. (Male #050, "John," nineteen-year-old Rolling 60's Crip)

Several subjects also mentioned that race has a major bearing on how they got along with the police. Black officers, for example, were viewed positively by some subjects.

I get along with them nicely, but see we have a lot of white policemen and we got black policemen. Some of the black policemen seeing it from our point. (Male #005, "Antonio," nineteen-year-old 6th Street Hoover Crip)

Other subjects, however, were extremely negative about black policemen, especially when they were perceived as "showing off" for their white fellow officers.

MALE #021, "40 Ounce," sixteen-year-old 107 Hoover Gangster Crip: But the white police, bad.
MALE #022, "8 Ball," fifteen-year-old 107 Hoover Gangster Crip: Black police too, especially.

021: I like the white police more when they around blacks because black police just want to show off and kick you all around and stuff.

INT: So if the black police are alone they are worse to you than the white police.

021: No. The black police alone they cool. When they get around the white police they trying to prove theyself or something.

022: When the white and black police together the white ones are more cool than the black ones are. That's what it seems like to me because the black ones try to show off too much.

I hate black cops. They be trying to show off in front of white cops. They come down harder on you than the white cops do. (Male #039, "Kaons BIC," seventeen-year-old Compton Gangster)

They [black police] try to show off in front of them, show off in front of the white cops. (Male #054, "Cedric," sixteen-year-old 62 Brim Blood)

Some subjects castigated the police for not doing their job properly; two expressed the opinion that the police need to be harder on gang members.

The police now I think they got scared. You got your teenagers now 13, 14 using handguns and pistols and stuff. That's like police got so they don't give a damn what's going on in this society. That way you can get rid of some of the population. Something like that. Police just ain't doing their job because if you try to stop a gang fight like 37 on 37, shit you need the police out there trying to break it up but there's going to be some killing there. (Male #017, "Billy," twenty-one-year-old North Side Crip)

I just think here in St. Louis they are not strict enough. That's how I see it. Cause if they was they could put a stop to this wannabe stuff. They could stop the shipments coming from California really if they wanted to. (Male #020, "Lil Thug," sixteen-year-old Gangster Disciple)

Several subjects also boasted that the police cannot or did not bother them.

They don't trip. They know in Laclede Town not to be tripping. (Male #033, "Larry," eighteen-year-old Thundercat)

Cops ain't nothing. They can't stop us out there. (Male #036, "NA," eighteen-year-old Compton Gangster)

Just as most of our subjects and their gangs had bad relations with the police, they also had high levels of involvement with them. Fifty-three subjects said they came into daily contact with the police, and nine said they had interactions at least once a week or every weekend.

> Every day. Every other hour! (Male #071, "B Daddy," seventeen-year-old Inglewood Family Gangster Blood)

This high level of involvement is due, at least partly, to police surveillance (or harassment, according to our subjects) of gangs.

> They see a group of people and they stop us and check us. See if we have dope. (Male #010, "Jason C.," fifteen-year-old Compton Gangster)

> Like a dude will be sitting on a porch and ain't bothering nobody. They come up and start checking you and stuff to see if you got any dope. Sometimes they make you pull your pants down, take your shoes off, socks off, coat, jacket, hat and all that. (Male #055, "Chris," seventeen-year-old Hoover Crip)

Those gang members who hung out daily in public places – parks, playgrounds, street corners, fast-food emporiums – quickly become noticeable to police patrols and subject to regular scrutiny and engagement.

> When you gang banging they looking for you every day. The police up at Skate King and they try to harass you too much. (Male #015, "Karry," fifteen-year-old Crenshaw Gangster Blood)

> We stay in one place all day. Stand on the corner or something. The police always ask what's up. They'll take our rag talking about they own our street. We laugh at them. (Male #028, "Killa 4 Ren," fifteen-year-old 187 Crip)

Only two subjects said they "never" came into contact with the police, although thirty-one did not answer this question.

Our subjects obviously do not like the police. Even those who said that their gang had "good" relations often meant only that they themselves were not being harassed at this particular time. This attitude is not surprising, of course. Gang members, after all, regularly commit crimes that the police are sworn to detect and prevent. Most of our gang subjects are also adolescents, who do not take kindly to any authority, especially one that is ready, willing, and licensed to use physical force. In some sense, the police are just another one of the many "threats" that drive our subjects into gangs and keep them there after they have joined. Besides these reasons, the police forces of the St. Louis area are predominantly white and our subjects predominantly black, a volatile contrast in American urban areas for the last forty or fifty years. The presence of black police officers does not alleviate this conflict; in fact, it may only make it worse. But it is not surprising that our subjects report high levels of negative interactions with police forces. As we have already discussed, and as the next section examines, the police have good reason to encounter and keep tabs on this group of St. Louis adolescents and young adults.

"Shit, I Can't Even Count That": Arresting Gang Members. The gang members we interviewed had regular contact with the police for very good reasons, they were substantially involved in serious crime and, as a consequence, had been arrested a lot. While nineteen of our subjects said they had never been arrested,[10] the mean number of arrests for the other eighty active members was just under ten. Some subjects seemed almost proud of the variety and quantity of their arrests.

> I got locked up for a UUW [unlawful use of a weapon], I had three possessions, I had a assault first, attempt to kill, I had, they tried to give me a robbery, they tried to give me a rape, but I turned myself in, that wasn't me. Conspiracy to distribute, conspiracy to sell. Trespassin. (Male #001, "Mike-Mike," twenty-year-old Thundercat)

> I been arrested say about, I don't know. I been arrested for drugs, stolen goods, burglary, robbery, CCW [carrying a concealed weapon]. (Male #003, "Jerry," eighteen-year-old Thundercat)

> Shit, I can't even count that. (Male #013, "Darryl," twenty-nine year-old Blood)

With others, however, it was like pulling teeth to catalog their arrests.

> INT: Have you ever been arrested?
> MALE #063, "Bobtimes," sixteen-year-old 6 Deuce Blood: Yes.
> INT: What for?
> 063: Assault.
> INT: Is that it?
> 063: Driving a stolen vehicle.
> INT: Anything else?
> 063: Trying to do a 187 [homicide]
> INT: So you basically got a CCW [carrying a concealed weapon]?
> 063: Yeah.
> INT: Anything else?
> 063: No.

As Figure 7.3 shows, their criminality began at a fairly early age; sixteen subjects had been arrested before they were thirteen years old (the lowest age of first arrest was eight) and the mean age of first arrest was fourteen.

INT: How old were you the first time you got arrested?
MALE #030, "Kenneth," nineteen-year-old Thundercat: About 9. Shooting pigeons with a BB gun downtown. You know how you are at that age.

Sixty-one subjects had been arrested within the year prior to our interview with them; and thirty-four within two months of our contacts.

About three weeks ago. I was on the south side and this guy had some static with my cousin. My cousin hit him in the mouth and he came running over there to us with a gun like he was going to shoot us. We all got out and started shooting at him. I hit him on the shoulder and I got to go to court for that next month. (Male #034, "Lil Gene Mack," eighteen-year-old 19th Street Rolling 60's Crip)

[It was for] reckless driving. Yesterday. (Male #039, "Kaons BIC," seventeen-year-old Compton Gangster)

[My most recent arrest:] They got me for the assault. They have had me for the shooting but they couldn't find the gun. We got in a fight with some dudes up on Cherokee. One of them pulled out a gun so I got in my

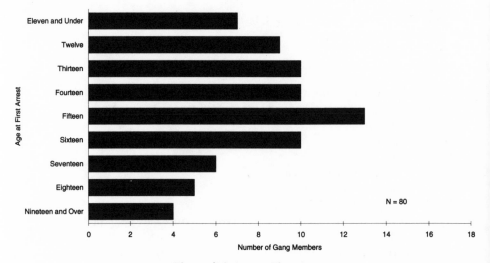

Figure 7.3 Age at First Arrest

trunk, we got out a shotgun and started shooting at them. They was just some dudes. They looked like dope fiends. (Male #091, "Paul," eighteen-year-old 107 Hoover Crip)

Fifty-three subjects said they were with the gang (or another member of the gang) at their last arrest; only eighteen said they were alone.[11] In some cases they claim to have been arrested just for being gang members.

Gang activity, that's a charge now, gang warfare. If you have a rag in you pocket they lock you up. If they see that you have a blue tattoo of your nickname on your left arm, they say you a Thundercat and they lock you up. (Male #030, "Kenneth," nineteen-year-old Thundercat)

Or because of mistaken identity.

They got mad cause I got accused of a drive-by shooting that I didn't do. They kept me for a week but they didn't find a gun so they let me out. (Male #015, "Karry," fifteen-year-old Crenshaw Gangster Blood)

If anything, these gang members are underarrested. Their narratives abound with criminal activities, and no matter how much boasting and bragging they may have done to impress (or scare) their interviewers, there is enough truth in their stories to suggest they too often commit serious crimes with impunity.

Firing a weapon and attempted murder. (Male #019, "Anthony," twenty-two-year-old Disciple Crip)

If they would have caught me it would have been for attempted murder. (Male #027, "G-Loc," fifteen-year-old Gangster Disciple)

Assault 1st, tampering, carrying concealed weapon, parole violation, reckless driving. I've been locked up a whole lot of times from all that. In the last two years I have been locked up 22 times. (Male #039, "Kaons BIC," seventeen-year-old Compton Gangster)

We have not counted the total number of crimes our ninety-nine subjects told us they had committed (and they almost certainly did not tell us all of them), but just from reading the interview transcripts, it is apparent that there are tens of homicides mentioned; scores of shootings (both successful and attempted); armed robberies, burglaries, and auto thefts; and hundreds of nonweapon assaults. Given the social characteristics of our subjects and the neighborhoods they live in, this pervasive involvement in illegal activities comes as no surprise.

> Assault, armed robbery, I got picked up on some murders too. (Male #036, "NA," eighteen-year-old Compton Gangster)

And the number of less serious crimes – vandalism, graffiti painting, underage drinking, petty theft, shoplifting, reckless driving – is probably even higher.

> I been arrested about 32 times. I'm talking about being an adult. As a juvenile I can't even count them. (Male #033, "Larry," eighteen-year-old Thundercat)

> One time I got arrested for dancing in the street. It was in front of my house. (Female #046, "Lady Tee," sixteen-year-old 74 Hoover Crip)

> Curfew, unlawful assembly. About 25 times. We get caught spray painting and all that junk. (Male #058, "Roach," fifteen-year-old Pine Lawn Organization Blood)

Our subjects' most recent arrests ranged from homicide to disturbing the peace, with the most common crime being assault (seventeen subjects). They were more likely to have been arrested for a violent crime than any other category. However, gang members often are unsure about what it is they are arrested for or what the difference is between an arrest – being taken into custody – and being charged or booked for a crime.

> Burglary, car theft, pressing us about the guy who got shot, I don't know, some other things. (Male #016, "John Doe," fifteen-year-old Crenshaw Mobster Blood)

> Jacking cars, fighting, carrying a concealed weapon. The latest one was for cussin' out a cop. Whatever the fuck that's supposed to mean, they arrested me for that bullshit. (Male #092, "Derone," twenty-one-year-old Rolling 60's Crip)

On occasion, they seemed wildly confused about levels of jurisdiction.

> Seven main arrests with federal charges. The others are like curfew or something like that. That ain't no real big charge. (Male #015, "Karry," fifteen-year-old Crenshaw Gangster Blood)

Seventy percent of our subjects, at the time we interviewed them, had been arrested more than once. As several quotes above show, many gang members can rattle off, in quick succession, their charges – when they can remember the total. And several said that they "couldn't count," "over fifty," or similar indications of very high numbers of arrest.

"Most of the Time I'm Found Not Guilty": Being Convicted and Doing Time. A conservative estimate of our subjects total arrests would be well over eight hundred. But only thirty-seven subjects said they had been convicted, and the total number of their convictions (at least those they could or did report) was only forty-nine. They often seemed confused about what a conviction might be, a surprising confusion given their obvious familiarity with the juvenile and adult criminal justice systems.

INT: Did they ever convict you of anything?
MALE #002, "Eric," sixteen-year-old Thundercat: Like, what you mean?
INT: Have you ever been found guilty?
002: Yeah. . . . Possess, I mean assault. Longest I ever stayed in Juvenile was two months.
INT: So you've been found guilty more than once or just one time?
002: Just one time. Like they'll drop the charges or somethin like that.

I ain't been arrested like convicted. I only been convicted twice but I been arrested about 32 times. I talking about being an adult. As a juvenile I can't even count them. (Male #033, Larry, eighteen-year-old Thundercat).

And it is not only gang members who are confused. Coding and recoding our questions about convictions and time served failed to resolve some minor discrepancies in our statistical portrait of conviction and imprisonment experiences. While thirty-seven subjects said they had been convicted, only thirty-four said how many times they had been convicted, thirty-nine gave us their age at first conviction, thirty-seven could tell us their sentence when first convicted, and thirty-six could tell us what they had been convicted for.

The median number of convictions for the thirty-four subjects who answered the question is only one, and the high is five, but we suspect that it may be higher, both because of the confusion mirrored in the above accounts and because some subjects probably have forgotten convictions for minor offenses that did not include jail or juvenile detention time.

INT: Have you ever been convicted?
MALE #003, "Jerry," eighteen-year-old Thundercat: What, for time?
INT: For time or just convicted.
003: Yeah, I did four or five months. This was doing like juvenile time.

MALE #035, "Edward," eighteen-year-old Hoover Gangster Crip: Once.

INT: What were you convicted for?

035: Well twice, I have been convicted twice. Once for unlawful use of a weapon. One was for stealing an automobile.

INT: So you have never been convicted of any of these arrests?

MALE #057, "Smith & Wesson," fifteen-year-old Neighborhood Posse Blood: What are you talking about?

INT: You go to court and the judge pronounces you guilty.

057: No.

The median age of first conviction is sixteen, and the range is from thirteen to twenty. Given both the ages of our subjects and the early onset of criminality among them, it is not surprising to learn that most gang members in our sample were first convicted as juveniles.

Well I was convicted for one robbery [when I was a juvenile]. I did like about 8 or 9 months. (Female #006, "Yolanda," nineteen-year-old 23rd Street Hoover Crips)

Our subjects had been convicted of at least twelve different crimes, with assault being the modal category (nine convictions) followed by weapons violations (six convictions for either UUW or CCW),[12] drug possession (five subjects), and stolen vehicle charges (three convictions).[13] These are not necessarily the first convictions for our subjects, or the most serious, but are probably only the first ones that they thought of mentioning, for whatever reasons of saliency.

I just got out. I got caught two times possessing alcohol, once when I was 16 and once when I was 18. I had a lot of misdemeanors like standing on the corner. All them misdemeanors add up, I'm on probation. (Male #065 "BK Kill," nineteen-year-old North County Crip)

The longest sentence received by one of our gang members on a first conviction was for five to ten years, but the median and modal category was less than six months (sixteen subjects). Seven subjects had received probation; four had received sentences of six months to one year.

When I got caught with the weed at school I was a juvie. They let me go, my mom came and got me and they let me go, man. (Male #012, "Lance," twenty-year-old West Side Mob member)

These light sentences are not surprising, given that our subjects' first arrest was usually as a juvenile and that their earliest charges probably were fairly minor.

Only seven subjects had sentences of more than one year (one subject for one to two years, five subjects for two to five years, one subject for more than five years). Three subjects were coded as receiving "other" sentences when first convicted, which meant that they were vague about the time or conditions of their sentencing.

Our subjects also seemed confused about serving jail or prison sentences. Forty subjects, for example, said that they had "done time" at some point in their life, but only thirty-two could tell us what they had done it for, only thirty-seven subjects could tell us how many times they had served such sentences, and only thirty-one subjects told us where they were incarcerated.

> Yeah. I went to the Workhouse but that ain't being convicted to the penitentiary. They let me out of there. (Male #039, "Kaons BIC," seventeen-year-old Compton Gangster)

> INT: Have you ever been convicted? Did they find you guilty of any of them?
> MALE #063, "Bobtimes," sixteen-year-old 6 Deuce Blood: No.
> INT: Have you ever done time?
> 063: Three months.

In many cases, no doubt, gang members were conflating pretrial detention, or overnight holdings in juvenile detention facilities, with an actual correctional sentence.

> Three days at Central [the main lockup], that's how long I was in detention. (Male #025, "Tony," seventeen-year-old 107 Hoover Gangster Crip)

Gang members were, after all, in and out of detention facilities fairly frequently.

> I was at juvenile detention then I got old enough and I got out last Wednesday and got out again today. I had got out August 1 and then I had got locked right back up on August 16. (Male #039, "Kaons BIC," seventeen-year-old Compton Gangster)

The median number of incarcerations is again one (mentioned by thirty-four subjects), only three said they had served more than one sentence (one subject said he served two terms and two subjects said they had been incarcerated five times). But our subjects probably have spent more time in detention facilities than these numbers indicate. These quotes, for example, come from subjects coded as having only one incarceration.

[I've been to the juvenile home] at least 12 [times]. (Male #015, "Karry," fifteen-year-old Crenshaw Gangster Blood)

I went to the DYS for a month. I was in jail for 11 months. (Male #072, "Blood," fifteen-year-old Swan Park 59 Blood)

The most frequent charge for which our subjects had done time was assault (ten subjects), followed by armed robbery (five subjects), drug possession and weapons violations (four subjects each), and arson and stolen vehicle (two subjects each).

Bank robbery. [I did five years on that]. (Male #013, "Darryl," twenty-nine-year-old Blood)

The arson incarcerations illustrate the confusing morass of our subjects' discussions of arrest, convictions, and incarceration; no subjects mentioned it as a crime for which they had been convicted and there were very few mentions of arson as a crime they had committed or been arrested for. Single subjects also mentioned being incarcerated for burglary, commercial sex prostitution, manslaughter, peace disturbance, and "other."

Those gang members who had been incarcerated predominantly served their time in juvenile settings and jails. Sixteen subjects, out of thirty-one who answered the question, said they had "done time" in juvenile detention facilities (thirteen at Juvenile Hall in the city, three in the county). Another ten had been jailed in county or city jails in the St. Louis region (nine at the Workhouse and one at Hogan St., a juvenile detention facility). Only five subjects admitted to doing time in state penal institutions (three at the Adult Correctional Institution, one in California, and one at a state prison).

Needless to say, many of our subjects were not model prisoners.

But uh one day cause I was too bad in Juvenile they just put me up out of here cause I was startin a gang riot up in there cause, man, we use to have unit fights, you know, be whoopin on people, throwing plates and stuff, throwin tables, have unit fights, we use to run it. Whoop on a youth leader, make me mad, cause I don't like to be hollered at, my mamma don't do much hollerin at me, I don't really like when she do much hollerin at me, but when the other person try to holler at me that really gonna make me go overboard. Just say, send him to confinement. They send me to confinement, and if I act crazy, they try to shackle me down. One day the uh, one of these youth leaders tried to whoop me and the man knew I was serious, I looked em in his eye, I say, man if you hit me wit that belt while all my clothes off, I be up here after work soon as I get out and I'm killin you. He didn't touch me cause he seen I was serious in the eye. I don't play that stuff, don't put your hands on me boy, you don't know me. Shackle me down, you can't move or nothin. (Male #002, "Eric," sixteen-year-old Thundercat)

I was up there. I was up in Booneville. It was like dorms up there. They put me in a house with Slobs. In the whole house there was about 20 Crips but the rest of them was Slobs. My partner had a big old nine and a one on the back of his arm and another partner had a six and an O on the back of his. In *Colors* they had a gate where they was on this side and we on that side. We throwing up signs and they spit on us. They would throw some water on our side or throw matches and burn a bed or something. It was wild. (Male #033, "Larry," eighteen-year-old Thundercat)

Many subjects, however, expected to end up someday in state penitentiaries, just like many of their parents, their older brothers, cousins, and fellow gang members.

Everybody said we gotta slow down cause we started losing people. We got one a victim of murder already, he's gone, and then another one, so now it's like half and half. Half the guys in jail, half the guys gone. (Male #003, "Jerry," eighteen-year-old Thundercat)

Most of my kind stop cause they either been in the penitentiary or they got beat up or somebody got killed or something like that. (Male #018, "Maurice," twenty-year-old 107 Hoover Gangster Crip)

INT: What do you see yourself doing in a year?
MALE #024, "Hamilton," sixteen-year-old Crip: Time in the pen.

St. Louis gang members spend a lot of their time interacting with the criminal justice system (not as much, of course, as they do interacting with each other).

I been in it since I was 12. That's about seven years and I have been through some of everything, penitentiary, juvenile homes and all that stuff, shooting, robbery, everything. (Male #030, "Kenneth," nineteen-year-old Thundercat)

Outside of their gang and school experiences, gang members have more frequent contact with the criminal justice system than with any other social institution. But while their attitude toward school is often positive, or at least neutral, gang members' feelings about the criminal justice system and its officials are usually highly negative. The quote that

began this section – "I hate the motherfuckers" – is echoed throughout
our interview transcripts. And while it was directed at the police, it can be
extended to other officials, prosecutors, judges, jail and prison guards,
juvenile counselors, parole and probation officers.

This is not a novel observation on our part. Our subjects' lives are
filled with criminal activity from before they became gang members. And
once they join and become active, the threats of violence that pushed
them into their gang remain. But "being down" also pushes members to
become more visible and vulnerable to police and legal attentions, as well
as more deserving of it. They are often keenly aware of the pulls and
pushes of this life, its stupidity and danger, but, as "Lil Thug" said:

> It's like a thing that I'm used to. I can't get out of it really. (Male #020,
> sixteen-year-old Gangster Disciple)

"Getting Paid": Jobs, Legal Money, and Future Jobs

> INT: What kind of jobs could you get if you wanted to work?
> MALE #083, "Winchester," fourteen-year-old Rolling 60's Crip: I sell
> dope!

The gang members we talked with had all spent time in school and 80
percent or more had been arrested at least once, but less than a fifth of
our subjects were involved in the legitimate labor market when we interviewed them. Only seventeen subjects said they were employed, and the
jobs they held were overwhelmingly in service or retail industries at the
lowest level. But even when they were not entry-level jobs, our subjects
soon lost them.

> I was taking algebra, chemistry. Then I got shot. I went to East St. Louis
> for a visit. I was at the wrong place at the wrong time and I got shot. I went
> on and graduated then I went to Job Corps. That worked out. I came back
> and was working for Chrysler. They got to striking out there and I got
> jumped on. Couple of grown men jumped on me out there cause I didn't
> know nothing about no picket line and all that. They jumped on me out
> there. My boss laid me off out there and didn't never call me back. I tried
> to succeed on everything else but couldn't, nothing go my way so I just
> went down the wrong road. (Male #037, "Big Money," twenty-two-year-
> old Compton Gangster)

The low level of participation in the labor market is due to a variety of
factors, including the relative youth of our subjects . . .

Lately I have been looking for a job so I can have some money. Basically any kind like fast food or the mall or something. I just turned 16 and last year I had better things to do. (Female #046, "Lady Tee," sixteen-year-old 74 Hoover Crip)

. . . the lack of available jobs in a declining rust-belt city . . .

That's why we make money [i.e., sell drugs], we going looking for a job and can't never find nothing. (Male #026, "Chill," fifteen-year-old Hoover Gangster Crip)

. . . a lack of acceptable skills and personality traits . . .

I quit my job at Popeyes in the city on Page. That was about two months ago. I was dropping the tickets in the grate. This little girl, she walked past me and bumped my hand and it went in the grease. I yanked it out real quick and my hand was burnt. I put butter on my hand. She was standing there, ha, ha, laughing so I hit her. It made the manager mad. We sat down and talked it out. He said he was going to put me on suspension for a week. I just said no, I quit. Plain and simple. I can get me another job. (Male #020, "Lil Thug," sixteen-year-old Gangster Disciple)

[I had a job] at McDonald's sweeping up floors. I get tired of people trying to tell me what to do. (Male #057, "Smith & Wesson," fifteen-year-old Neighborhood Posse Blood)

. . . their race and presumed criminal tendencies.

Yeah, I'm a young black and most people know young blacks like they ain't nothing but drug dealers or gang bangers. When young blacks really try to succeed they get turned down and they be on they way, drugs be the only way of making money. (Male #037, "Big Money," twenty-two-year-old Compton Gangster)

All of these factors are consistent with the underclass position of the majority of our subjects. Manufacturers, retailers, and service industries have migrated out of the city – especially from those neighborhoods where our subjects live – and entry-level, unskilled, part-time jobs have also migrated with them. Public transportation to places outside the city limits is slow, infrequent, or unavailable, and inner-city residents find it difficult to follow jobs out to the suburbs or across the rivers. Our subjects also appear to lack personal networks that could lead them into the above ground job market. High unemployment and underemployment in these areas has eroded both social contacts and social capital.

But the main reason most of our subjects do not work is because they are gang members, whose lives and time are focused on street and peer-group interactions and activities that they find more rewarding.

> Because we don't want a job. If I get a job I have to move out. (Male #021, "40 Ounce," sixteen-year-old 107 Hoover Gangster Crip)

> I was trying to find me a job. I can get out of the gang that way. I mean I'm not going to stop hanging with the guys I'm in the gang with. That's why I'm trying to find me a job or get back in school. I can't get back in school so I got to find me a job. (Male #034, "Lil Gene Mack," eighteen-year-old 19th Street Rolling 60's Crip)

Gang life, with its threats and violence, as well as the lure of drug sales and other criminally acquired money, creates a drop in and drop out relationship with work for many of our subjects. The transitory nature of our subjects' work experiences is testimony to the pervasive influence of the gang and its ability to reduce the involvement in and effect of social institutions.

> [I was working in a kitchen] bout four months. (Male #001, "Mike-Mike," twenty-year-old Thundercat)

> I worked at first but I'm looking for a job now though. Nothing special, I used to paint and drywall now and then and used to be a prep cook. Any job as long as I make money I'm all right. I used to work at Wendy's. (Male #005, "Antonio," nineteen-year-old 6th Street Hoover Crip)

> I had one last summer. I was working with tires, like a junk yard. They paid me about $20 a day, $20 each evening. I worked at nine and then went home about 8 but we didn't work all the way through, we have resting. (Male #009, "Marrien," fifteen-year-old Compton Gangster)

> I only worked two weeks there [MacDonald's] anyway, no, four weeks and got two checks. One was for $196 and the other one for $70. (Male #039, "Kaons BIC," seventeen-year-old Compton Gangster)

Most jobs that subjects could hold were part-time, low-wage, unskilled labor of some sort, jobs that our subjects often belittled.

> Yeah. I'm working at the airport with my father. [For] about $3.80. Just cleaning up offices and stuff. (Female #006, "Yolanda," nineteen-year-old 23rd Street Hoover Crip)

> I work for a pizza and a restaurant joint. I work there 14 or 10 hours a day. Making pizzas or making dough. (Male #018, "Maurice," twenty-year-old 107 Hoover Crip)

MALE #029, "Randell," seventeen-year-old Thundercat: I worked at Six
Flags. $3.80. I worked about two hours a day.
INT: Was it worth your time going out there?
MALE #029, Randell: No.

Some subjects mentioned having much better paying and skilled jobs at
some times.

Well I used to work at the Federal Building. Secretarial. When I graduate
I am going to back to them. Cause I want to work year around, not just a
part-time job. (Female #006, "Yolanda," nineteen-year-old 23rd Street
Hoover Crip)

Income from these jobs was not great. Although four subjects said
that they earned between $200 and $300 a week (for full-time work), the
mean income reported for the sixteen subjects who supplied figures was
$142. (The range was from $35 to $300, the mode was $150, and the
median $125 to $130). But given the intermittent nature of our subjects'
hours and job tenure and the chaotic and spontaneous character of their
life, we assume that these figures fluctuate rather wildly at times.

Our subjects not only are unrealistic about potential and actual drug
income, they appear to be sadly deluded about future jobs and income.
We asked gang members what kind of money they wanted to be making
when they were about thirty, and what kind of job they might have to
earn it. Some subjects were fairly realistic about their possibilities (if
sometimes a little hazy about their math) and had rather everyday aspira-
tions.

I want to bring home about $200 a day. About $18.00 an hour, either
setting tile or doing electronics. (Male #009, "Marrien," fifteen-year-old
Compton Gangster)

I can tell you how much I would make an hour, about $20 an hour. That's
good. That's for nursing. You can get that for nursing. (Female #047,
"Baby," fifteen-year-old Rolling 60's Crip)

Working at like Boatmen's [a local bank] or something. Somewhere other
than a carwash or flipping burgers. (Male #020, "Lil Thug," sixteen-year-
old Gangster Disciple)

Be an auto mechanic. (Male #026, "Chill," fifteen-year-old 107 Hoover
Gangster Crip)

I want to go into cosmetology. $45,000 a year. (Male #029, "Randell,"
seventeen-year-old Thundercat)

Other subjects, however, dreamed big.

> About $100,000 a year at least. I would really like to play basketball or be an accountant. (Male #045, "C-Loc," seventeen-year-old Rolling 60's Crip)

> About $100,000 or $200,000. Probably playing football. (Male #008, "Robert," fourteen-year-old Compton Gangster)

> A good paying job. Fashion design. (Male #010, "Jason C.," fifteen-year-old Compton Gangster)

These jobs, and this labor market, are unable to control the behavior and values of this group of generally poor urban residents. They often lack the skills, workplace discipline, and future orientation that would allow them to keep jobs, even the poor-paying, rather meaningless ones they can obtain. And their income from working is laughable when compared to their (ludicrous in their own way) estimates of what they make selling drugs. After all, if you can make up to $15,000 a week selling drugs, why work flipping burgers? In sum, it isn't only the earnings that places the legitimate job market at a competitive disadvantage with selling drugs, it is the nature of work, with its requirements of structure and discipline, that conflict with the values of life in the gang.

"I Go to Church at Easter and Christmas": Gang Members and Legitimate Social Organizations

We have mentioned this several times, but it is worth repeating: before joining their gang, eighty of our subjects participated in legal groups (church, clubs, scouts, sports), but after they "got down," sixty of them dropped out of such organizations. The attractive pull of the gang and of peers obviously is very strong, stronger, in most cases than those of church, neighborhood clubs, or sports. In addition, the intensity, duration, and frequency of interaction for the remaining twenty subjects is not great.

Not surprisingly, involvement in religious organizations was minimal. However, one subject noted his efforts to balance the demands of the gang with those of his religion. "Mike-Mike," as he was familiarly known, may be an atypical subject in some regards, but his mixture of gang involvement and token or part-time participation in "legal organizations"[14] seems fairly typical of those subjects who continued to be involved in legal groups.

I run the Thundercats, that's over in Laclede Town and plus I'm a Muslim. I go to the Temple every Saturday. Well see, it's like this, I have to take a little time off from being with the Muslims and a little time off from being with my gang. (Male #001, twenty-year-old Thundercat)

It is interesting to observe that five of the seven female members we interviewed were churchgoers, and several were involved in more than just attending services.

I go to church like twice a month. (Female #006, "Yolanda," nineteen-year-old 23rd Street Hoover Crip)

I'm in the church choir. Practice on Wednesday. (Female #007, "Tina," fourteen-year-old Hoover Crip)

FEMALE #046, "Lady Tee," sixteen year-old 74 Hoover Crip: I go to church every Sunday with my grandmother.
INT: Why do you go?
046: I don't know.
INT: Mostly for your grandma?
046: No. I just go. I like church. Well I like our church. I don't think I would like just any church. I don't go for no after church Sunday school, none of that.

I'm in a [church] choir. (Female #078, "Tina," fifteen-year-old Treetop Blood)

Only one male who mentioned church participation was more than a simple attender. Ironically, he admitted to engaging in drug sales and other crimes and had ten arrests. He appeared to give the appearance of wanting to "play all the angles" and admitted that he liked to sing.

MALE #038, "G.O.D.," nineteen-year-old Compton Gangster: Yeah, I go to church every Sunday. Sing in the choir.
INT: You sing in a choir group?
038: Yeah, and usher boy.

One male subject seemed defensive about going to church, sharply telling the interviewer that "I go because I want to go."

INT: What kind of stuff do you do there?
MALE #010, "Jason C.," fifteen-year-old Compton Gangster: Listen to the minister.
INT: Ok, so mostly going to church.
010: Yeah.
INT: Do you go most of the time?

010: I go every Sunday.

INT: Do you think of yourself as religious or not?

010: I don't know.

INT: Do you just go because your family goes?

010: I go because I want to go.

INT: You don't go with your family?

010: They go.

Other male churchgoers seemed more like our first subject, dividing their time "away from the gang" between church and nonchurch activities.

INT: What are some of the things you do without the gang?

MALE #036, "NA," eighteen-year-old Compton Gangster BIC: Go to church and lounges.

INT: You go to church on Sunday right.

036: Right.

INT: When do you go to lounges?

036: Thursday, Friday, and Saturday nights.

Church, yeah, I go to church every Sunday and work, that's about it. (Male #045, "C-Loc," seventeen-year-old Rolling 60's Crip)

In general, female gang members seem to be less exclusively involved with the gang and more involved with other groups than male members.

After school talent show and plays and stuff. Spirit club. (Female #007, "Tina," fourteen-year-old Hoover Crip)

Sometimes, we got this center that we go to and all of us be up there. Like recreation center it's right in there. It's the neighborhood association. They send you to camp every year. (Female #011, "Lisa," fifteen-year-old Compton Gangster)

We got a group of people in the neighborhood that talk to us. It supposed to be something for us to do. We go up there on Saturday nights do craft things, they take us skating, they take us to shows. It's supposed to be something for us to do to get off the streets. In the summer they have camp for us. It's pretty nice. They ought to do it on Friday nights too. It only costs $2.00 for the whole year. We sit around up there and talk about gangs. The leader, his name is Bruce. He talk about gangs and drugs. We talk about the other groups and getting together with the other groups for dances. We only go to the dances when they in our neighborhood. It's like a church group. We not going in they neighborhood. (Female #046, "Lady Tee," sixteen-year-old 74 Hoover Crip)

Religious activities were only slightly less popular than organized sports. Two members said they were still on school teams (basketball in both cases) and five other subjects mentioned involvement in community sports groups of some sort.

Operation 10 in the neighborhood [a city basketball program]. (Male #009, "Marrien," fifteen-year-old Compton Gangster)

No, sometimes I box at clubs. (Male #082, "Dough Boy," fourteen-year-old B Gangster Disciple)

Several subjects mentioned rather ironic club associations they were involved with. Numerous gang members during our earliest interviews mentioned that they went to the "Herbert Hoover" Boys and Girls Clubs in the city. It would be easy to mistakenly consider these clubs as the source for set names ("107 Hoovers," etc.) but these clubs predate the current emergence of gangs in St. Louis.

MALE #010, "Jason C.," fifteen-year-old Compton Gangster: Yes. I still go to Herbert Hoover.
INT: What's Herbert Hoover?
010: Boys club, play baseball, soccer, football.

Another member described playing on a police-sponsored softball team.

INT: How did you get involved in this softball team?
MALE #050, "John," nineteen-year-old Rolling 60's Crip: From Operation Teamwork with the police.
INT: The police run this thing?
050: Yeah.
INT: Do they know you are in a gang do you think?
050: Last year we used to get into fights so I guess they do.
INT: So the police actually run this softball team?
050: Yeah.
INT: So you don't mind being involved with the police?
050: No.

As a general rule, however, our subjects drop their associations with legitimate organizations, preferring the excitement and interactions of gang life to the tamer pursuits of church, sports, scouts, or "crafty things." Such group pursuits, after all, do not protect members from the generalized and specific threats they faced before and within the gang. There are hints, however, that female members (and younger, more recent members) appreciate the services and interactions of nongang groups, but in most cases, such groups do not seem to pull members away from their life on the street.

Conclusion

Gang involvement dramatically increases the social isolation of our subjects to a disturbing degree. After all, they are already profoundly separated from many social institutions in the surrounding society because of their race, poverty, and residence. The relative lack of legitimate social institutions in their neighborhoods, low levels of parental involvement, a weak labor market offering largely unrewarding jobs, and dangerous and violence-prone streets all contribute to our subjects' withdrawal from legitimate social pursuits.

But these conditions alone do not explain the social isolation of gang members. Two-thirds of our subjects had either graduated from high school or were still attending school, and 80 percent had participated in nongang groups prior to initiation. Why have they dropped out? To answer that question we need to consider the threats and violence that have propelled our subjects into the gang and keep them in it, as well as the attractiveness of drug sales, the excitement of street life, and adolescent peer pressure from their fellow gang members and friends.

We have already shown that joining a gang in order to be protected from threats – to have some back-up – perversely only increases the level of threats and the probability of violence in our subjects' lives. And, just as perversely, because gang membership insulates members from nonmembers and social institutions, the level of threats and violence is increased. Legitimate social institutions that provide relatively safe arenas of activity are forced to distance gang members from their activities and drop them from their clientele. These processes illustrate that gang membership leads to isolation both as the gang assumes a more dominant role in the lives of its members and as social institutions actively exclude such members from their activities.

Schools do not want students who sell drugs, fight with rivals, show disrespect for teachers and staff, and carry weapons. Employers would rather not hire young men and women who wear gang colors, throw signs, and say "what's up cuz." And neither do churches, scout troops, sports teams, and neighborhood clubs want these people. Gang members and gangs bring danger to their environs and the people around them. Legitimate social institutions, therefore, distance gang members from their provinces, just as gang members distance themselves from such nonstreet life activities.

The one major exception, of course, is the criminal justice system, which is forced to step up its interest and attention in individuals who join gangs. But attention also diminishes gang members' safety and life chances and increases (or adds other kinds of) threats. Police harassment and surveillance, arrests, jail and holdover stays, prison time, probation, and parole cut peoples' ties to their society and to institutions. Such bonds are further reduced by defying or resisting police officers or being an inmate in prison or jail.

Gang membership creates a world of peer-oriented, temporary, and unstable groups for our subjects, which not only results in isolation from legitimate public organizations but also drives them away from nongang peers. As we discuss in the next chapter, gang membership also distances our subjects from their families and relatives.

"My Mom Doesn't Know": Gang Members and Their Families

THERE IS LITTLE systematic research that examines the link between family characteristics, values, and processes and gang membership. Some speculate that female-headed households make it more likely that young men will decide to join gangs, and that the decision to join a gang represents an attempt to find male role models unavailable in the nuclear family. An alternative suggestion holds that many urban families are unable to provide for the basic economic needs of their children and that gangs fulfill that need. Yet other approaches emphasize that adolescence is a time of increasing independence from the family, when family ties are weakened and those to peers and street culture become stronger. In each case, however, there is much more speculation than actual research.

We believe it is important to understand gang members and their families in the context of the neighborhoods they live in. By and large, the members of our samples lived in neighborhoods with few resources. Schools were plagued with difficulties (created in part by members of our sample), housing stock had declined, jobs in the legitimate economy had vanished, and recreation opportunities were hard to find. But not only had the power of formal social institutions been eroded, other mechanisms had lost their ability to control the behavior of neighborhood residents as well. Key among this latter group were neighborhood social control and the family. Viable neighborhoods, with functioning legitimate opportunity structures, go a long way to provide effective controls on behavior, especially for young people. Within the context of declining neighborhoods, families – generally headed by poor single women – often stood alone in their efforts to control the behavior of their children. Living in neighborhoods with limited economic and social capital and generally lacking in these themselves, the families we observed fought a difficult battle up a steep hill.

In this chapter, we address family issues by contrasting the perceptions of active gang members about ties to their family with the perceptions of family members. We emphasize the process of learning about and responding to gang membership on the part of family members, as well as the steps taken to "normalize" gang membership and activities within the context of family membership. Throughout, we examine closely the role that "family values" – beliefs about the importance of the family, its permanence, and moral legitimacy – play in the lives and relationships of gang members and their relatives.

Family Background Variables

We begin our analysis by examining the family structure and characteristics of the sample of active gang members. Thirteen of the ninety-nine active gang members live with both parents, and twenty-five lived away from both parents. This latter group tended to be older. The remainder of the sample (fifty-five individuals) lived with either their mother (fifty) or their father (five). These variations in family structure are not particularly surprising, as they have become commonplace in neighborhoods characterized by high levels of poverty, unemployment, and population change. However, what these aggregate data mask is the residential mobility of gang members. Many subjects reported that they "stayed" (maintained a primary residence) with one parent but spent time at a number of different locations throughout the course of a week or month.

But gang members can be parents and form families independent from their parents. Eighteen of our subjects were parents, and five more told us that their girlfriend was pregnant at the time of the interview. Two-thirds of those with children (twelve out of eighteen) did not live with their children. Despite this, all but one member of this group told us that they saw their children every day or nearly every day. Furthermore, none of our subjects were married. The vulnerability of the institution of marriage among poor, inner-city residents has been well documented in other quarters (Wilson 1987; Hacker 1992), a finding that receives support in our limited sample.

We now examine the impact of having a family member in a gang, especially a parent, on decisions to join the gang. Considerable evidence has been amassed that gangs in Los Angeles have a strong intergenerational structure (Vigil 1988; Moore 1978, 1991). However, there is little evidence of an intergenerational character to St. Louis gangs. This is hardly surprising, given the recent reemergence of gangs in the city. Twelve members of our sample indicated that their father had been a gang member, and one reported that both his parents formerly were members of the Blackstone Rangers when they lived in Chicago. Other Chicago gangs were identified as the affiliation of their parents, including the Disciples. "NA," an eighteen-year-old Compton Gangster, said that his father ran with a gang, an experience that gave him insight into his sons behavior.

> INT: What did he [your father] say when he heard [you were in a gang]?
> MALE #036, eighteen-year-old Compton Gangster BIC: I told him it wasn't a gang, it was a social club.
> INT: What did he say to that?
> 036: Don't be lying to me, boy.

In some instances, gang members were opposed to being members of the gang their parent had belonged to. The reasons for not wanting to affiliate with the same gang, in this instance, were more of style than substance.

> INT: Was your father ever a member of a gang?
> MALE #014, "D. C.," eighteen-year-old Disciple: He's a member of an old gang. You ever heard of the Mohawks? They used to be on the south side. He used to be a member of the Mohawks. I be messing with my girlfriend up at the bar and I be talking to these Crips. My father said, when I was in a gang we used to wear mohawks and long dangling earrings. He not put no mohawk on my head. I ain't walking around with no long dangling earrings.

While thirteen gang members knew that one of their parents was formerly affiliated with a gang, a number knew that their parents were involved in crime. Despite the fact that we did not ask specifically for gang members to tell us about their parent's criminal involvement, eight told us that their father was a criminal, but not a gang member.

> INT: Was your father a member of a gang?
> MALE #010, "Jason C.," fifteen-year-old Compton Gangster: We got pictures of him, he was a pimp. He used to be one of those. We got a whole lot of pictures.

> Na, my father was a criminal, just a criminal. He used to, uh, make bad checks, rob places and stuff. (Male #002, "Eric," sixteen-year-old Thundercat)

The modal response, accounting for over 80 percent of respondents, was that they either were unsure about the gang status of their parents or that their parents had not been gang members. In another, the response was somewhat different.

INT: Was you father a member of a gang?
MALE #042, "Leroy," seventeen-year-old Rolling 60's Crip: Oh no. He's a police officer.

There were no circumstances in which a son or daughter had joined their parents' gang, nor did they received any urging to join that (or any other) gang from their parents.

The picture is considerably different when we examine the role of family members of the same generation – especially brothers – on the decision to join the gang. Just under half of our sample (45 percent) told us that they had a brother in a gang. One-third of this group told us that their brother encouraged them to join.

INT: Why did you join?
MALE #031, "John Doe," sixteen-year-old Thundercat: Cause my brother was in it mostly.

INT: Did he have anything to do with you joining the gang?
MALE #052, "Jonathon," fifteen-year-old 107 Hoover Crip: He talked me into it, and then I just joined.

Sometimes the influence was indirect, operating through the instrumental advantages of gang membership.

INT: Did you have anything to do with him [your brother] joining?
MALE #092, "Derone," twenty-one-year-old Rolling 60's Crip: He just saw me making the money and everything else. He said, can I join, and I said yeah.

One subject who had several brothers in a gang stated they did not influence his decision to join because they lived in another city. "Lil B-Dog" (male #070), a fifteen-year-old Inglewood Family Gangster, had three brothers who were gang members in California and one in Chicago. In another instance, "Maurice" (male #018), an eighteen-year-old 107 Hoover Crip, told us he had an older brother in a gang but that he was a "slob," the pejorative term used by Crips to refer to Bloods. The majority of individuals with a brother in a gang (just over two-thirds) told us their brother did not influence them to join. Indeed, only 40 percent of those with a brother in a gang joined the same gang. This can be attributed in large part to the age grading and loose structure of St. Louis gangs.

The majority of our sample (55 percent) did not have a brother in a gang. These individuals typically directed their efforts toward discouraging gang membership.

> INT: What about the younger one [brother], does he. . .
>
> MALE #002, "Eric," sixteen-year-old Thundercat: Naw, he a criminal, he a little bitty somethin, but I don't get along wit em cause I see who he try to be like and then he claim that he can't stand me but yet he try and do everything I do. I mean he got caught wit a couple of my guns, got caught wit some dope, and he only eleven years old. And that's messed up.

> INT: Is your brother a member of a gang?
>
> MALE #033, "Larry," eighteen-year-old Thundercat: I be telling him I don't want him in it. He be going to school and talking about "What's up Cuz," and all that. I be tellin' him, don't try to follow in my footsteps.

> INT: Do you have a brother who has been a member of a gang?
>
> MALE #005, "Antonio," nineteen-year-old 6th Street Hoover Crip: No. He won't or I'll hurt him. He tried. He wanted to be a Disciple. I said, no brother.

One member told us that their brother was not in a gang, that he was "just wild" (#012). Another said:

> He say he don't wanna be in no gang. He say he just wanna sell drugs. (Male #001, "Mike-Mike," twenty-year-old Thundercat)

Two others disclosed that their brother had left the gang, in one instance, "to make something out of his life, to get a job" (#010).

Clearly, there is variation in the impact of having a brother in a gang. In only a minority of cases did individuals end up in the same gang as their brother. Perhaps this reflects the friendship-based, peer orientation of most St. Louis gangs. Because they hung out with different friends, gang members of the same family were likely to end up in different gangs. Equally interesting were the responses that indicated gang members would actively discourage gang membership on the part of brothers. Perhaps these were idealized responses, reflecting subjects' perceptions of their expected role rather than their actual relationship with their brothers.

We now introduce the sample of relatives of gang members we interviewed. These twenty-four individuals are a diverse group, as shown in Table 8.1. They include two whites, nine women, and ten different gangs. Six different family relationships are represented in this sample:

Table 8.1 *Relative chart*

ID #	Relation to gang member	Gang	Race	Sex	Age
R001	Brother	Bloods	B	M	20
R002	Cousin	104 Piru Bloods	B	M	20
R003	Cousin	Crips	B	M	19
R004	Sister	Pine Lawn Organization	B	F	16
R005	Sister	Rolling 60's	B	F	17
R006	Brother	Gangster Disciples	B	M	19
R007	Cousin	Southside Mob	B	M	14
R008	Cousin	Bloods	B	M	14
R009	Cousin	Treetop Bloods	B	M	15
R010	Mother	107 Hoover Crips	B	M	36
R011	Cousin	Bloods	B	M	14
R012	Cousin	Crips	B	M	17
R013	Cousin	Rolling 60's Crips	B	M	18
R014	Cousin	Crips	B	M	17
R015	Mother	Rolling 60's Crips	B	F	44
R016	Mother	Bloods	B	F	44
R017	Father	Bloods	B	M	44
R018	Mother	Crips	B	F	32
R019	Stepmother	Bloods	B	F	23
R020	Aunt	Bloods	B	F	30
R021	Mother	Disciples	W	F	45
R022	Father	Disciples	W	M	46
R023	Mother	Bloods	B	F	37
R024	Father	Bloods	B	M	37

two brothers, nine cousins, two sisters, one aunt, seven mothers, and three fathers. Throughout this chapter, we will compare the responses of these relatives to those of gang members.

Do They Know? Finding Out About Membership

Gang members and their families interact in a variety of roles. Learning about and acknowledging gang membership represent new roles in the relationship between gang members and their families. In the following sections, we trace the steps in this relationship – learning about membership, responding to membership, the effect on the family, whether the gang is like a family, and future relationships between gang members and their family.

Gang members generally preferred to hide their gang membership from family members, especially their mother and younger siblings. This is not surprising, as gang membership typically entails involvement in criminal activities not willfully disclosed to family members whose respect is valued. Many gang members attempted to conceal their membership because they professed that it would be "easier" on their mother that way or that she wouldn't have to worry if she didn't know. We suspect that failing to disclose membership was also easier for gang members, as they were less likely to be chastised or receive sanctions at home. And for their part, parents often denied that their son or daughter was a gang member, instead choosing to believe they were simply involved with the wrong friends. The response of relatives and children is not surprising in this regard. Nor is it unique to St. Louis gang members. "Monster Kody" (Shakur 1993), a notorious Los Angeles gang member, disclosed that in his early days as a gang member he and his mother had a tacit understanding about his gang membership. Despite numerous arrests, being shot, and years of membership, Kody and his mother did not directly acknowledge his status as a gang member to each other for some time. Parental denial of criminal involvement on the part of their children is not unique to gang members. When Abdul Salameh was charged in the 1993 bombing of the World Trade Center in New York City, his mother's response was that her son "wasn't involved."

Despite their efforts at keeping their membership from their family, 21 percent of our sample of active gang members reported that their family knew about their membership. There was considerable variation in the family member who knew about membership. In Figure 8.1 we report the frequencies that display which family member knew about their gang membership. Brothers (79 percent) and sisters (66 percent) were more likely to know about gang membership than any other relative. This is not surprising, given the age-graded structure of activities, friends, and opportunities among most city residents. Sixty-one percent of mothers were aware of gang membership, though often that awareness represented only the grudging acknowledgement of gang status by mother and child. Interestingly, fathers (38 percent) were not as likely to know about gang membership as were uncles (41 percent) and aunts (39 percent). In large part, this is due to the fact that most gang members no longer lived with their fathers and, in some cases, had no contact at all with them. Finally, 31 percent of grandparents knew about gang membership.

We asked gang members how relatives learned about their gang mem-

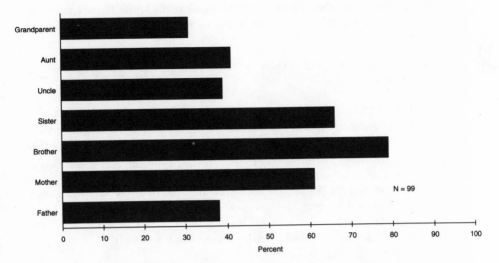

Figure 8.1 Relative Who Knew of Gang Membership

bership. Here again, there was considerable variation. Four members of
our sample indicated that they were "up front" about their membership
with relatives. These individuals indicated that members of their family
"knew from the beginning" (#063), or:

> INT: Who all knows you are a banger?
> MALE #088, "T-Loc," twenty-one-year-old Grape Street Crip: Everyone,
> my mother, brothers, sisters, uncles, aunts.

One told us that members of his family "respected" what they were doing
(#091) and warned them to be careful.

Many members of our sample were less certain that their family knew
about membership. These individuals indicated that either their family,
themselves, or both were unwilling to recognize the fact that they were in
a gang. A number of gang members told us that their mother "might
know," "probably knew," or "had a feeling" about their membership,
attesting to the shared, though unspoken, understanding between mothers and gang members about status. The difficulty in admitting gang
membership to a family member or in recognizing membership in the
behavior of a family member is evident in the following responses.

> INT: Anybody in your family know?
> MALE #021, "40 Ounce," sixteen-year-old 107 Hoover Gangster Crip:
> They don't want to believe it, but they think so.

My father thinks I'm in a gang, but he don't really know. He been talking to me about it. (Male #025, "Tony," seventeen-year-old 107 Hoover Gangster Crip)

They probably suspect it. (Male #048, "Corkey," sixteen-year-old Rolling 60's Crip)

These responses were the exceptions, however. For the most part, the families of gang members found out their children were in gangs as a consequence of some external symbol of membership. Often this had to do with gang signs. In most cases, such recognition did not come easily.

INT: When did the people in your family find out that you were in a gang?
MALE #020, "Lil Thug," sixteen-year-old Gangster Disciple: When I was fourteen cause I was starting leaving town. I was heading here and there. My mother asked me why I wore black so much.
INT: What did you tell her?
020: I lied to her. I said it's just that black is my favorite color. Then it came to me that I should tell her the truth.

I guess I started coming forward with it and would start talking about it. For a long time I was wearing my hat deep to the right and they said, "Why do you wear your hat like that?" I was like, personal business. (White male #099, "Joe L.," eighteen-year-old Insane Gangster Disciple)

INT: Does anyone in your family know you are in a gang?
WHITE MALE #100, "J Bone," nineteen-year-old Insane Gangster Disciple: Yeah, my mother does.
INT: Did she figure it out or did somebody tell her?
100: She figured it out. She asked other people about the way I'm doing things and dressing and they told her that probably what it is.

For other relatives, the signs of membership were easier to identify, particularly when they involved violence or contact with the police.

INT: Does your family know that you are a member of a gang?
MALE #030, "Kenneth," nineteen-year-old Thundercat: No. They got ideas; they know I got locked up and that I shot a gun. They don't know that I am an actual real gang member. They wouldn't understand if I told them.

INT: When did your mother find out?
MALE #035, "Edward," twenty-year-old Hoover Gangster Crip: I used to keep everybody's guns at my house, and everybody came over there to get them.

INT: When did your parents find out?

MALE #015, "Karry," fifteen-year-old Crenshaw Gangster Blood: I'd say, maybe a year and a half ago when I came back from California. That's when *Colors* [the movie] and all that stuff came out. It used to be that I could walk around with my red rag around my head and nobody know. But if you do that now, you going to get killed.

About one in five members of our sample told us that their family was unaware of their status as a gang member. In most cases, gang members in this category attempted to hide their membership from their family. Some of these individuals acknowledged that members of their family could identify the signs of membership, yet ignored them.

INT: Do your parents know that you are in a gang?

MALE #037, "Big Money," twenty-two-year-old Compton Gangster: Yeah. My mother. I don't acknowledge it in front of her. I don't bring none of my friends around or nothing like that. Everything I do I keep on the street.

Other gang members expressly tried to keep their membership from family members.

I keep it away from them. As far as they know, I just have a lot of friends. The way they carry theyself, they can't really tell. (Male #019, "Anthony," twenty-year-old Crip)

And even when family members are informed of membership, it is not always taken seriously.

INT: But your mother still doesn't know?

MALE #001, "Mike-Mike," twenty-year-old Thundercat: I told her yesterday, though, say mamma, you know I'm running a gang? Get out of here, you ain't runnin nothin. You out there sellin that cocaine.

Accounts provided by family members parallel the comments of gang members. Typically family members learned of gang membership through symbols of the gang. In some cases, the signs of membership were displayed quite openly, making their identification quite easy.

INT: How did you find out your cousin was in the gang?

MALE #R002, twenty-year-old cousin: It shocked me really. He just came home and started talking about it. He said I'm gonna get initiated tomorrow. He came home, he had his little tattoo, had his little color rag, they gave him a little gang name. Right now, they call him Redrum, murder spelled backwards.

INT: How did you learn about his gang membership?
FEMALE #R010, thiry-six-year-old mother: From pictures, his behavior, his friends that he started to spend time with.

In one case, a female Blood admitted her membership openly to her parents, the police, and authorities at juvenile court (#R016, forty-four-year-old mother).

Other relatives learned of gang membership through such things as "colors," "hand signs," and "gang talk." These visible signs made it more difficult to ignore the obvious, that their relative had affiliated with a gang. Recognizing the symbols, however, was not always easily accomplished, in part because of a lack of knowledge, but also because of a reluctance to believe that a relative may be a gang member.

INT: Did he try to hide it from your momma?
#R001, twenty-year-old brother: Yeah, he tried to hide it from her a little bit, but she was overlooking it.

INT: How long ago did you discover that she was in it [a gang]?
#R017, forty-four-year-old father: About two years.
INT: She told you or you all kind of discovered it?
R017: We discovered it and then she admitted to it. Had my wife buy her all these red Nikes and all that, she [my wife] didn't know.
INT: She [your wife] just thought red was her favorite color?
R017: Yeah.
INT: Then her mama said, why do you want all this red?
R017: Right, That's when it all surfaced.

In other cases signs of membership were more disturbing. The aunt (#R020) of a Blood reported that she saw the signs of membership but never really put them together until she and her husband were approached by someone in the neighborhood who told them "to get a black suit and a black dress [for a funeral], I knew then that it was real." Most relatives were aware that the gang member in their family had been arrested. In a few cases, the arrests were for minor kinds of trouble, such as shoplifting, skipping school, and driving without a license. For most though, arrests were for more serious offenses. One subject (#R001) reported that his brother had been arrested for "[selling] drugs, taking cars, assault, mainly those." Two cousins (#R012, #R014) knew that the gang member in their family had been arrested for murder. And in listing her nephew's many arrests, an aunt (#R020) added the qualifier "so far," anticipating future troubles with the law.

What Was Their Response?

Once a relative learned of membership, active gang members were faced with efforts to intervene in their lives. Sixty percent of gang members whose family knew about their membership reported that their family had taken steps to encourage them to quit the gang. An equal percentage said that their family did not support their gang membership. In only one case did a gang member report that family members (other than those who belonged to a gang themselves) liked the fact that they were in the gang. This was true even for those few members who reported that they provided their family with money from drug sales and other crimes. But there was some support for membership, thirty-two gang members told us that someone in their family supported their decision to become a gang member. In twenty-five of these cases, it was a brother or cousin who themselves were gang members. The role of girlfriends and boyfriends in this process is interesting. Though not relatives, such persons are close to gang members, spend considerable amounts of time with them, and influence their behavior. Sixty percent of those with a girl or boyfriend reported that this person urged them to quit the gang, a percentage similar to that reported for relatives. Gang members told us that their parents were most active in family efforts persuade them to quit the gang. Thirty-six percent of the active gang members whose family tried to get them to quit their gang said their mother was the person most active in such efforts; 20 percent indicated it was their father. Brothers (14 percent), and sisters (10 percent) were next most likely, with aunts, uncles, and grandparents representing the remainder of those family members who attempted to get them to quit the gang. These data paint a picture in which gang membership continues despite the disapproval of individuals significant to gang members, their family, boyfriend, or girlfriend, highlighting the diminished role of primary relationships in establishing patterns of social control.

Having established that most gang members faced opposition to their status from relatives, we next examine the ways in which the family supported gang membership. In most cases the family did not provide support. These sentiments are captured in the comments of "G-Loc," (male #027, fifteen-year-old Gangster Disciple) who said, "Nobody [supports me] but my boys," and other gang members who acknowledged no support from family members, only fellow gang members. Only rarely did subjects say that members of their family supported their gang membership. Such support was of a generalized nature, primarily found in the actions of brothers who could be counted on when they were needed to respond to trouble (#012) or for parties (#083) or simply not to criticize the member for belonging to the gang (#049). Other forms of support were more direct.

INT: How is it that he [your cousin] is supportive?
MALE #071, "B Daddy," seventeen-year-old Inglewood Family Gangster: He encourage me and front me.
INT: Does he front you with product [cocaine] or money?
071: Both.

In another case, "Larry" (male #033, eighteen-year-old Thundercat) reported that his grandparents helped him when he got locked up.

When I get locked up for possession or something I call them and they down there. I been in like 35 times and all 35 times I done got out on bond. Before I got papers, my bond was like $5,000. I said to my grandmother, "Can you pay $5,000?" She said sure and I got out.

We now examine the steps family members took to discourage gang membership. There was considerable diversity in these efforts. However, most things done by family members are typical of the struggles of families to control the behavior of their younger members, including talking to them, putting them out of the house, threatening violence, and, in some cases, resorting to outside help. In most instances, these steps were as successful as efforts to curb the behavior of adolescents in general – not very.

Most parents chose first to talk to their children about their misbehavior. The members of our samples (active gang members and relatives) were no different in this regard. By a margin of over three to one, attempting to deal with gang membership by talking about it outnumbered any other response.

He [my uncle] be talking about it but I don't pay no attention. (Male #025, "Tony," seventeen-year-old 107 Hoover Gangster Crip)

We [my father and I] sat down and we talked about it. He told me what it was all about. For about two weeks I wasn't hanging with them. It's hard. (Male #034, "Lil Gene Mack," eighteen-year-old 19th Street Rolling 60's Crip)

INT: What did they do when they found out that you were in a gang?
MALE #035, "Edward," twenty-year-old Hoover Gangster Crip: Told me to watch myself, don't do anything stupid.

INT: Who said that?

035: My mom. Asked me to get out of it.

INT: Why didn't you do it?

035: I don't know. I wasn't the kind of person that listens.

INT: What did she do, what did she say, just don't do it?

035: She cried, begged.

INT: It didn't do any good?

035: No.

INT: What did your parents do when they found out that you were in a gang?

MALE #015, "Karry," fifteen-year-old Crenshaw Gangster Blood: Tried to talk to me. Tried to get me out of it. They say what you going to get out of a gang? You ain't doing nothing but killing yourself. If the KKK came you going to want to fight with them. You always see black fighting black.

INT: Were they angry?

015: Yeah, confused, frustrated. She tried to take me to little meetings at the YMCA and stuff about gangs. They tried to read books, they asked for help. Took me to juvenile.

Other families responded to gang membership by attempting to keep their child in the house, away from other gang members. This strategy is also common among parents searching for methods to protect their children from getting involved with the "wrong crowd."

Yeah. Like if I had something to do that day they would say it's family day. You have to work here. I was falling for it for awhile then it just hit me. Then it was talk, what you are doing is wrong. I said well, ok, I let you live your life why don't you let me live mine. They said because what you are doing is not living your life, you living the fast life. That's exactly how they put it. You living the fast life. I said, ok, I see it as I'm living the fast life as selling drugs, but being in a gang I don't see that as being the fast life. (Male #020, "Lil Thug," sixteen-year-old Gangster Disciple)

In another case, relatives attempted to take the gang member away from the neighborhood for extended periods of time.

MALE #014, "D. C.," sixteen-year-old Disciple: My relatives, especially my mother, she tried to keep me away from the crowd I was running with.

INT: What did they try to do?

014: When they first heard about it they was kind of shocked. They had to try to deal with it. It was something that I wanted to do back then. They would say, "What do you want to do?" I would say please get out of my face or I will be forced to do some bodily harm. They don't understand. They will learn one day.

One gang member (#033) disclosed that his mother kicked him out of the house when she learned of his membership. Other parents simply stopped trying to get their children to leave the gang. "Lance" (male #012), a twenty-year-old member of the West Side Mob, explained:

My parents just say fuck it. He ain't going to listen. He going to do what he want to do.

In some cases, efforts to diminish gang activity created the potential for violence. "NA" (male #036) said that his uncles intervened at the behest of his mother to try and talk some sense in him. "NA" reported that he was ready to fight them because of their criticism of his friends. And in another instance, "Mike-Mike" (#001) disclosed that his uncles had threatened to kill his little brother if he didn't get out of the gang. When earthly efforts failed to produce results, many parents resorted to calling on heavenly sources of help. Four gang members told us that their family had all but given up on them and were left to "pray" for them to leave the gang.

Family member responses about steps taken to end gang membership were more measured and well thought out. In most instances, family members revealed that they had taken several steps to deal with the gang affiliation of their relative. Typically, these steps progressed from confrontation to talking to seeking outside help, such as meeting with doctors, counselors, psychologists, the church, the juvenile court, and probation. None of the relatives reported that these efforts were successful.

INT: What steps have you and your husband taken to try to deal with things in the house?

#R016, forty-four-year-old mother: From the police to the juvenile courts. Juvenile said they will not remove her from our premises unless they had accurate proof that she was a threat. She can go so far, they gave us a sheet of paper to write down everything that she supposed to do and how she going about obeying our rules. I've gone to the point of trying to put her in a Catholic organization. I've had her in [the hospital] where I work in the psych ward.

I have been to counseling with that boy ever since 13. We would go to Washington University. He had psychiatrists and all that but he just had a mind of his own. He was gonna do what he wanted and be what he wanted to be. He just couldn't stop it. (#R019, thirty-three-year-old mother)

Some relatives reported that active gang members were unwilling to attend counseling sessions or were uncooperative or disruptive when they went. This further frustrated their efforts to deal with gang membership. One parent (#R017) lamented the difficulty in having his child put away, even after considerable violence at his house as a consequence of his daughter's membership in the gang.

The responses of our sample of family members may not be typical of those of most parents who discover they have a relative in a gang.[1] However, these individuals share in common with other parents the frustrations of dealing with gang membership and the dilemmas it presents for family relationships. Their children were generally uncooperative with the services they arranged, and often found the services to be unresponsive to their needs. Despite seeking high-quality expert help, not one relative reported success in reducing the level of gang involvement or withdrawing their family member from the gang. This should not be surprising. Intervention generally occurred two years or more after the initiation of gang membership. Intervening at that point is less likely to be successful in reducing gang involvement than would earlier intervention. In addition, these relatives were fighting an uphill battle against the lure of friends and the street. These two forces are powerful "pulls" in the lives of all adolescents, especially those whose economic and neighborhood circumstances resemble those of our subjects. Finally, these efforts may have been unsuccessful because the family had lost its moral sway over the gang member. Faced with the decision whether to accede to the authority of the streets or that of their family, gang members chose the street. And in large part, their families had limited social capital to use in pulling them back from the influence of the street. Unable to dissuade the gang member from further involvement, families were left to deal with the consequences of having a relative in a gang, our next topic.

How Has Membership Affected the Family?

There was considerable cleavage between the responses of gang members and relatives over how gang membership had affected the family. Every relative was able to recount, often in considerable detail, the negative consequences of having a gang member in the family. The majority of gang members (60 percent), on the other hand, felt that their membership had not affected the family. However, both groups agreed that the consequences of membership for the family have been negative. Each focused their responses to these questions on threat, the threat posed to the house and other family members by having a gang member present. The vast majority of gang members who responded that their membership had not affected the family gave a single word answer when asked what affect their membership had had on the family: "None." In other cases, they offered rationalized accounts of their gang or the threat it posed for their family.

> INT: Has your family been affected by you being in a gang?
>
> MALE #039, "Kaons BIC," seventeen-year-old Compton Gangster: The kind of gang we in really ain't no trouble cause it just like deep friendship. They come over and we go to my house and cut the grass or something. All of us together that way. We can go to my mother's house and cut the grass, clean up the house or something just like they do everybody else house.

This account was provided by a gang member who participated in gang shootings and had five arrests for serious crimes. And one suspects that seventeen-year-old gang members are no easier to convince to mow the lawn than are other seventeen-year olds. Lisa (female #011, fifteen-year-old Compton Gangster) indicated that her family had not been affected by her membership and that she was still treated the same. However, recognizing the threat having gang members present at the house may pose, she also said that other gang members didn't come over because, "I don't want anybody in my family to get hurt."

A substantial minority of our subjects were not ambivalent about the effects of gang membership. Consistent with the role of threat in the lives of gang members, the predominant effect on the family was violence or threatened violence. Because gang members pose threats to other gangs, they become targets for retaliatory violence that is often indiscriminate about its victims. This illustrates the double-edged nature of threat for gang members: they create violence and are targets of violence, targets that may involve other members of their family.

Six gang members told us that their family residence had been shot as a consequence of their gang membership. This further illustrates the threat that gang members pose, not only to themselves and other gang members, but also to those with whom they share a residence or hang out with. In one case, such a threat was present, though shooting was avoided. "John Doe" (male #031, sixteen-year-old Thundercat) graphically described his family's brush with rival gang violence.

> INT: Has your family been affected by your membership?
>
> 031: We had to move out of Laclede Town cause my brother killed one and shot two others. There was a leak down through one of the girls

that stay down there. My mother and me came home one night and we was going in the house and my brother had hid all the guns in the vacant house next door cause the police was watching our house. We came in about three in the morning and when we came in there was people from another gang waiting.

INT: Next door or in your house?

031: In the vacant house on the opposite side of us.

INT: Did they shoot?

031: Well they really didn't get a chance. They was coming down the steps and I was trying to get my mother out of the house. When we went to the front door there was one right there. She got on the phone and called the police.

Other families weren't so fortunate.

INT: What kind of stuff did you bring on her [your mother]?

MALE #015, "Karry," fifteen-year-old Crenshaw Gangster Blood: People knocking on the door late at night, shooting on the street, selling rocks out of the house, police breaking down the door.

INT: They shot your parents' house up?

MALE #065, "BK Kill," nineteen-year-old North County Crip: Yeah, it was three or four in the morning. They shot up the back. I was outside. Dudes creepin in my backyard. There was about six or seven.

One gang member initially indicated that his family hadn't been affected in any way by his gang membership, that there was "no static brought to the house" except for one time.

I was out with my sister and her friend was sitting up on the front porch and I went around the corner to get my hair cut, and the dudes thought I was on the corner with some of my friends, and they shot down at my house. My sister and her friend went in the house. She came over to the house where I was and she was crying. (Male #084, "Rolo," sixteen-year-old Rolling 60 Crip)

Gang members whose house had not been shot at posed a threat to the safety of their families, many of whom sought to distance themselves from the gang member. An Inglewood Family Gangster Blood (#060) indicated that his grandmother did not like him to visit, because she lived in Crip territory and his presence at her house would make it a target for violence. The threat for gang involvement need not include violence and often extends to the inclusion of younger siblings.

INT: How has your family been affected by your membership in the gang?

MALE #021, "40 Ounce," sixteen-year-old Hoover Gangster Crip: My mother, she scared. She try to keep me off the streets and stuff. She say I'm going to become a statistic and stuff.

INT: How about your younger brothers and sisters, do they [your family] try to keep them away from you?

021: My sister, she be going around the house and throwing up signs. I said you better cut that stuff out.

INT: You trying to discourage her?

021: Yeah, she might go around the wrong person doing that stuff. My little sister is five and she be running around, C-World. My little bother is running around saying, "hey dude, what's up with that color, you got the wrong color on."

INT: How old is he?

021: Six.

Such threats produced fear on the part of parents for the safety of the gang member as well as other members of the family. A number of families moved in response to the threat of violence or placed their child in the voluntary school desegregation program for the specific purpose of removing them from their neighborhood and friends.

While gang members create threats, they also provide protection from a number of threats for family members. "Joe L." (white male #099) an eighteen-year-old Insane Gangster Disciple, reported that his sister viewed his gang membership as an advantage.

Cause if anybody gives her any problems up at that pussy ass high school, I'll be down there in a minute.

And, "Billy" (male #017), a twenty-one-year-old North Side Crip:

I have gang members watch out for my mother and them. I come around every once in a while just to check up on everything.

Other gang members reported that their relatives weren't scared because neighbors knew that gang members would look out for them. And one gang member (#033) furnished a gun for his grandparents safety.

While the threat of violence provided more tangible negative results, it also produced symbolic effects. Two gang members reported that their families had lost respect because of legal troubles stemming from their gang membership. "Kenneth" (male #030, nineteen-year-old Thundercat) reported, "I'm the only one in my family that ever been in jail. That was bad." Another "Money Love" (male #101), a twenty-year-old Insane Gangster Disciple, said that his mother "got on my case for smoking [shooting] that person I did. She got on my case hard about that." These were exceptions, though, as most gang members could identify more tangible means in which their family had been affected by their gang membership.

This domain, effect on the family, produced similar responses from family members. Four family members reported that their house had been shot as a result of their relative being a gang member.

> Yeah, like one night we were sleeping, it was about 3:00 in the morning and I heard a loud gun shot and I was so shocked I couldn't move and then I ran out my room and our house was all shot up like bullet shots and him [her brother] running in the house. They [rival gang members] was in our backyard looking for his friend. (#R004, sixteen-year-old sister)

A father also reported that the house had been shot.

> And then both of my front room windows were shot, bullet holes went through them. (#R024)

It is not surprising relatives felt under stress as a consequence of having a family member in the gang. One father (#R022) described it [gang membership] as "trauma," while a mother (#R021) indicated that it "caused a lot of tension." Another relative (brother, #R006) described gang membership as a "weakness" that caused him to lose respect for his brother. In two cases, relatives reported that the gang member had been kicked out of the house.

An exception to the strongly negative appraisals of the effect of gang membership was reported by a cousin (#R002) who indicated that he was safer and could walk wherever he wanted because his relative was in a gang. This individual provided a tangible example of such protection.

> They back me up. Like when my car got stolen. It took me about ten minutes to find it. All I did was get on the phone, call a couple of my boys from the city, told them, got up a posse, and looked for my car. I had Crips chasing the car everywhere. We caught the guys with my car, they was in trouble. They was getting an initiation to the hospital. (#R002, twenty-year-old cousin)

A sister reported that having a brother in a gang provided advantages to her, like money.

> If I need some money they'll give it to me. But I would rather not get it because I know where it's coming from. (#R005, seventeen-year-old sister)

Family members and gang members agreed that gang membership produced negative consequences for the family. In most instances, both groups pointed to the increased threat of violence, including completed acts as well as potential threats. This underscores the centrality of violence to the gang. Gang membership puts families under the threat of violence. Even in neighborhoods where the risk for violence is high, gang members and their relatives knew that gang membership increased the chances for violence directed against members of their family. Despite this, we received no reports that such experiences caused gang members to leave their gang or consider moving away from the house to reduce their families' exposure to violence. These examples highlight the strength of the bonds between the gang and its members. Such a finding suggests that the gang may be more important to gang members than their family. In the next section, we examine this issue.

Is the Gang Like a Family?

Adolescence is a period of asserting independence from the family and other institutions. At the same time, peers exert greater impact on the choice of behaviors. Where peers organize and can provide resources, their ability to influence behavior is even greater. Against the backdrop of weakened family structure and declining family influence, gangs are a potent force in shaping behavior in underclass neighborhoods. The loss of social capital in underclass families makes adolescents especially vulnerable to challenges to the legitimacy of family authority. Some have argued (Brown 1978; Abrahams 1970) that gangs are attractive because they provide male role models absent for many urban youths. And because life in the gang is a life under threat of violence, solidarity among gang members increases while their isolation from the family (among other institutions) increases. These circumstances suggest an ascendant role for the gang and declining importance of the family. In this section, we examine the relative importance of the gang and the family.

One way to measure the relative importance of the gang and the family is to ask gang members to choose between them. Answers to this question provided one of the most lopsided responses received throughout the study. Eight-nine percent (seventy-three out of eighty-two) of those responding to this question reported that if forced to choose, they would choose their family over their gang. The two most frequent reasons offered for this choice were: (1) the family cares for me more ($N = 37$, half of those who chose their family over their gang) and (2) blood relations are more important than gang affiliations ($N = 31$, 43 percent of that group). The reliance on affective reasons for choosing the family is evidence that, despite its problems and despite the many attractive features of gang affiliation, the family retains its role (if not function) in the lives of gang members. But the limited social capital created by families has been diminished by the growth of the underclass and the concomitant loss of jobs, social opportunities, and traditional means of social control. Indeed, the traditional patterns and practices of familial social control appear to have all but vanished for many of these youths and their parents.

Despite allegiance to their family, the gang provided things like money and support for involvement in crime for most gang members that the family did not. This can be linked to a number of factors. First, gang members spent considerably more time with gang members than with their family. While this pattern (spending more time with peers than parents) is generally typical of adolescents, it appears to be especially pronounced among the gang members we interviewed. Only 16 percent of our sample reported that they spent less time with their gang than their family, and 42 percent told us that they spent "much more time" with gang members than with family. Second, the gang provided understanding about things that the family did not, a response offered by 80 percent of gang members. This is not atypical of most adolescents, who, at a time of increased independence from parental control, feel they are better understood by peers than parents. In describing ways that the gang provided support that resembled a family, just over a quarter (26 percent) identified material support, such as money or clothes. Only twelve percent reported that the gang approved of criminal activities when their family did not. The largest category (59%), though, could not identify a way that the gang provided support that was like a family.

Forcing gang members to choose between their family and their gang caused them to contrast the relative importance of competing values in their lives. For most gang members, the gang was a place to find protection, companionship, and understanding. Their family, however, represented something deeper, a commitment that most saw as transcending life in the gang. Among those who chose their family over the gang, the modal responses emphasized the family role in birth, nurturing, and caring.

INT: If you had to choose between your gang and your family, which would you choose?

MALE #004, "Anthony," seventeen-year-old Thundercat: My family.

INT: How come?

004: Because the gang is there don't mean nothing. The gang might fall out from under me. If you fall out with your mother, she still there.

INT: If you had to choose between the gang and your family, which would you choose?
MALE #005, Antonio," nineteen-year-old 6th street Hoover Crip: My family.
INT: Why?
005: Because the gang ain't doing nothing for me. My family, I get along well with my family. My mother, my father love me, my little brothers look up to me. I know that. The gang, they don't love me.

INT: If you had to choose between your family and the gang, which one would you take?
MALE #084, "Rolo," fifteen-year-old Rolling 60's Crip: My family, really.
INT: Why?
084: Because I grew up with them, that's my kin blood.

Others emphasized the permanence of the family.

Because if it really came down to it I know they [my family] love me. Your family always do. Your friends won't always be there but your family will. (Male #045, "C-Loc," seventeen-year-old Rolling 60's Crip)

Cause they [my family] always gonna be around. I don't think the gang will always be around. (Male #058, "Roach," fifteen-year-old Blood)

My family, cause I'm always going to stand by them, always. I'm always going to stand by them because I know they are going to be there at the last minute. The gang ain't going to do that. (Female #006, "Yolanda," nineteen-year-old 23rd Street Hoover Crip)

Others mentioned that the family was "blood," representing a stronger tie than to the gang. And violence was ever present, often playing a role in defining the choice between the family and the gang.

Most people on the street don't care too much about you. They'll help you fight and stuff, but that's your own blood, your family. (Male #027, "G-Loc," fifteen-year-old Gangster Disciple)

Cause my family would be there. They was with me longer than these guys. But they give the same support. If you don't have anyone in your corner there isn't any choice but to go to the gang. If I had a choice to go to either one, I would go to my family. There is some guys that would not go with their family, they would go to the gang. That's a short life. It's a short life anyway, but that's even shorter. (Male #034, "Lil Gene Mack," eighteen-year-old 19th Street Rolling 60's Crip)

The gang don't do shit for me, get me killed. I love my family. (Male #065, "BK Kill," nineteen-year-old North County Crip)

"D. C." (Male #014) a, sixteen-year-old Disciple, made his case for the family quite emphatically, saying, "Because you gonna need your mother before you need your gang. If it came to that I would tell the gang to kiss my ass."

A handful of members, however, did choose the gang over their family. By and large, members of this group were older, had been gang members longer, and were living away from home. Given this, it is not surprising that they chose the gang over their family; in a sense, their actions had already affirmed that choice, a point made by "Darryl," at twenty-nine the oldest member of our sample. Two of these individuals indicated their decision was based on being too deeply involved in the gang to make any other choice. The younger of the two, highlighted the lack of supervision found in the gang.

> INT: How come you would have chosen the gang [over the family]?
> MALE #015, "Karry," fifteen-year-old Crenshaw Gangster Blood: Because I could do anything I wanted to do. I didn't have no rules. I could leave at 8:00 in the morning and not come back until 2:00 the next night. Didn't have nobody to answer to. I could wake up in the morning and eat potato chips and go to sleep that night eating pizza and french fries.

And another member emphasized the permanence of gang membership.

> INT: If you had to choose between your gang and your [family], which would you choose?
> MALE #033, "Larry," eighteen-year-old Thundercat: Well, I'm in it to win it. They just have to take me out. I'm in and I can't get out, there's no way out. I can't say that I'm out of the gang.

The contrast between the responses of active gang members and relatives is quite informative. Almost all family members responded that their gang-involved relatives would choose the gang over the family. In part, this must reflect the fact that these gang members had been involved in their gang over quite a period of time and that their relatives had exhausted several means of attempting to encourage them to leave the gang. Family members identified two major reasons why their relatives chose the gang over their family: money and support for involvement in illegal activities. Family members saw these as two arenas where they were incapable of competing with gangs and identified them as the primary reason why the gang would take precedence over the family.

INT: If he had to choose between staying with the gang or staying with the family, which would he choose?

#R012, seventeen-year-old cousin: He would choose to stay with the gang because he prefers to stay over in my mother's neighborhood. He says it's boring where we live, he bored stiff.

Probably the gang because they've got his mind, they've got it. (#R020, thirty-year-old aunt)

One mother (#R021) reported that she asked her son if he was a member, and that he had told her forthrightly that he would choose the gang over the family

and that nothing will make him give up his gang. That once you're in it, you're in it for life. I said what about your family? Aren't you a member of the family for life? That's what he tells me, that he would choose his gang.

But she detected some ambivalence in his answer.

But I really don't believe him because he still lives at home and gets very upset when you ask him if he would like to leave.

Other parents displayed ambivalence in answering this question. The role of violence emerged in discussions of their children's preference for gang or family. The knowledge of violence on the part of parents underscores, yet again, the central role that violence has come to play in the lives of gang members.

INT: If he had to choose between the gang and your family, do you have any idea how he would choose now?

#R022, forty-six-year-old father: I don't know. Of course, I'm viewing it from a very prejudicial and very biased view because he's my son. I would assume that if a gang member told him that he had to shoot me or the gang leader that he would shoot the gang leader.

We interviewed (separately) both parents of a sixteen-year-old female gang member. Their daughter was pregnant by a second gang member, having given birth to the child of a different gang member the year before. The parents experienced violence at the house – from their daughter as well as other gang members – and exhausted the social service agencies available to them. They differed in their appraisal of their child's ultimate loyalty.

> INT: If she had to choose between the family and the gang, what would she choose, do you think?
> #R016, forty-four-year-old mother: Actually I believe she would choose her family. I just don't believe that she would go against her family when it come to it. I think she still cares for us, she just got mixed up with the wrong crowd.

Her father expressed a somewhat different viewpoint.

> Yeah, it's a funny thing, these kids and these gangs. They more loyal to the gangs than they are to they family. I had always heard that to get out of the gangs you have to kill a family member or something like that. We want to do what we can for her. We don't hate the kid. But all at the same time, I basically don't really want her around me as long as she's affiliated with this. It's caused problems in the family, her gang affiliation and the babies and stuff like that. It's caused problems between me and my wife. (#R017, forty-four-year-old)

The most hopeful response was offered by the thirty-seven-year-old mother of a Blood. Unfortunately, her responses were only hypothetical, because her son had been killed three weeks prior to our interview. This mother expressed with certainty the view that her son would chose her over the gang because she was the person who really cared about him. This was a sentiment also offered by many of the active gang members of the reasons why they chose their family.

> I'm the only one that's gonna help him and I'm his mother. Only person that care about him is me. (#R023)

Relatives and active gang members identified many aspects of the gang that were like a family. However, few were willing to concede that the gang was a family. Family attributes linked to the gang included such things as caring for members, understanding them when they were in trouble, or providing for them financially. However, the depth of the commitment of the gang to an individual was recognized as being somewhat more shallow than that of the family. The permanence, nurturing, and "blood" relations of family members were seen as stronger and, in the long run, more compelling features of the family. However, it is clear from this section that gangs had attained a significant foothold in the lives of their members. What remains to be seen is the perceptions of gang members and family members about their future, the concluding topic of this chapter.

Future Relationships with Family

We now consider perceptions of the future held by gang members and the families of gang members. We first examine gang members' views of their future relations with family, specifically their parents. We then review family members' perceptions of their gang-involved relatives future. We conclude by examining another aspect in the future of gang members' lives, whether they want their children to join a gang. These three perspective allow us to assess perceptions of the future and speculate on the role such perceptions may play in the behavior of gang members.

The majority of gang members, 74 percent of those who answered the question, responded that they expected relations with their family to be good in the future. The next largest category chose the response "don't know" in assessing how they would get along with their family in the future. Only 8 percent thought such relationships would be bad, and 3 percent said they currently had no relationship with their family. These responses do not fully represent the breadth of views on this issue. Many of those who expected to have good relations with their family in the future described the nature of such relations in rather ambiguous or poorly articulated terms.

> They, they probably gonna be wonderin why didn't I get out [of the gang]. (Male #001, "Mike-Mike," twenty-year-old Thundercat)

> I really don't know for real. (Male #093, "Lil P," sixteen-year-old Crenshaw Mob Gangster Blood)

> I hope it be alright. I don't want nothing to change because of what I am. If it comes to that I'll have to deal with it. (Male #084, "Rolo," sixteen-year-old Rolling 60's Crip)

> It be cool as long as they don't find out I'm in the gang. The only person that really know I'm in a gang and have shot somebody is my mother. (Male #101, "Money Love," twenty-year-old Insane Gangster Disciple)

Gang members who said that relationships would be good generally based that assessment on the status of their current relationship. One of them, however, offered an ominous tone to his description.

INT: What do you think your future relationship will be with your family?
MALE #036, "NA," eighteen-year-old Compton Gangster BIC: It will straighten out because I'll be dead or straightened up. I will still have my friends because I won't leave them in hard times. Not like, "fuck you, I ain't going to hang with you no more."

INT: How do you think your relations will be with your family in the future?
MALE #039, "Kaons BIC," nineteen-year-old Compton Gangster BIC: Yeah, I always have got along with them. My family is real close. Whenever I get in trouble, like if I get locked up for a shooting, I get my mother, she be by my side.

Some who foresaw good relations with their family offered idealized versions of that relationship. These individuals recognized the troubles that their arrests, involvement in violence, and impact on the neighborhood created for their family. Despite this, many felt that these travails could be brushed aside in the future. "Antonio" (male #005, nineteen-year-old 6th Street Hoover Crip) told us that things were bad between him and his mother but that in the future when she asked him to come over and help her with chores at the house, he would do so. He expected that this would bring them closer.

Those gang members who described future relations with their family as bad or deteriorating chose rather strong language.

INT: What do you think your future relationship will be with your family?
MALE #041, "C. K.," twenty-year-old Blood: Even more fucked up. I swore when I make it, they can kiss my ass. I'll leave all my money to charity.

INT: What do you think your future relationship will be with your family?
MALE #013, "Darryl," twenty-nine-year-old Blood: None.
INT: You wrote them off and they wrote you off?
#013: Yeah.

The generally positive views of future family relations by gang members were not matched by relatives' assessments of gang members' futures. A number of family members indicated that they did not expect much of a future for their gang-involved relative. Indeed, the modal category was represented by those relatives who expressed the view that the gang member in their family would either be dead or in jail. When asked about her brother's future in five years, one sister (#R005) said, "I hope they still alive." Another (#R010, thirty-six-year-old mother) told us, "One year from now, the way things are looking, if he's still alive, probably in some legal trouble."

> INT: What do you think her future looks like?
> #R017, forty-four-year-old father: Within a year she could be dead. I'm a realist. I've found out over the last few years that I'm a realist and I say what I believe. I believe that at the rate she's going, in the next two years she could very well be dead.

Others used such terms as "shitty" (#R011), "down the drain" (#R023), "on shaky ground" (#R006), or said that they expected to be burying their relative in the future (#R019).

But not all family members expressed the same level of fatalism about their relatives' future. A cousin (#R007) expected a "very bright" future for his cousin, indicating that he expected him to be "a straight-up businessman or straight-up student of college." Another cousin expected his gang-involved relative to be successful at any number of careers.

> He wanna be an auto mechanic or aerospace, like airplanes and stuff like that or probably an attorney, a criminal prosecuting attorney. He won't defend nobody. (#R011)

Only one relative, a teenaged cousin, anticipated their relative leaving the gang within the year.

Our final measure of future commitment to the gang comes from one of the last questions we asked during interviews. We simply asked whether gang members would want their son to join a gang when they grew up.[2] This question drew the most lopsided response of any question we asked. Ninety-eight percent of those answering the question (eighty-seven out of eighty-nine) indicated that they did not want their son to join a gang. The responses to this question were often very strongly worded, and many gang members focused on the violence associated with gang membership as a reason to keep their son out of the gang.

> Cause to me a gang is dangerous, I can tell you that. I wouldn't want my son to go the same way I'm going. (Male #020, "Lil Thug," sixteen-year-old Gangster Disciple)

> Cause you don't go nowhere in no gang. You either end up dead or in the penitentiary. (Male #030, "Kenneth," nineteen-year-old Thundercat)

> I don't want my kid out there doing dope, selling dope. I want him to make something out of himself. I don't want my kid to come in no gang man. There's only one way out. You are going to die or go to jail. That's it.

Die or go to jail, that's the only way to go. (Male #012, "Lance," twenty-year-old West Side Mob member)

Others pointed to the "hardness" of gang life and wanted their son to avoid the difficulties associated with it.

I wouldn't want him to be in all kinds of trouble like I do. (Male #024, "Hamilton," sixteen-year-old Hoover Gangster Crip)

At the end you don't get nothing out of no gang. Someday all the girls going to be gone, all your Blood partners going to be gone, all the money going to be gone. Then what are you going to have? The world changes so fast. It's dumb to be grown and be gang banging, it's stupid. (Male #015, "Karry," fifteen-year-old Crenshaw Gangster Blood)

Another gang member (#028) told us he would tell his son there "wasn't no such thing as a gang."

The two individuals who said they wanted their son to become a gang member reflected the role of threat in the lives of many urban residents. Both said they wished their son to join a gang because of the protection it would provide.

WHITE MALE #100, "J Bone," nineteen-year-old Insane Gangster Disciple: Because I want to raise him up to be hard and take care of himself.
INT: Do you think you could teach him that without being a member of a gang?
100: Yeah, but he'll be even harder if he's in a gang.

These responses suggest several conclusions about the future life of gang members. Most gang members expect good future relationships with their family. But family members generally did not foresee a positive future for their relatives. Finally, gang members were almost unanimous in their desire to keep their sons (and presumably their daughters) out of gangs. Taken together, these observations indicate a more hopeful outlook on the part of gang members than relatives. Perhaps these differences can be linked to age. Most members of our active gang sample were younger than the relatives we interviewed, and their outlook may reflect the perceived invincibility and strength of youth.

This chapter has examined a number of stages in the relationship between gang members and their families. In a sense, we have moved from the earliest link between gangs and their families – parental membership – to the final link – whether their gang membership would be passed on to the next generation. Throughout, the responses of gang members and their relatives offered several potential avenues for intervention. Despite the challenges faced by their families and the problems created by gang membership and activities, most subjects identified areas where intervention into gang life and gang activity could have a positive impact. In the concluding chapter, we examine these and other potential areas of intervention to reduce gang involvement.

"There's Only Two Ways to Leave the Gang, Die or Move": Responding to Gangs

THIS BOOK HAS examined the group process and values of the gang within the context of social institutions. We have done this by focusing on the gang member's perspective, highlighting the insights of gang members regarding the nature of gang membership, the structure of the gang, gang activities, and relationships with social institutions. In this, the concluding chapter, we discuss strategies for responding to gangs. We begin by reviewing what gang members told us about how to stop people from joining gangs and how to eliminate their gang. Then we examine the responses of a number of ex-gang members to questions about leaving their gang. Following this, the salient cultural and institutional features of the gang are highlighted for their role in responding to gangs. Next we discuss a number of gang intervention strategies in light of our findings. We conclude by considering the role of social capital in gang formation and membership.

In order to respond to gangs, both their proximate and fundamental causes must be addressed. Examining both levels can only be accomplished through purposive institutional and community actions that ultimately have an effect on the values that are the underpinning of the gang. The proximate, or immediate, causes of gangs include the threats gangs generate, their values that reinforce violence, and the lack of legitimate activities in the neighborhoods where most gang members live. The fundamental causes that must be addressed include racism, unemployment, the lack of jobs, and the demise of the family in urban America. The increasing concentration of these problems in a common location makes this task all the more complicated. Neither set of causes will be remedied easily. Because of its part in generating gang membership and promoting violence, the role of threat must figure prominently in policies targeted at gangs.

Institutional approaches to dealing with gangs must be guided by a variety of principles. Huff (1991) pointed out that gangs are typically viewed as independent variables, causes of problems. When gangs are viewed in this way, efforts to deal with them typically have a more proximate focus and are targeted toward law enforcement interventions. Steps to reduce the problems gangs present for society must recognize that gangs are also dependent variables; that is, gangs are a consequence of a variety of factors that have a foundation in fundamental causes. Such factors call for comprehensive, integrated approaches to dealing with youth problems. Youth gangs are comprised of individuals who have needs for a wide variety of services. Another question is whether to address gangs or their criminal, disruptive behavior. It is possible to focus on the cultural, social, or imitative aspects of gangs and disregard their criminal behavior. Our recommendation is to respond to the crimes of gang members, especially their violence, not to the group nature of the affiliations these individuals maintain. Most importantly, policies should not encourage activities that provide the gang with resources or control over activities that would strengthen the organizational structure of the gang. When the gang structure is integrated into the response to gangs, negative consequences are likely to result. A final principle that must guide gang policy and programs is the need to experiment and evaluate. Because we don't know what works, and because the nature of gangs is highly variable across time, neighborhoods, and cities, local innovations in gang response should be encouraged and supported. Each innovation, though, must be evaluated so that the knowledge base regarding successful interventions can be expanded in meaningful ways.

Leaving the Gang

Just as defining a gang and establishing criteria for membership are problematic, determining when and whether membership has ended also is difficult. Does it mean, for example, the termination of relationships with gang members? Or alternatively, does leaving the gang mean the cessation of illegal activities associated with the gang, such as selling drugs or participating in gang fights? For example, an individual may claim to be a gang member but refrain from committing crimes or hanging out with gang members for an extended period of time. On the other hand, individuals may claim that they are no longer affiliated with the gang but continue to hang out with or commit crimes with gang members. Because many friendships predate gang membership, terminating such relationships is not always easy or straightforward and may not occur even when gang membership has ended. The comments of an ex-gang member we interviewed in the course of our study illustrates these the complexity of this issue.[1]

> INT: Have you told them? Did you tell the guys in the gang, "I'm done, I'm finished."
>
> EX001: Yeah.
>
> INT: What did they say?
>
> EX001: They say, why you wanna leave? I told them I'm tired man, everybody getting killed.
>
> INT: What did they say when you told them that?
>
> EX001: Say all right, brother, you gonna leave us.
>
> INT: Do you still hang around with them?
>
> EX001: Some of them.

Further complicating the retirement issue are the perceptions of rival gang members and institutions such as the police or schools. Despite claims to have left the gang, past antagonisms between the "former" gang member and rival gang members may persist. Such antagonisms may get played out on the street and have the effect of drawing the "former" member back into the gang or lead the ex-member to depend on the gang for protection. In particular, when rival gangs seek to retaliate for past violence, they are unlikely to consider that a gang member claims to have left his or her gang. Hence, the threat that compels individuals to join the gang often persists well beyond the time they have decided to leave their gang. In this case, the behavior transcends one's status as a gang member. Social institutions may be no more likely (or willing) to forget prior gang affiliations. Police and school officials may not be aware of the decision of individuals to leave the gang or may not take such claims seriously, and records may not be purged of prior gang status. In such cases, the institution continues to treat the individual as a gang member. When representatives of official agencies (e.g., police, school) identify an individual as a gang member, they are sending a powerful signal to rival gang members as well as to people in the community about the gang involvement of that person. Such a symbol may have consequences for how that individual is treated.

More importantly, the threat that initially propelled individuals toward their gang remains. Thus the very mechanism responsible for decisions to join the gang continues to dominate the lives of those who have decided to leave it. These factors complicate the process of leaving the gang as well as our ability to know who has left the gang.

> INT: I'm not trying to hassle you about this but I can't quite decide if you're still in a gang or not.
>
> EX003: To put it down in writing, I would say yeah instead of I don't know or in between, I'll just say yeah [I have left the gang].
>
> INT: But you don't fight with them any more?
>
> EX003: No.
>
> INT: And you don't hang with them very much anymore it doesn't sound like.
>
> EX003: If one of my boys came up shot or killed I would try to find out who did that. I believe who kill, deserve to die.

These comments from an ex-gang member illustrate the often tenuous nature of gang membership and the difficulty of distinguishing between active and ex-gang member status. Perhaps it is the acknowledgement of this complication that led many of our gang members to express the view that "there are only two ways to leave the gang, move or be killed."

Responding to Gangs

A central premise of this book is that the gang member's perspective is crucial to understanding the gang values and the group processes that characterize life in the gang. Consistent with this approach, we asked gang members: (1) how they would propose to stop individuals from joining a gang and (2) how to get rid of their gang. We then asked the active gang members about the reasons given by people who had left their gang, as well as the steps taken by ex-gang members to leave their gang.

Stopping Individuals from Joining Gangs. During the course of interviews, many gang members expressed the belief that it is impossible to leave the gang. A number of subjects told us that the only way to exit the gang was to be killed. Such beliefs have their foundation in the role of threats of violence for maintaining gang solidarity and membership in the face of threatened formal and informal sanctions. Despite such statements, the majority of active gang members (63 percent) told us they knew at least one person who had left their own gang. Interestingly, fewer than half of these individuals (45 percent) could tell us why the person left. However, among those who could do so, 60 percent indicated that the ex-gang member had just "grown out of the gang." That is, the contingencies of adult life such as a job, family responsibilities, or age led the individual to leave their gang.

The observations of gang members about the best way to stop individuals from joining gangs can be grouped into four main categories: (1) talk to individuals about the hazards of life in the gang, (2) provide stricter punishments or discipline for those considering joining the gang, (3) provide activities such as jobs, sports or community centers, and (4) no steps can be taken to prevent individuals from joining gangs.

The majority of gang members told us that the best way to stop individuals from joining gangs was to talk to them about the risks of membership. Most of these recommendations took the form of "informational" interventions, providing prospective gang members with information about what life in the gang is "really" like.

INT: What would be the best way to stop kids from joining gangs?
MALE #065, "BK Kill," nineteen-year-old North County Crip: I would talk to a group of kids and tell them about it. You can talk to kids if you been a member.

Well I was thinking that you get a lot of gang members together, go around to the public school, take a look. Tell them [the students at the school] about being in a gang. Let them see the gang thing, tell them about the shooting. (Male #014, "D. C.," sixteen-year-old Disciple)

These comments reflect the centrality of violence in the life of the gang. Those who recommended violence as a means to prevent individuals from joining the gang emphasized the ever present threat of violence and seemed to believe that simply being aware of the risks would deter most young people from deciding to join a gang.

Let them know how it is, what's the consequences. You can be alive one minute then bam. Somebody might see you in your colors and shoot you. (Male #038, "G.O.D.," nineteen-year-old Compton Gangster)

Let them know how hard it is, let them know people do die. Like a lot of brothers over here are getting killed over what somebody said or what somebody else said and they get killed over this shit. (Male #088, "T-Loc," twenty-one-year-old Grape Street Crip)

Despite expressing these beliefs, some gang members recognized that simply talking to prospective members about the hazards of joining the gang wouldn't be enough to discourage them from joining.

> MALE #022, "8 Ball," fifteen-year-old 107 Hoover Gangster Crip: You have to talk to them so you have to catch them at an early age and show them. Bring in some guys that got shot up in a gang, "Look what happened to me, a broken jaw or broken bones and stuff." You got to talk to them. There was a movie called *Scared Straight* and I looked at that and that kind of changed my mind about everything.
>
> INT: But you are still in the gang.
>
> 022: Yeah because I didn't trip off that because I was young then. I keep telling myself that I'm going to stop, that's what I be saying. I'm going to try to stop, but that's hard to do. You got your reputation.

The second largest category of responses about how to keep people from joining gangs included those pointing to the need to provide more effective sanctions for gang members. A number of these gang members identified a key role for parents to play in both watching and disciplining their children.

> INT: What would be the best way to stop kids from joining gangs?
>
> MALE #031, "John Doe," sixteen-year-old Thundercat: Parents will have to come down a little harder. Keep a close eye on them, don't let them hang out. When you tell them don't go out and they sneak out you have to show them then that you really meant no sneaking out.

> They mommies and fathers don't let them live off the street and be there to watch them. Don't ever let them leave their eyesight. When they go to school, come up to school and check them out there. Just check up on them. Talk to them about drugs and all that kind of stuff. You got to know what they gonna run into ahead of time before it do happen. (Male #068, "CK," sixteen-year-old 104 Piru Blood)

In some cases, the recommended interventions took on a more ominous tone, and violence was seen as the most effective deterrent to gang membership. One gang member offered that the best way prevent young people from joining gangs was to "slap them upside the head" (Female #046, "Lady Tee," sixteen-year-old 74 Hoover Crip). Others were equally explicit.

> Say for instance there's a party going on and your mother tell you, you can't go but your partner say he want you to go. That's peer pressure. They gonna go with what they boys say over what your parents say. Grab

them motherfuckers by the throat, but still give them room to breathe. (Male #092, "Derone," twenty-one-year-old Rolling 60's Crip)

The third recommendation for combatting the decisions of young people to join gangs focused on the need for more activities, specifically sports and jobs. Such distractions as "football" (#005), "pool tables" (#029), and neighborhood activities were offered in this context. One gang member explained:

Have a lot of public activities like ball games. Like our section has a little basketball team and baseball team. Have stuff like that. Have little rallies, stuff like that, little parties. (Male #037, "Big Money," twenty-two-year-old Compton Gangster)

However, these activities are widely practiced by gang members and would be unlikely to deter gang membership on the part of others. Using the gang as a means of prevention or intervention has been tried and found to produce negative outcomes time and again (Klein 1971; Short and Strodtbeck 1974; Spergel 1994). Other people in this category recognized the significance of jobs in preventing individuals from joining gangs. Despite the fact that many of the members of our sample and many prospective gang members were below the legal age of employment, jobs remained a popular prevention recommendation.

INT: What would you say is the best way to stop kids from joining gangs?
MALE #015, "Karry," fifteen-year-old Crenshaw Gangster Blood: They need jobs, man. Kids don't have a job. When they get out on the street what are the black kids going to do in a black neighborhood? They can't get no jobs, they see people around them with all these cars. They don't want to sell dope, man. If they could get a job they would have their little clothes; do it the honest way, man, and legal.

A final small group of active gang members reported that either they didn't know how to prevent individuals from joining a gang or that it was impossible. One subject (#016) said that he "hadn't thought about it," while another (#042) stopped in midsentence and admitted "I don't know." Others in this category said that "there ain't no best way, a person can only decide for his self" (#039). Finally, "Bullet" (male #060), a twenty-year-old Ingelwood Family Gangster Blood, told us:

You really can't keep them from joining. If they want to be in one, they gonna be in one.

Getting Rid of Gangs. When we shifted the focus from preventing individuals from joining gangs to eliminating or getting rid of gangs themselves, the answers we received from gang members became more pointed. We expected to find recommendations targeted at the basic causes of gangs such as racism, unemployment, and education as well as more immediate solutions such as detached workers, recreation centers, and job training. Instead, the modal response was that violence would be the most effective means of eliminating gangs. Twenty-five of the ninety-nine members of our sample told us that the only way to get rid of their gang would be to use violence, a response confirmed by gang members in their conversations with the field ethnographer. This finding under-scores the central role violence plays in understanding the gang members' perspective. Violence is so integral a part of gang culture that gang members' recommendations about ending gangs include elements of violence. For many gang members, life in the gang has become coter-minous with violence; for one, even the offer of jobs was not viewed as sufficient to undermine the gang.

> INT: What would be the best way to get rid of the Thundercats?
> MALE #033, "Larry," eighteen-year-old Thundercat: Smoke us all.
> INT: Kill you all?
> 033: Yeah.
> INT: We couldn't give you guys jobs?
> 033: No, just smoke us.

Others recommended using extreme levels of violence to get rid of their gang.

> INT: What would it take to get rid of your gang?
> ESC#035, "Edward," twenty-year-old Hoover Gangster Crip: Whole lot of machine guns. Kill us all. We just going to multiply anyway cause the Pee Wees gonna take over.

> INT: What would be the best way to get rid of the 60's?
> MALE #042, "Leroy," seventeen-year-old Rolling 60's Crip: Kill us all at once. Put them in one place and blow them up.

The second largest response category, which included twenty-four members, told us that there was no way to get rid of their gang, that it simply had become too strong.

The Perspectives of Ex-Members. In the course of our fieldwork with active gang members, we encountered a number of ex-gang members.

Early in the project we decided to interview these individuals as well, hoping to learn from their experiences as former gang members. In all, we interviewed twenty-four such individuals: their average age was nineteen, two years older than that for our sample of active members; twenty-two of them were black males, two were black females. Half of these individuals had left their gang in the preceding twelve months. We put two specific questions to the ex-members that bear on the issues examined in this chapter. Specifically, we were interested in knowing why they left the gang and the process by which they left their gang. We now turn our attention to these two issues.

There are a number of possible reasons for individuals to leave their gang. Maturational reform, family obligations, getting a job, and moving to a new town are all reasons that may bear on such a decision. However, none of the individuals we interviewed offered these as the reason why they left their gang. One consistent response characterized the answers of this group; they left their gang as a consequence of experiencing violence, either directly or indirectly. All twenty-one of the individuals who answered this question told us, flat out, that their experience with violence had been the primary motivation for leaving the gang. In seven cases the violence was experienced directly: three of these individuals had been shot, one had been stabbed, and three others had been beaten badly by members of a rival gang. Fourteen others reported that a friend in their subgroup within the gang had been killed. Few other topics we discussed with gang members elicited such consistent responses.

INT: Why did you decide to leave the gang?
EX001: Cause everybody was getting killed and shot for no reason. I said one day it's gonna be one of us. I just quit.

Well after I got shot, I got shot in my leg. You know how your life just flash? It like did that so I stopped selling dope, got a job, stayed in school, just stopped hanging around cause one day I know some other gang member catch me and probably kill me. (EX003)

INT: Why did you leave?
EX008: At first it was fun and then it just got kind of stupid cause too many people was getting killed and stuff.

These responses underscore what has become a central theme of this book: gang members put themselves at considerable risk by joining their gang and engaging in gang activities. It is a cruel irony that many gang members became part of their gang for protection against the violence of

rival groups in nearby neighborhoods, only to find that the gang ampli-
fied the violence they already were exposed to. In each case where the
decision to leave the gang was motivated by violence, ex-gang members
identified the source of the violence as external to the gang. Violence
that is internal to the gang, especially during group functions such as an
initiation, serves to intensify the bonds among members. A similar case
occurs with respect to "mythic" violence; the retelling or embellishment
of stories of violence committed against or threatened by rival gangs.
However, when violence by external gangs is real and is experienced by
the individual gang member or a close friend, the impact appears to be
far different. Rather than increasing gang solidarity, this type of violence
appears to have the effect of splintering off individual gang members.
We cannot specify with precision the mechanism by which this works, nor
can we isolate other factors that may affect such decisions. However, the
period immediately following violent confrontations with rival gangs appears to be one with potential for intervening in the lives of gang members. When some intervention occurs immediately following exposure to
violence, before the gang can cast it in a light favorable to the gang and
be used by the gang to increase solidarity, individuals appear most likely
to leave their gang. We have argued that violence or its threat is crucial to
understanding gangs: why they form, how they keep their members, and
why they spread. It also appears that violence, especially when experienced directly or by someone they are close to, can have the reciprocal
effect of loosening the ties to the gang.

The responses of ex-gang members also provide insight into the process of leaving the gang. The sample of active members uniformly held
that leaving the gang could be accomplished only with great sacrifice.
The most consistent responses to this question emphasized that in order
to leave, an individual must be "beaten out" (a process similar to being
"beaten in" to the gang) or must shoot a close relative, usually a parent.
In general, the ex-gang members we interviewed scoffed at these notions, particularly the obligation to shoot a parent as a condition of
leaving the gang. In fact, the disjuncture between the experiences of ex-
gang members and the beliefs expressed by active gang members could
hardly be greater. Thirteen of the nineteen ex-gang members who answered this question told us that they "just quit" their gang, four indicated that they moved to another state where they were not known as
gang members, and two told us they had been "beaten out" of their gang.

The responses of ex-gang members who said that they "just quit" are
instructive. They underscore a point made earlier about the strength of

ties between the individual and the gang – such ties are weak and the authority of the gang is generally effective only when the individual's preferences for action are consistent with those of the gang.

> I just quit. I stopped hanging out with them. There was about three of us that quit, we just stopped hanging out with them and everything. (EX001)

> INT: How did you get out?
> EX007: You just stop claiming.
> INT: That's all?
> EX007: See, that's stupid shit. Them young people. They fickle minded, they don't know shit. I ain't got to kill shit [to get out of the gang].

> It ain't really like that. Some of them [active gang members] be funning saying they got to kill they mother but some of the stuff is true. How I really got out of it, I just got me a little job, stopped hanging with them. (EX011)

For some, the threat of violence remained but never materialized, suggesting that its primary purpose was to deter individuals from leaving the gang without actually being carried out.

> INT: How did you leave?
> EX016: I just stopped socializing with them. I was threatened to get killed after I left, but it didn't really faze me. I didn't leave, I just faded away from it.

The responses of those who had moved as a means of leaving their gang reflect the role of threat in maintaining gang ties. One individual who had moved from California to St. Louis to get out of his gang, indicated that you can never really leave your gang, only move away from it. A primary motivation for him to do so was his belief that the only way to leave the gang was to kill his mother, and as he said, "I can't get out of it. I ain't killing my mother."[2] Two individuals had been beaten out of their gang. One of them (EX004) suggested that the beating administered at the time of leaving the gang was more severe than at the time of entry. This makes sense for purposes of organizational survival, as any group must make it easier to get in than to get out in order to maintain its viability.

These findings underscore two of the main contentions made throughout this book about group process and gang values. First, the gang is a loosely organized confederation of individuals bound together through common actions, experiences, symbols, and allegiances. It is the symbolic and affiliational aspects of the gang that bind members together, not its formal or institutional authority. Subgroups within the gang make a stronger claim for the allegiance of members than does the larger gang. Second, the threat of violence, real or mythic, is ever present for gang members. Such threats play a substantial role in the decisions of gang members; indeed, we have argued that threat is a primary motivation for the decision to join the gang and often compels members to leave their gang.

It is against this backdrop that decisions to leave the gang must be viewed. Because the ability of the gang to extract allegiance from members is circumscribed, the gang can do little to prevent members from leaving. In this context, reports from ex-gang members that they simply quit or left their gang make sense. As an organizational entity, the gang was unable to offer strong enough incentives – or threats – to keep members or to prevent individuals from leaving. For these reasons, most who wanted to do so simply stopped associating with individuals in their gang. And because life in the gang is, at its heart, life under threat of violence, it should not be surprising that many individuals who left their gang report that the decision to do so was motivated by violence. The ability of violence to motivate individuals to join the gang and strengthen the bonds of membership has an upper limit. When that limit is exceeded, its ability to maintain ties to the gang evaporates and individuals leave the gang.

The Culture of the Gang

Understanding the gang means understanding gang culture. Elements of gang culture include the symbols, values, and traditions of the gang. Most critical among these are the values of the gang. Gang values play a critical role in the lives of gang members because the institutional structure of the gang is so weak. Unable to rely on formal rules, sanctions, or lines of authority to guide the behavior of members, values play the primary role in identifying goals and shaping behavior. The values of the gang and the values of gang life provide important symbolic links between gang members. This is evident in the language and dress of most gang members, reflecting a preference for specific colors, phrases, and apparel. These outward symbols transmit a gang identity recognized by fellow gang members, rivals, and most nongang adolescents. More important than the identity portrayed by these external symbols are the shared meanings they convey. By identifying himself (or herself) as a member of a specific gang set, a member communicates a set of behavioral expectations about how they will act and incurs a set of expectations about how others will respond.

The gang formed as a response to the threat of violence, a threat that compelled neighborhood men and women to join the gang and expose themselves to violent victimization even as they engaged in violence themselves. For this reason, violence is an important part – in our minds and in the words of our respondents the most important part – of gang culture. The centrality of violence to gang culture is evident from the first stages of gang membership (initiation) through drive-by shootings, shootouts with rival gangs, and (for many gang members) the decision to leave the gang. Life in the gang is a life under threat of violence coupled with the willingness to use violence. The proximity of firearms and other munitions reinforces the central character of violence to gang members.

Violence is not the only element of gang culture. Other values play an important role in gang life, values that reflect the age and socioeconomic status of gang members. Loyalty to other members – especially those within one's subgroup – is a key gang value. Thus "being down," or supportive of other members, is a crucial element of gang culture. But such loyalty has its limits. Autonomy from external authority – police, school, adults, family – is also a value accorded considerable weight in gang life. Autonomy from such institutions is likely a necessary prerequisite for joining the gang. The gang members in our sample had few prospects in the job market and were generally free of its constraints. The age, race, and socioeconomic status of gang members are critical to the formation and maintenance of such values. Their exclusion from mainstream society as a consequence of their location in the racial, socioeconomic, and age stratification patterns of American society clearly contribute to the ability of the gang to call on the loyalty of members as traditional social institutions are unable to do so. In large part, the lack of relationships, social capital, inhibits the integration of gang members into the American mainstream.

But gang culture cannot be understood apart from the larger culture within which it exists. Messner and Rosenfeld (1994) demonstrated that the values of the American Dream permeate all levels of American society, a point underscored by Nightingale (1993), who argues that the greatest dilemma for underclass youth is their strong commitment to the tenets of the American Dream. Thus gang members have a desire for cars, clothes, and success goals common throughout our society. These values create expectations for economic success and material possessions that their position in and relationship to institutional structures (the job market, schools, family, the legal system) cannot fulfill or control. It is within this broader cultural context that the gang exists.

However, there are two more proximate cultural sources that strongly influence the gang. The first is popular culture, a substantial influence on the values and behavior of youth gangs. Through popular culture – movies, music videos, audio recordings, television, and other media – gang symbols are transmitted and made readily available to a broad audience. Popular culture, not gang migration, is primarily responsible for the names, symbols, and affectations of St. Louis gangs that mimic their Los Angeles counterparts. Thus, St. Louis gang names take on prefixes like Inglewood, Crenshaw, and Compton,[3] the colors red and blue, and a distinctive preference for certain weapons. This form of transmission is not purposive; rather it is imitative in a manner similar to the transmission of most fads among adolescents.

The second proximate cultural source affecting gang values is street-life culture. Indeed, it is the influence of the culture of the street that distinguishes the urban gang members we interviewed and observed from their suburban or rural counterparts who may be similarly exposed to gang images in popular culture. The values of the street emphasize toughness and "getting over," obtaining a share of available rewards as expeditiously as possible and "by any means necessary." Viewed in this context, selling drugs is ideally suited to life on the street; it has a large market, requires few skills, little capital investment, and offers a quick payoff. The short-term focus of life on the street is also evident in the lack of long-term trust people are willing to place in institutions or others, inhibiting the development of relationships – social capital – that may be instrumental in preventing gang membership. Thus the view exists that people can't be trusted and, when possible, should be exploited. These values play an important role in creating a culture of the gang, contribute to its level of social organization, and insure its continued isolation from mainstream institutions.

Gangs as Institutions

We contend that gang values are the primary determinants of life in the gang. And while it is our argument that the institutional structure of the gang is weak, it is not without effect. Indeed, the gang is more than its culture alone; the roles, rules, and authority structure within the gang do have consequences for the actions of its members. Here we discuss leadership, role differentiation, and rules.

Leadership within the gang has a situational character that is dynamic. Few gangs have a single identifiable individual who occupies the role as leader for an extended period of time. In part, this reflects the fact that subgroups within the gang more effectively set priorities and direct behavior than does the gang as a whole. Because allegiance to a small number of friends is stronger than that to the gang, the ability of a leader to control gang members is diminished. But the values of the street also prohibit a leader from effectively assuming control of gang members. The autonomy from authority so highly prized on the street inhibits effective leadership.

Role differentiation is also underdeveloped within the gang. This reflects three realities about gangs in St. Louis. First, St. Louis is an emerging gang city, where gangs reappeared in the mid-1980s.[4] As a consequence, specific roles may not have had ample time to develop and become institutionalized. A second reason for the lack of specific gang roles can be traced to the fluid nature of gang membership. As has been documented earlier, gang members come and go, whether as a consequence of being shot, or imprisoned, or as part of a conscious decision to reduce involvement in gang activities. The fluidity in membership prevents the stability required for roles to develop and become more formal. Finally, life on the street requires generalists, people capable of fulfilling a variety of roles equally well rather than specializing in a single role. Street life mitigates against hierarchical structures that spawn role differentiation. Given the transitory nature of gang membership, role specialization within the gang makes little sense.

A third institutional characteristic of the gang is its ability to demand loyalty from its members. This encompasses proscriptive constraints on members' behavior as well as prescriptive commands to fulfill certain expectations. Here too, the ability of the gang to channel the behavior of its membership is weak. Rules of a general nature abound; the specific requirements for enforcing such rules are harder to find. Guidelines about drug use, the appropriate dress, and the proper locus of loyalty were identified in some form by most of our subjects; justifications for violating these guidelines were equally plentiful. Thus, in the final analysis, gangs are relatively ineffective as institutions in the promulgation and enforcement of these rules.

The weak institutional structure of local gangs has many sources. As noted above, in emerging gang cities, the institutional structure may develop later, following and depending upon the creation of gang culture. But the role of street life culture in mediating the institutional authority of the gang cannot be ignored. Most of the gang members we interviewed grew up enmeshed in the culture of the street and were committed to its ideals well before they embraced those of the gang. It is also the case that institutional structures comprised of and originating with adolescents (recall that the average age of our sample was seventeen) are seldom highly differentiated, formal-rational organizations. Finally, the members of our sample have not been effectively integrated into or controlled by institutions. Institutions such as the family, school, job market, and legal system have had little effect on the lives of these individuals. Thus gang members have little expertise – certainly far less than their same-aged peers – in developing and maintaining relationships with closure, trustworthiness, and mutual dependence. There is little reason to expect the gang to emerge as a strong institution or to be successful in controlling the lives of people who have already demonstrated resiliency to the power of institutions.

Policy

The Spergel and Curry Models. The typology of intervention strategies developed by Spergel and Curry (1993) provides a means of organizing our discussion of policy interventions targeted at gangs. Their respondents represented 254 law enforcement and social service agencies nationwide and were part of the National Youth Gang Suppression and Intervention Program. Spergel and Curry (1993) found five strategies used by respondents: (1) suppression, (2) social intervention, (3) social opportunities, (4) community mobilization, and (5) organizational change. Suppression included typical law enforcement and criminal justice interventions such as arrest, imprisonment and surveillance. It was the primary strategy for 44 percent of respondents. Social intervention, employing crisis intervention, treatment for youths and their families, and social service referrals was used in 32 percent of the cities. Eleven percent of the cities indicated that they had employed organizational change as their primary intervention strategy. Organizational change included the development of special task forces to respond to gang problems. Community mobilization was described by 9 percent of cities as their dominant reaction. This strategy emphasized interagency cooperation and typically led to better coordination of existing services. The provision of social opportunities, reported by 5 percent of cities, stressed education and job-related interventions. Ironically, in cities with chronic gang problems, the strategies employed least often (social opportunities and community mobilization) were reported as most effective.

Suppression was the primary strategy used in most cities. Typically, it depends on the use of law enforcement resources such as arrest, prosecution, and imprisonment that responded to the proximate causes of gangs. Clearly such an intervention must be part of an overall set of responses that respond to the illegal actions of gang members. But by itself, suppression is unlikely to have much effect on the growth of gangs or the crimes committed by their members. But suppression efforts should not be organized in ways that accord increased status or recognition to gangs. As Klein (1995) has observed, the formation of specialized police gang squads is unlikely to make the police more successful in apprehending gang members following the commission of a crime. And such units may have the latent negative consequence of "creating" a larger gang problem through overidentification and conferring increased status to gang members among their peers. Law enforcement strategies are likely to exacerbate the racial disproportionality of arrest. An additional outcome of increased arrest, prosecution, and incarceration of gang members will be the growth of prison gangs. Gang members commit a large number of criminal and delinquent acts – many of them violent – that afford law enforcement the opportunity to intervene. However, cities that follow suppression policies exclusively will do little to address the long-term consequences of gangs.

Social intervention focuses on intervening in times of emergency and is particularly relevant as a response to threats of violence. The use of crisis intervention and the provision of social services to gang members and their families receives support from the findings of our study. These are largely proximate strategies, designed to address needs of a more immediate nature. As gang members are frequently victims of violence or witness a friend's victimization, crisis intervention services would appear to be especially promising. In the short term, those who have been shot or seen a friend be shot find the strength of their allegiance to the gang tested. Over the long term, such experiences solidify the ties among gang members. These observations call for a crisis intervention response immediately following a violent victimization. Ideally, such responses would be available at emergency rooms and could be mobilized by law enforcement or other community groups. The goals of such an intervention should include the separation of gang members (to forestall the development of gang interpretations of the violence as heroic, routine, or admirable) and provision of mentoring and other social services.

Social intervention has another component, especially as it involves families. Many of the gang members in our sample attempted to deceive their parents about their membership in the gang. This was especially true in the early stages of membership. This suggests a role for parents in attenuating the early stages of membership. Because the families of most gang members we interviewed faced a number of challenges, most had few resources to draw upon. The provision of support for these families must be a significant part of any response to gangs. And because most members of our sample had siblings or other relatives in a gang, family interventions hold broad promise.

Organizational change requires the mobilization of a broad consensus to address gang problems by the formation of task forces. It is targeted at the proximate causes of gangs and cannot solve gang problems in and of itself. It is most likely the case that organizational change will either lead to an awareness of the problems gangs create and mobilize efforts to address them, or lead to a new set of relations among agencies and groups who respond to such problems. To be successful, organizational change must have the support of the community and groups in those neighborhoods where gangs operate. Ideally, support from both local politicians and the private sector can be integrated into these approaches. This is typically a response that occurs early in the cycle of responding to gangs; chronic gang cities have seen a number of efforts to develop consensus around interventions.

Community mobilization attempts to better coordinate existing services to meet the needs of gang members. Unlike the three preceding strategies, community mobilization begins to address the fundamental causes of gangs and gang membership. It does so by coordinating and targeting services so that they more effectively meet the needs of gang members. Most cities have a wide range of services in place to respond to the institutional problems faced by gang members. However, it is rarely the case that such services are integrated or offered in ways that would prove effective in serving the needs of gang members. Recall that, by and large, active gang members in our sample had little experience or ability to interact with social institutions. While this often included their most immediate social institution, the family, it extended to others. In particular, schools, community agencies and groups, churches, public health efforts, and agencies of the criminal and juvenile justice system need better coordination among their myriad services. Referrals across agencies require careful case management; the end goal must be to enhance links between individuals and the social institutions to which they must relate.

Social opportunities approaches concentrate on expanding job prospects and educational placements for gang members. These efforts, more than any other, tackle the fundamental causes of gang formation and gang membership. Because social opportunities approaches address factors responsible for the creation of an urban underclass and the resultant dislocation of a large group of urban residents, they hold the greatest long-term prospects for success. Such efforts include the creation of jobs, job training, and residential placements that attempt to reshape values, peer commitments, and institutional participation. The fundamental premise of such approaches is that they will create new values among gang members by integrating them into legitimate social institutions. In this way, such interventions directly zero in on a strongly felt need among most adolescents, the need to affiliate with a set of peers in age-graded activities. And because the demands of such institutional affiliations are extensive, the opportunities to cause threats and feel the need to respond to threats is circumscribed.

But the task of creating and supporting such efforts is substantial, and failures are likely to be plentiful. Programs attempting to integrate individuals with little history of successful participation in institutional life will inevitably encounter resistance. Because of their integration into life on the street, the individuals likely to benefit most by such interventions will find the least to like about them. Few of the gang members we spoke with had successful job experiences. Indeed, most lacked even the most basic necessities required to hold a job – acceding to authority, punctuality, waiting for financial rewards, and starting out with menial tasks. And to paint an even bleaker picture, the costs of such interventions will be great. Intensive programs require equally high levels of commitment of human and financial capital. However, there are a variety of reasons why implementing such approaches makes sense. The costs – social and financial – of other approaches will be far greater in the long term. And current gang members represent powerful role models for young people growing up in their neighborhoods. Absent this level of intervention, we risk losing a generation of youth to the streets and the gangs that dominate them.

A fundamental problem, the lack of social capital among gang members, must guide any gang intervention. As Sampson and Laub (1993) note, the accumulation of social capital is often a necessary precondition to "turning points" in the life course, such as jobs, marriage, or desistance from crime. Thus this is an important first step that must precede or accompany intervention programs that emphasize social opportunities. Coleman (1988) identified three elements of social capital: (1) obligations and expectations, (2) the exchange of information between parties, and (3) norms accompanied by sanctions. Gang members clearly lack social capital, especially sets of relationships between themselves and those who may be in a position to influence their involvement in the gang. Indeed, gang membership is initiated in the presence of limited social capital, capital that diminishes over time as the gang member becomes increasingly involved in gang activities to the exclusion of other social roles and relationships. Social capital, especially as it is embodied in relationships with individuals from legitimate social institutions, is critical in reducing the influence of gangs. As Short (1990) observed, social capital provides links between gang members and the legitimate world that in turn enhance the development of human and financial capital. These links to the legitimate world – and the obligations it requires – compete with life in the gang, providing alternative paths for gang members enmeshed in life on the street. The social disapproval inherent in strong relationships with legitimate social institutions and adults is often lacking for individuals who have grown up under the influence of street-life culture, increasing the likelihood of gang involvement and inhibiting an exit from the gang. In short, absent social capital means there is no way for gang members to get from there (the gang) to here (life outside the gang). Enhancing the social capital of gang members, and others in their neighborhoods at risk for gang involvement, must be a task high on the agenda for gang intervention.

Conclusion

We have underscored the centrality of violence to life in the gang. From entrance to exit, violence is ever present in the form of threat – threat from rival gangs and the threat created by gang members themselves. Yet there is an ironic quality to threat, in that it compels individuals to join their gang, increases their level of activity and commitment to the gang, yet is cited by many as the reason why they left the gang. Threat causes us to look away from values as initial causes and look toward the objective circumstances of life under threat of violence, the need to affiliate with a gang for protection and the resulting isolation from social institutions. Values compound these problems for the poor minority urban residents we interviewed. However, values play a significant role in shaping the lives of gang members and their responses to gangs, social institutions, and everyday life. Enhancing the social capital of gang members provides a means to address both the cultural and institutional factors that make gang life compelling.

Notes

Chapter One

1. We have faithfully reproduced the words of gang members in quotes throughout the book. Where quotes were unclear, we have added words in brackets to clarify the meaning and added grammatical marks for the same purpose. For each quote, we use the gang member's ID number, gang name, the name of their gang, their age, and sex. White subjects are specifically identified by race. The interviewer is denoted by the initials, INT. See the Chart in Chapter 3, page for ID numbers and gang names.

Chapter Two

1. That is, in researching burglars or intravenous drug users, one seldom finds organized groups engaged in ongoing conflict with other burglars or IVDUs. Thus, moving the sample from one burglar to another or one drug user to another does not present the problem one faces in attempting to do the same with gangs. Because of the violent and sometimes lethal antagonisms that exist between gangs, it was generally not possible to move across a large number of networks of gangs. One exception was the case where brothers were members of rival gangs.
2. A number of subjects expressed concern that we might be part of a sting operation designed to draw gang members to a specific location and arrest them. Such concerns are not without foundation, as law enforcement officials often use stings, and offenders are wary of such tactics.
3. Verification of eligibility can be confirmed through other means as well. During several interviews, the subjects' "beeper" went off. They made a note of the number that appeared on the beeper, told us that it was a

"customer," and asked to use the phone to call them back. We declined to allow them to use the phone, as that would have been directly contributing to illegal activity, something we had decided explicitly not to do.

4. The concern about family members, especially parents, discovering the extent of gang involvement is an important finding. This receives a full discussion in Chapter 8.

5. A study such as this can be fraught with ethical dilemmas. Our commitment was to have no foreknowledge of a crime, and we told subjects not to give us any details of offenses they had planned. In addition, we told subjects not to provide specific details of violent crimes, such as dates, addresses, or victim identification.

6. The lone exception to this was our first two subjects who chose to drive themselves to the interview site in a brand new white Mustang 5.0 with red pin striping.

Chapter Three

1. In this table, we first list the project number, corresponding to the order in which subjects were interviewed. Following that we list the name that they gave us and the name of their gang. This entry is followed by the race, age, sex, and age at time of joining the gang. The final three columns report their participation in illegal activities, whether they sold drugs, committed other crimes, and the number of self-reported arrests.

2. A "posse" is an incursion into the neighborhood of a rival gang.

3. These forces produce a variety of responses. Noted paleontologist Stephen Jay Gould, commenting on the popularity of dinosaurs following the release of the movie Jurassic Park, observed, "You just need a little push to kick the positive feedback machine of human herding and copying behavior into its upward spiral (especially powerful in kids with disposable income" 1993, 51). A similar process – fueled by popular culture – has occurred among young people who emulate gang symbols, clothing, and behavior.

4. Subjects discussed their "wills," documents that existed among gang members or were of "mythic" character.

5. This subject and the field-worker maintained contact for several months after the interview. So thorough was this white gang member's integration into the street culture of his (predominantly black) gang, that the field-worker told us that if he closed his eyes and listened to him talk, he thought the subject was black.

Chapter Four

1. The level of imitation is substantial, adopting gang names, individual names, colors, and hand signs. While attending a national conference on

gangs in 1991, we showed a slide of the names of gangs from whom we had recruited gang members. A researcher from Los Angeles said (facetiously) that we could not have those names as they were taken from street names used by Los Angeles gangs.

2. Larry Hoover had a parole hearing in 1993 for release from prison in Illinois. His request for parole was denied (Kass 1993).

3. This is not particularly surprising given the young age of our subjects.

4. The code 3-11 refers to C, the third letter in the alphabet, and K, the eleventh letter in the alphabet.

5. Laclede Town was the replacement for Pruit-Igoe, the twin towers that were blown up by HUD in the 1960s. Pruit-Igoe was decried as a failed model for federally subsidized housing because its high-rise design was linked to high crime rates and the development of squalid conditions. Ironically, most of Laclede Town, a low-rise townhouse development located on a large expanse of land near downtown, was closed because of the failure to control crime.

Chapter Five

1. This subject, a twenty-nine-year-old Blood from Los Angeles, had come to St. Louis from California after the arrests of members of the Moorish Science Temple – a local mosque whose members had been convicted of federal drug charges – in order to get the drug market back in shape. He is not typical of our subjects – but he may be an "ideal" for many of them – a real L.A. Blood.

2. An assertion we cannot verify since, in order to ensure confidentiality we did not ask for date of birth or real names – necessary for record searches. Our suspicion is that almost all of our subjects have been taken into police custody – without necessarily being booked or charged at some point in time.

3. In our interviews this question was usually asked: "Were you alone or with the gang at the time of your last arrest?" We wanted to know whether the subject had committed the crime while alone or with the gang, but our subjects' responses can be interpreted as referring to either or both the crime and/or the arrest.

4. There were a total of 142 mentions by these eighty subjects, with the most popular being sport groups of some sort – 55 mentions of school sports, another 18 of community sports groups.

Chapter Six

1. This usually meant being able to buy more drugs for resale.

2. Six of our subjects were arrested most recently for drug possession and four for selling drugs.

3. We borrow this phrase from the title of Nancy Scheper Hughes' book about Brazilian favelas.
4. This is a rather old trophe. Aristophanes – parodying the opening paragraphs of Herodutus – wrote on the causes of the Peleponnesian War that "and thus for the sake of three whores the whole of Greece was set aflame."
5. To be honest, one subject admitted that he had accidentally shot himself.

Chapter Seven

1. Familial interactions and involvement also drops dramatically, as we discuss in Chapter 8.
2. These subjects mentioned 142 activities, the most popular were sports groups of some sort. Fifty-five subjects, for example, mentioned school sports and another eighteen subjects mentioned community sports groups.
3. This assumes that our subjects were telling the truth about their grades – there is not much reason to lie about grades in high school when shootings and fights were disclosed in the same interview. However, "doing well" may have meant "passing" or its equivalent to many of these students, only two of whom said they were getting mostly As and seven who said they were getting mostly Bs.
4. These subjects mentioned eleven different schools, including two county schools where the subjects who answered were attending as desegregation students. These answers reflect our subjects' perceptions of where their own particular clique attended school.
5. Twenty-one subjects said that their school did not know they were gang members, but these subjects may be deluding themselves on this point.
6. Although, as we have already noted, guards, teachers, and other staff may also be "customers."
7. Thirty subjects said that weapons were not used at school and thirty-one did not answer this question.
8. Impressing girls, of course, may have serious consequences that are parallel to and reinforce gang-related criminal behavior.
9. Nineteen subjects, after all, said they had never been arrested.
10. Our subjects often appear to be rather unclear about legal definitions and procedures – with respect to arrest, booking, charging, conviction, pretrial detention versus sentenced time. However, they do know something about dealing with the police. In order to ensure confidentiality and maintain trust we did not ask for date of birth from our subjects, an item that (along with their name) could be used to access their police records. Our suspicion, however, is that almost all of our subjects have been taken into police custody – without necessarily being booked or charged – at some point in time.

11. In our interviews this question was usually asked: "Were you alone or with the gang at the time of your last arrest?" We wanted to know whether the subject had committed the crime while alone or with the gang, but our subjects' responses can be interpreted as referring to either or both the crime and/or the arrest.
12. Unlawful use of a weapon and carrying a concealed weapon.
13. The other thirteen convictions included one for manslaughter, two for armed robbery, two for burglary, two for stolen property, two for drug sales, one for destruction of property, one for peace disturbance, and two convictions for other (unstated) charges.
14. Many of the leaders of the "Muslims" he mentions were arrested within six months of his interview on federal and state charges of, among other things, murder, criminal conspiracy, and drug distribution.

Chapter Eight

1. Their willingness to be interviewed is evidence of their commitment to finding solutions for gang involvement. It is not surprising that parents who seek outside help would also be willing to be interviewed for a project that attempted to understand gangs and formulate responses to gang problems.
2. We chose "son" over "daughter" because of the preponderance of male gang members in St. Louis, and more respondents had experience with male gang members.

Chapter Nine

1. In the course of our fieldwork, we interviewed twenty-four ex-gang members. To qualify as an ex-member, individuals had to admit prior gang membership and acknowledge that they had been out of their gang for a period of three months or more.
2. Despite hearing such stories dozens of times, we never confirmed an instance in which a gang member killed a parent. This suggests that such stories are apocryphal.
3. These are cities in the Los Angeles area with high levels of gang activity often depicted in movies or music videos.
4. See Spergel and Curry (1993) for an excellent discussion of the distinction between "emerging" and "chronic" gang cities.

References

Abrahams, Roger D. 1970. *Deep Down in the Jungle: Negro Narrative Folktales from the Streets of Philadelphia.* Chicago: Aldine.

Anderson, Elijah. 1994. "On the Streets." *Atlantic Monthly* May: 81–94.

Asbury, Herbert. 1928. *The Gangs of New York.* Garden City, NJ: Alfred Knopf.

Bessel, Richard. 1987. *Life in the Third Reich.* New York: Oxford University Press.

Biernacki, Patrick and Dan Waldorf. 1981. "Snowball Sampling: Problems and Techniques of Chain Referral Sampling." *Sociological Methods and Research,* Volume 10: 141–163.

Bookin-Weiner, Hedy, and Ruth Horowitz. 1983. "The End of the Gang: Fad or Fact." *Criminology,* Volume 21: 585–602.

Bowker, Lee and Malcolm Klein. 1983. "The Etiology of Female Juvenile Delinquency and Gang Membership: A Test of Psychological and Social Structural Explanations." *Adolescence,* Volume 18: 740–751.

Brown, Waln K. 1978. "Black Gangs as Family Extensions." *International Journal of Offender Therapy and Comparative Criminology,* Volume 22, Number 1: 39–48.

Burns, John. 1993. "Gangs in Sarajevo Worry Diplomats." *New York Times,* October 4, A3.

Bursik, Robert J. 1993. "Comments on *Islands in the Street.*" Presented to the 1993 Meetings of the American Sociological Association.

Bursik, Robert J. and Harold G. Grasmick. 1993. *Neighborhoods and Crime: The Dimensions of Effective Community Control.* New York: Lexington.

Campbell, Anne. 1984. *The Girls in the Gang.* New York: Basil Blackwell.

Cloward, Richard and Lloyd Ohlin. 1960. *Delinquency and Opportunity.* New York: Free Press.

Cohen, Albert K. 1955. *Delinquent Boys*. Glencoe: Free Press.

Coleman, James. 1988. "Social Capital in the Creation of Human Capital." *American Journal of Sociology*, Volume 94: S95–S120.

Community Development Agency. 1993. *Neighborhood Demographic Profiles*. City of St. Louis.

Curry, David, Richard Ball, and Robert J. Fox. 1994. "Gang Crime and Law Enforcement Record Keeping." *Research in Brief*. Washington, DC: National Institute of Justice.

Dacus, J. A. and J. W. Buel. 1878. *A Tour of St. Louis or The Inside Life of a Great City*. St. Louis: Western Publishing Company.

Decker, Scott H. and Kimberly Kempf. 1991. "Constructing Gangs: The Social Construction of Youth Activities." *Criminal Justice Policy Review*, Volume 5, Number 4: 271–291.

Dunlap, Eloise, Bruce Johnson, Harry Sanabria, Elbert Holliday, Vicki Lipsey, Maurice Barnett, William Hopkins, Ira Sobel, Doris Randolph, and Ko-Lin Chin. 1990. "Studying Crack Users and Their Criminal Careers: The Scientific and Artistic Aspects of Locating Hard-to-Reach Subjects and Interviewing Them about Sensitive Topics." *Contemporary Drug Problems*, Volume 17: 121–144.

Emerson, Robert. 1983. *Contemporary Field Research*. Boston: Little Brown.

Esbensen, Finn and David Huizinga. 1993. "Gangs, Drugs and Delinquency in a Survey of Urban Youth." *Criminology* Volume 31: 565–590.

Federal Bureau of Investigation. 1991. *Uniform Crime Reports, 1990*. Washington, DC: USGPO.

Gould, Stephen Jay. 1993. "Jurassic Parked." *New York Review of Books*, Volume XL, Number 14: 51–56.

Hacker, Andrew. 1992. *Two Nations: Black, White, Separate, Hostile, Unequal*. New York: Scribners.

Hagedorn, John. 1988. *People and Folks*. Chicago: Lake View Press.

Hagedorn, John. 1991. "Back in the Field Again: Gang Research in the Nineties." In C. Ronald Huff (ed.), *Gangs in America*, 240–259. Newbury Park, CA: Sage.

Hernon, Peter. 1990. "Gang Wars." *St. Louis Post-Dispatch*, September 21: A1.

Horowitz, Ruth. 1983. *Honor and the American Dream*. New Brunswick, NJ: Rutgers.

Huff, C. Ronald. 1991. "Denial, Overreaction and Misidentification: A Postscript on Public Policy." In C. Ronald Huff (ed.), *Gangs in America*, 310–317. Newbury Park, CA: Sage.

Jackson, Pamela Irving. 1991. "Crime, Youth Gangs, and Urban Transition: The Social Dislocations of Postindustrial Development." *Justice Quarterly*, Volume 8: 379–398.

Kass, John. 1993. "Hoover Case Is the Tip of Gangs' Political Iceberg." *Chicago Tribune*, August 15: C1.

Katz, Jack. 1988. *Seductions of Crime.* New York. Basic Books.

Klein, Malcolm. 1971. *Street Gangs and Street Workers.* Englewood Cliffs, NJ: Prentice Hall.

Klein, Malcolm. 1995. "Gang Cycles." In J. Q. Wilson and Joan Petersilia (eds.), *Crime,* 217–236. San Francisco: ICS Press.

Lerman, Nicholas. 1991. *The Promised Land: The Great Black Migration and How It Changed America.* New York: Vintage Press.

Loftin, Colin. 1984. "Assaultive Violence as a Contagious Process." *Bulletin of the New York Academy of Medicine.* Volume 62: 550–555.

Maxson, Cheryl and Malcolm Klein. 1985. "Differences between Gang and Nongang Homicides." *Criminology,* Volume 23: 209–222.

McCall, George. 1978. *Observing the Law.* New York: Free Press.

Messner, Steven F. and Richard Rosenfeld. 1994. *Crime and the American Dream.* Belmont, CA: Wadsworth Publishing Company.

Miller, Walter. 1958. "Lower Class Culture as a Generating Milieu of Gang Delinquency." *Journal of Social Issues,* Volume 14: 5–19.

Miller, Walter B. 1992. *Crime by Youth Gangs and Groups in the United States.* Washington, DC: U.S. Department of Justice, Office of Juvenile Justice and Delinquency Prevention.

Moore, Joan W. 1978. *Homeboys: Gangs, Drugs, and Prison in the Barrios of Los Angeles.* Philadelphia: Temple University Press.

Moore, Joan, W. 1991. *Going Down to the Barrio: Homeboys and Homegirls in Change.* Philadelphia: Temple University Press.

National Institute of Justice. 1993. *Street Gangs: Current Knowledge and Strategies.* Washington, DC.: U.S. Government Printing Office.

Nightingale, Carl Husemoller. 1993. *On the Edge: A History of Poor Black Children and Their American Dreams.* New York: Basic Books.

O'Connor, Mike. 1994. "A New U.S. Import in El Salvador: Street Gangs." *New York Times,* July 3: A3.

Padilla, Felix M. 1992. *The Gang as an America Enterprise.* New Brunswick, NJ: Rutgers University Press.

Quicker, John C. 1983. *Homegirls: Characterizing Chicana Gangs.* San Pedro, CA: International Universities Press.

Raab, Selwyn. 1994. "New Group of Russian Gangs Gains Foothold in Brooklyn." *New York Times,* August 23: A7.

Reuter, Peter, Robert MacCoun, and Patrick Murphy. 1990. *Money from Crime: A Study of the Economics of Drug Dealing.* Santa Monica, CA: Rand.

Riis, Jacob A. 1892 (1971). *The Children of the Poor.* New York: Arne Press.

Riis, Jacob A. 1902. *The Battle with the Slum.* Montclair, NJ: Patterson Smith.

Sampson, Robert and John Laub. 1993. *Crime in the Making.* Cambridge: Harvard University Press.

Sanchez-Jankowski, Martin. 1991. *Islands in the Street.* Berkeley, CA: University of California Press.

Sanders, William B. 1994. *Gangbangs and Drive-bys: Grounded Culture and Juvenile Gang Violence*. New York: Aldine.

Shakur, Sanyika. 1993. *Monster*. New York: Atlantic Monthly Press.

Sheldon, Henry D. 1898. "The Institutional Activities of American Children." *The American Journal of Psychology*, Volume 9, Number 4: 425–448.

Short, James F. 1974. "The Level of Explanation Problem in Criminology." In R. Meier (ed.), *Theoretical Methods in Criminology*, 51–72. Beverly Hills, CA: Sage.

Short, James F. 1990. "Gangs, Neighborhoods and Youth Crime." *Criminal Justice Research Bulletin*, Volume 5: 1–11.

Short, James F. Jr. and John Moland Jr. 1976. "Politics and Youth Gangs: A Follow-up Study." *Sociological Quarterly*, Volume 17, Number 2: 162–179.

Short, James F. Jr. and Fred L. Strodtbeck. 1974. *Group Process and Gang Delinquency*. Chicago: University of Chicago Press.

Skolnick, J., T. Correl, E. Navarro, and R. Robb. 1988. "The Social Structure of Street Drug Dealing." *BCS Forum*. Office of the Attorney General, State of California.

Spergel, Irving. 1966. *Street Gang Work: Theory and Practice*. Reading, MA: Addison-Wesley.

Spergel, Irving. 1994. *Gang Suppression and Intervention: Problem and Response*. Washington, DC: Office of Juvenile Justice and Delinquency Prevention.

Spergel, Irving and G. David Curry. 1993. "The National Youth Gang Survey: A Research and Development Process." In Arnold P. Goldstein and C. Ronald Huff (eds.) *Gang Intervention Handbook*, 359–400. Champaign, IL.: Research Press.

Stephens, Ronald D. 1993. "School-Based Interventions: Safety and Security." In C. Ronald Huff *Gangs in America*, 219–256. Newbury Park, CA: Sage.

Suttles, Gerald. 1972. *Social Construction of Communities*. Chicago: University of Chicago Press.

Taylor, Carl. 1993. *Female Gangs*. East Lansing, MI: Michigan State University Press.

Tedeschi, James T. and Richard B. Felson. 1994. *Violence, Aggression, and Coercive Actions*. Washington, DC: American Psychological Association.

Thrasher, Frederick. 1927. *The Gang*. Chicago: University of Chicago Press.

Thornberry, Terrence, Alan Lizotte, Marvin Krohn, Margaret Farnworth, and Sung Joon Jung. 1991. "Testing Interactional Theory: An Examination of Reciprocal Cause Relationships among Family, School and Delinquency." *Journal of Criminal Law and Criminology*, Volume 82: 3–35.

Vigil, James Diego. 1988. *Barrio Gangs*. Austin, TX: University of Texas Press.

Whyte, William F. 1943. *Street Corner Society*. Chicago: University of Chicago Press.

Wilson, William J. 1987. *The Truly Disadvantaged.* Chicago: University of Chicago Press.

Wright, Richard and Scott H. Decker. 1994. *Burglars on the Job.* Boston, MA: Northeastern University Press.

Wright, Richard, Scott H. Decker, Allison K. Redfern, and Dietrich L. Smith. 1992. "A Snowball's Chance in Hell: Doing Fieldwork with Active Residential Burglars." *Journal of Research in Crime and Delinquency.* Volume 29, Number 2: 148–161.

Yablonsky, Lewis. 1962 (1973). *The Violent Gang.* Baltimore: Penguin.

Zimring, Frank. 1981. "Kids, Groups and Crime: Some Implications of a Well-Known Secret." *Journal of Criminal Law and Criminology.* Volume 72: 867–885.

Index of Gang Members, Relatives, and Ex-Members

Anthony, Male #004, 92, 112, 125, 133, 161, 167, 191–2, 251–2

Anthony, Male #019, 113, 156, 196, 213, 239

Antonio, Male #005, 109, 126, 145, 154, 156, 162, 164, 190, 193, 196, 205, 207, 208, 222, 234, 252

B Daddy, Male #071, 98, 210, 242

Baby, Female #047, 68, 191, 208, 223

Big Money, Male #037, 62, 121, 131, 137, 147, 169, 180, 198, 203, 208, 220, 221, 239, 267

Billy, Male #017, 68, 74, 87, 88, 97, 127, 139, 147, 148, 158, 163, 179, 209, 248

BK Kill, Male #065, 80, 94, 115, 129–30, 155, 198, 216, 247, 253, 265

Blood, Male #072, 103, 114, 195, 199, 218

Blue Jay, Male #087, 71, 79, 146

Bobtimes, Male #063, 80, 111, 118, 122, 211, 217

Bullet, Male #060, 66, 83, 87, 120, 125, 132, 136, 193, 267

C-Loc, Male #045, 76, 88, 96, 135–6, 224, 226, 252

C-Note, Male #089, 101, 200, 207

Cedric, Male #054, 209

Chill, Male #026, 135, 141, 221, 223

Chris, Male #049, 208

Chris, Male #055, 122, 210

CK, Male #041, 150, 161, 163, 257

CK, Male #068, 70, 81, 86, 97–8, 102, 133, 135, 138, 133, 197, 199, 266

Coke Cane, Male #080, 121, 122

Corkey, Male #048, 79, 91, 116, 124, 238

Darryl, Male #013, 70–1, 82, 92, 110, 113, 117, 179, 194, 202, 211, 218, 257

David, Male #051, 96, 137, 169

DC, Male #014, 97, 98, 120, 135, 156, 199, 205, 232, 243–4, 253, 265

Derone, Male #092, 77, 80, 86, 122, 133, 145, 146, 147, 155, 162, 171, 176–7, 182, 198, 214, 233, 266–7

Dough Boy, Male #082, 99, 101, 115, 159, 194, 202, 227

Edward, Male #035, 142, 146, 188, 215–16, 238, 242–3, 268

8 Ball, Male #022, 66, 120, 192, 197, 201, 208, 266

Eric, Male #002, 56, 83, 87, 109, 123, 127, 150, 154, 174, 177, 182, 198–9, 200–1, 203, 215, 218–19, 232, 234
Ex-member #001, 263, 269
Ex-member #003, 264
Ex-member #007, 271
Ex-member #008, 269
Ex-member #011, 271
Ex-member #016, 271

40 Ounce, Male #021, 120, 131, 187, 195, 197, 202–3, 207, 208, 222, 237, 247–8

G-Loc, Male #027, 101, 131, 147, 213, 241, 252
G.O.D., Male #038, 74, 123, 126, 127, 131, 138, 149–50, 157, 199, 225, 265
Gunn, Male #086, 82, 175, 197

Hamilton, Male #024, 179, 194, 219, 259
Hell Bone, Male #079, 194

J. Bone, White Male #100, 79, 111, 259, 238
Jason C., Male #010, 66, 145, 146, 147, 158, 190, 210, 224, 225–6, 227, 232
Jerry, Male #003, 75, 104, 105, 109, 121, 124, 145, 165, 174, 184, 199, 205, 211, 215, 219
Jimmy, Male #053, 178, 180, 208
Joe, White Male #099, 70, 126, 138, 144, 148–9, 238, 248
John, Male #050, 77, 86, 89, 164, 178, 184, 204, 208, 227
John Doe, Male #016, 214
John Doe, Male #031, 77, 81, 88, 92, 110, 132, 146, 149, 159, 233, 246–7, 266
John Doe, Male #094, 94, 99, 121
Jonathan, Male #052, 141, 145, 175, 233

K-Red, Male #061, 163
Kaons BIC, Male #039, 119, 147, 179, 196, 204, 207, 209, 212, 213, 217, 222, 246, 257
Karry, Male #015, 56, 67, 78, 79, 99, 104, 113, 153, 158, 161, 165, 190, 206, 210, 213, 214, 218, 239, 243, 247, 253, 259, 267
Kenneth, Male #030, 85, 102, 134, 151, 159, 161, 195, 196, 212, 213, 219, 238, 258
Killa 4 Ren, Male #028, 136, 162, 165, 169, 182–3, 210
Knowledge, Male #040, 67, 110, 124, 131, 137–8, 153, 165, 177, 178, 197

Lady Tee, Female #046, 80, 84, 107–8, 127, 172, 214, 221, 225, 226, 266
Lance, Male #012, 41, 62, 75, 78, 90, 96, 104, 130, 150, 167, 182, 190, 203, 205, 216, 244, 259
Larry, Male #033, 72, 91, 93, 96, 131, 136–7, 138–9, 147, 181–2, 197, 209, 214, 215, 219, 234, 242, 253, 268
LC, Female #096, 126, 129, 164
Lee Roy, Male #043, 100, 103, 193, 200
Leroy, Male #042, 62, 91, 126, 133, 138, 150, 151, 233, 268
Lil Gene Mack, Male #034, 136, 177–8, 183, 204, 208, 212, 222, 242, 252–3
Lil Thug, Male #020, 67, 69, 77, 96, 120, 135, 179, 196, 209, 220, 221, 223, 238, 243, 258
Lil-B Dog, Male #070, 164, 201, 233
Lil-P, Male #093, 68, 98, 104, 108, 133–4, 256
Lisa, Female #011, 66, 83–4, 125, 133, 226, 246

Marrien, Male #009, 85, 96, 120, 222, 223, 227
Maurice, Male #018, 67, 122–3, 125, 126, 139, 168–9, 195, 206, 207, 219, 222, 233

Mike-Mike, Male #001, 1, 82, 87–8,
102, 108, 124, 131, 148, 149, 165,
168, 169, 176, 194–5, 200, 206,
211, 222, 225, 234, 239, 244, 256
Money Love, Male #101, 79, 248–9,
256

NA, Male #036, 70, 87, 90, 100, 101,
106, 110, 112, 115, 119, 160, 181,
183, 194, 209, 214, 226, 232, 257

Paincuzz, Male #044, 93, 125, 174,
183–4
Paul, White Male #091, 98, 109, 157–
8, 212–13
Pump, Male #064, 99, 149

Randell, Male #029, 131, 156, 165,
223
Relative #001, brother, 240
Relative #002, cousin, 239, 249
Relative #004, sister, 249
Relative #005, sister, 249, 257
Relative #006, brother, 249
Relative #007, cousin, 258
Relative #010, mother, 240, 257–8
Relative #011, cousin, 258
Relative #012, cousin, 240, 254
Relative #014, cousin, 240
Relative #016, mother, 244, 255
Relative #017, father, 240, 255, 258
Relative #019, mother, 244
Relative #020 aunt, 240
Relative #021, mother, 249, 254
Relative #022, father, 249, 254
Relative #023, mother, 255
Relative #024, father, 249

Rellol, Male #090, 97, 100, 151
Roach, Male #058, 191, 207, 214, 252
Robert, Male #008, 76, 95–6, 105,
110, 112, 136, 155, 199, 224
Rolo, Male #084, 70, 72, 108, 116,
122, 123, 132, 175, 247, 256

Shon, Male #074, 172, 194
$hort Dog, Male #067, 115, 120, 125,
126, 129, 130, 158
Short Dog, Male #066, 90
Skonion, Male #032, 91, 102, 134,
157, 163, 198, 207
Smith & Wesson, Male #057, 66, 171,
174, 202, 216, 221

T-Loc, Male #088, 83, 151, 237, 265
Tina, Female #007, 84, 225, 226
Tina, Female #078, 82, 84, 133, 155,
162, 166, 175, 196, 225
Tony, Male #025, 68, 107, 130, 182,
217, 238, 242
Tony, Male #056, 181
2-Low, Male #085, 112, 197
Tyrell, Male #075, 112–13

Winchester, Male #083, 77–8, 111,
142, 146, 196, 200, 220

X-Men, Male #069, 71, 94, 103, 116,
122, 175, 194, 202

Yolanda, Female #006, 94, 97, 132,
136, 201, 216, 222, 223, 225, 252

Subject Index

action research, on gangs, 8–12
activities: as deterrent to joining, 267; constraints on, 120–2; with non-members, 141–3
adolescence, gangs and, 230
adolescents, group activities of and gangs, 5–6
adulthood, leaving gang as result of, 265
American Dream, and the underclass, 273–4
analysis software, 53–4
Anderson, Elijah, 21
armed robbery, 152
arrests: age at first, 128; gang members', 128, 211–14; kinds of, 213–14; mean number of, 211
auto theft, 126–7, 148–9

"beating in," 174
beating out, to leave gang, 270–2
blocked opportunities, 7
Bloods, in St. Louis, 57, 93
breakdancing, and gang origins, 87–8
brothers, of gang members, 233–4
burglary, 150–1

"cafeteria-style" delinquency, 10, 118–28
Campbell, Anne, 18–19
car jacking, 149
Chicago gangs, and St. Louis gangs, 88
Chicano gangs, in East Los Angeles, 13–14, 15–16
church, and gang members, 224–8
Cloward, Richard, 7–8
Cohen, Albert, 7
Colors, 86, 88–9; as source of gang rules, 102–3
colors, respecting gang, 102
community centers, and gang members, 226–7
community mobilization, gang intervention strategy, 276, 278–9
Compton Gangsters, drug sales by, 160
concerts, gang members and, 124–5
confidentiality, of interview data, 45–9
conflict, and role in gang life, 172
constraints on activity, 120–2
contagion, as explanation of violence, 185

convictions: confusions about, 215; nature of, 216; of gang members, 215–20

cowardice, consequences of, 180

crack cocaine, sales of, 166–7; quantities sold, 167

crack fiends, 168–9

crime: gang-motivated, 29; gang-related, 29

criminal justice system, and gang members, 189: arrests, 211–14; convictions, 215–16; incarcerations, 216–19; interactions with the police, 205–11

criminal profits, used for gang, 146–7

criminality, minor: disturbance of the peace, 129–30; drug use, 134–41; graffiti, 130–2; property crime, 132–4; vandalism, 130

Crips, 57; in St. Louis, 93

cruising, 126–7

culture: gang, 272–4; popular and gangs, 274

Curry, David, intervention strategies of, 276–80

data sources, 53–4

deaths, of subjects, 171

denial: on part of family members, 47–9; on part of parents, 236

drinking, and gang members, 125–6

drug addiction, and gang members, 137–41

drug customers, relations with, 168–9

drug fiends, 126–7

drug houses: as burglary targets, 148; gang involvement in, 165–6

drug profits: collective uses of, 158–9; individual uses of, 157–9

drug sales: as reason for being in gang, 153–5; at school, 195–8; by gangs, 17; customers of, 167–8; disorganized nature of, 161–2; earnings from, 155–9; extent of member involvement, 159–63; frequency of at school, 197; inter-gang variation in, 169–70; intra-

gang variation in, 169–70; neighborhood nature of, 167; non-monopoly of by gang members, 154–5; organization of, 160–6; products, 166–7; public concern about, 152–3; reasons for engaging in, 153–4; roles in, 160–2; sales quota, 159–60; stopping because of an arrest, 155; suppliers, 164–6; suppliers as leaders, 162–3; turf for, 163–4

drug turf, reactions to encroachment, 163–4

drug use: and gang members, 126; and violence, 139; by gang members, 134–41

drugs, as burglary target, 148

Dutchtown, characteristics of, 34–5

earnings, from drug sales, 155–9

East St. Louis gang: comparisons to, 183–4; gangs in, 88

ex-members, perspectives on leaving gang, 268–72

Fagan, Jeff, 29

Fairgrounds Park neighborhood, 186

family: contacting for interviews, 43–4; future relations with gang members, 256–60; permanence of to gang members, 252–3

fear, as constraint on activities, 124–5

female gang members, and church, 224–5

female gangs, 81–4; studies of, 18–19

female-headed households, as cause of gangs, 230

field contacts, ix, 27–8

field ethnographer, 29

fieldwork, with gangs, 28–9

fighting, frequency of, 175

firearms: accidents, 182; gang possession of, 175–6; mean number owned by members, 176; and schools, 201–4; uses of by members, 176 gambling, 129

gang: arising from friendship groups, 65; choosing between it and family, 250–4; compared to a family, 63; compared to family, 250–6; culture of, 272–4; defined in terms of criminal activity, 64; defined in terms of violence, 64; definition of, 29–31; forming in response to threat, 273; history of usage of term, 2–3; individual reasons for joining, 56–8; informal nature of, 271–2; money for, 74–5; positive reasons for staying in, 72–5; process of entry into, 67–9; protection by, 73; providing substitute for family, 251–2; pulls for joining, 65; pushes for joining, 65; reasons for joining, 64–7; research issue of, 54–5; support by, 75; symbols as aids to cohesiveness, 271–2; values of, 272–4; working definition of, 31

gang activities, as research issue, 54

gang colors, 1

gang family, as research issue, 55

gang formation: and status, 12; from friendship groups, 14; threat of violence, 10–11

gang initiation, 69–72; "beating in," 69–70; by tattooing, 71; functions of, 69; of females, 72; shooting rival in, 71

gang intervention programs: increasing delinquency, 9–10; schools, 195

gang members: activities in school, 190–2; activities with nonmembers, 141–3; age at first arrest, 212–13; arrests of, 128, 211–14; black police and, 208–9; brothers of, 233–4; characteristics of, 57; choosing gang over family, 253–4; church and, 224–8; community centers and, 226–7; compared to nonmembers, 127; constraints on, 120–2; contacting,

39–43; convictions of, 215–20; criminal justice system and, 189, 204–20; definitions of a gang, 62–4; desire to hide membership, 236; drinking by, 125–6; drug addiction of, 137–41; drug use by, 137–41; extent of involvement in drug sales, 159–61; families and, 230–60; family backgrounds of, 231; frequency of contacts with police, 209–11; frequency of drug use, 136–7; functions of white members, 80–1; future jobs, 223–4; future relations with family, 256–60; gang membership of parents, 232–3; graffiti and, 130–2; harassment of by police, 208; incarceration of, 215–20; income from jobs, 223; job searches by, 121; jobs of, 220–4; labor market and, 220–4; legal groups and, 188–9; loyalty toward gang, 275; minor criminality of, 128–34; minor theft by, 132–4; mothers of, 237–8; operational definition of, 31–2; parenthood of, 231; parents' response to membership, 232–4; peace disturbances by, 129–32; perspective of, ix; place of incarceration, 217–18; police brutality and, 206–8; positive assessments of family, 256–8; prison behavior of, 218–19; protection racketeering by, 149–50; race of, 78–9; relations with drug customers, 168–9; relations with family, x; relations with police, 205–11; relatives of, 234–5; relatives' knowledge of membership, 235–40; roles of female, 81–4; rules about drug use, 137–8; school reactions to, 193–5; sentencing of, 216–20; serious criminality by, 144–87; social institutions and, 187–229; social isolation of, 141–3; sons of joining gang, 258–60; sports and,

gang members (cont.)
227–8; suburban schools and,
191–2; underclass theory and,
189–90; use of heroin by, 136;
use of marijuana by, 134–6; vandalism by, 130–2; views on eliminating gangs, 261–8; views on
stopping new members, 261
gang membership: as research issue,
54; effect on family, 245–50;
knowledge of by relatives, 235–
40; negative effect on family,
245–6
gang problem: emerging, x; reality of,
29
gang rivalries, Crips versus Bloods,
92–3
gang subgroups, 114–16; activities of,
114–16; constitution of, 114
gang symbols, 75–8; clothes, 77; functions of, 75–6; spread of, 76;
tattoos, 77–8
gang turf, 111–14
gangs: allies, 94–5; amplifying of violence, 184; armed robbery by,
151–2; breakdancing origins of,
87–8; control of schools by, 192–
4; criminal profits and, 146–7;
drug houses and, 165–6; ex-
members of, 262–4; fundamental
causes, 261–2; imitation model,
86–8; importation model, 86–7;
information about as deterrent to
joining, 265–6; institutional approaches to, 262; institutional
characteristics of, 274–6; instrumental nature of, 91–2; intergang relations, 92–5; intergenerational structure of, 231–2; interracial, 78–9; intervention
strategies for, 276–80; junior,
105–6; leaders in, 95–100; leadership within, 275; leaving process, 262–4; media awareness of,
1; meetings of members, 103–5;
neighborhood affiliations of, 87–
8; neighborhood base of, 106–11;

organization of in St. Louis, 95–
106; organized for violence, 184;
origins of, 85–9; police and, 122;
policy responses to, 261–81; popular culture and, 274; post–World
War II, 7–12; providing male role
models, 250; proximate causes,
261–2; public interest in, 1–2; relations with neighbors, 122–3; relations with other cities, 89–92;
rivals, 92–4; role differentiation
in, 275; rules of, 100–3; St.
Louis, 57; selected for violence,
184–5; stopping individuals from
joining, 264–7; strategies for
eliminating, 268–72; street culture and, 274; studies of before,
1920s, 3–4; territorial nature, 13;
threat of violence and rules, 101–
2; unwritten nature of rules, 100;
violence and, 171–86; weak institutional structure of, 275–6;
working definition of, 57
grades, of gang members, 191
graffiti, 130–2; and initiations, 131;
reactions to tampering with,
131–2
Greater Ville, 95
guns, as burglary target, 148 (see also
firearms)

Hagedorn, John, 19–20
hanging out, as dominant gang activity, 10, 117–28
heroin: sales of, 167; use by gang
members, 136
Hit Man T, 180–1
homicide rates, of interviewees, 171
Hoover, Larry (aka King Hoover), 89
Horowitz, Ruth, 14–15
Huff, Ronald, on gang parents' denial,
47

incarceration: future expectation of,
219; of gang members, 215–20;
places of, 217–18

Inglewood Family Gangster Bloods, drug sales by, 160
initiations: shooting of rivals, 174–5; violence in, 174–5
intervention strategies, gang, 276–80
interview subjects: finding, 37–43; homicide rate among, 171; relations with, 45–9
interviews, ix; as primary data source, 29; conduct of, 49–51; ethical concerns about, 51–3; payment for, 51
isolation, from nonmembers, 141–2
issues for research, 54–5

jobs: and gang members, 220–4; deterrent to joining, 267–8; future and gang members, 223–4; income from, 223; looking for, by gang members, 121
junior gangs, absence of in St. Louis, 105–6

King David, 89
King Piru, 89
King, Rodney, verdict, results of, 94–5
Klein, Malcolm, 9–11
Kody, Monster, 236
Ku Klux Klan, 80, 95

labor market, and gang members, 220–4
Laclede Town, 109
leadership: drug contacts and, 97–9; in gangs, 95–100; perceived absence of, 95–6; size and age as determinants, 96–7; within gang, 275
legal groups, and gang members, 188–9
Loftin, Colin, 22–3
Los Angeles gangs: comparisons to, 183; relations with St. Louis, 86–9; romanticizing of, 91
loyalty, of gang members, 275
LSD, sales of, 167

marijuana, sales of, 166–7; use by gang members, 134–6
McCall, George, 28–9
meetings: informal character of, 103–5; of gang members, 103–5
middle-class flight, in St. Louis, 189–90
Miller, Walter, and lower-class values, 8
mobility, residential, 107
money, as reason for joining gang, 67
Moore, Joan, and field studies of gangs, 12–14

neighborhood: as place of entry into gang, 67–8; forced joining in, 110–11
neighborhoods, gang families', 230–1
neighbors, and gangs, 122–4
New York gangs, 4
nonmembers, activities with, 141–3

official agencies, ix–x
Ohlin, Lloyd, 7–8
107 Hoover Crips, drug sales by, 160

Padilla, Felix, 16–18
parents: response to gang membership, 232–4; stopping children from joining gangs, 266–7
partying, and gang members, 125–8
PCP, sales of, 167
peace disturbances, 129–32
police: assaults on by gang members, 207–8; black police and gang members, 208–9; brutality by, 206–8; control of streets by, 209–10; frequency of contacts with gang members, 209–11; gang members' relations with, 205–11; gangs and, 122; harassment of gang members, 208
Primo, use of by members, 136–7
prison gangs, 13
property crime, 145–52; frequency of, 145; planning for, 145–6

protection: as benefit of gang mem-
    bership, 110; as reason for joining
    gang, 65–6; need for, 23, 63
protection racketeering, 149–50

race, and school violence, 201
rank, gained by violence, 98–9
recruitment: of gang members, 64–5;
    physical coercion in, 106–7
relatives: as reason for joining gang,
    66–7; future relations with gang
    members, 257–60; interventions
    of with members, 242–5; inter-
    viewed for study, 234–5; knowl-
    edge of membership, 235–40;
    opposition to membership, 241–
    5; response of to membership,
    241–5; support of membership,
    241–6; views about choice be-
    tween gang and family, 253–6
research questions, 26
retaliation, 186
Riis, Jacob, 4
robbery, as initiation, 151
role differentiation: in gangs, 95–100,
    275; leaders, 95–8; other roles,
    98–100
routine activities, and violence, 185
rules, gang, 100–3; sanctions against
    breaking, 101–3; unwritten na-
    ture of, 100

St. Louis: characteristics of, 32–6; co-
    operation of police department,
    46–7; decline of industrial base
    in, 33; history of gangs in, 36–7;
    middle-class flight in, 32–3, 189–
    90; population decline in, 32; ra-
    cial isolation in, 34–5; study
    neighborhoods of, 34–7; study
    site, x; underclass formation in,
    34–7
Salameh, Abdul, 236
sales quota, for drug sales, 159–60
Sanchez-Jankowski, Martin, and gang
    fieldwork, 20

school: activities and gang members,
    190–2; attended by study sub-
    jects, 192–3; criminal activities at,
    195–204; drug sales at, 195–8;
    firearms at, 201–4; frequency of
    bringing firearms, 201–2; gang
    intervention programs at, 195;
    gang members at, 189, 190–204;
    kinds of drugs sold at, 196–7; ra-
    cial violence in, 201; reactions to
    gang members, 193–5; recruit-
    ment at, 68–9; staff complicity in
    criminal activities, 194–5; staff
    knowledge of gang membership,
    193–4; violence in, 198–204
selection, as explanation of violence,
    185
sentencing, of gang members, 216–20
serious crime, by gang members, 144–
    87: "beating in," 174; burglary,
    150; car theft, 148–9; drug sales,
    152–71; extortion of protection
    money, 149–50; property crime,
    145–8; robbery, 151; shooting,
    174–5, 176; weapons violation,
    176–7 (see also violence)
sex, and violence, 177–8
shooting rivals, 174–5
shoplifting, by gang members, 134
Short, James, 11–12
siblings, and knowledge of member-
    ship, 236
skating, 116
Smith, Dietrich, ix, 179
snowball sampling, 37–43
social intervention, gang intervention
    strategy, 276–8
social opportunities, gang intervention
    strategy, 276, 278–80
speed, sales of, 167
Spergel, Irving: and detached worker
    approach, 9; intervention strate-
    gies of, 276–80
sports, and gang members, 120,
    227–8
status, as reason for joining gang, 67
status frustration, 7

street-life, culture of and gangs, 274
Strodtbeck, Fred, 11–12
subgroups, of gangs, 6, 114–16; constitution of, 114
suburban schools, and gang members, 191–2
suppliers, of drugs, 164–6
suppression, gang intervention strategy, 276–7
symbols of gang, 75–8

theft, as part of initiation, 133, 132–4, 147–9
Thrasher, Frederic, x, 4–7, 171–2
threat: against family members, 247–8; defining gang for members, 63; role in leaving gang, 263–4; theoretical framework of, 20–6; violence and, 21–2
Thundercats: and armed robbery, 152; splintering of due to residential mobility, 107, 109
turf: defense of, 22, 111–14; drug sales on, 163–4; gang, 111–14; reasons for defending, 111–13; symbolic dimensions of, 112–13

underclass: American Dream and, 273–4; gang members and, 189; gangs and, 19–20; jobs and, 221–2

values, of gang members, 272–4
vandalism, by gang members, 130–2
Vigil, Diego, 14–15
violence: attitudes toward, 182–6; blase attitude toward, 183; causes of, 177–82; consequences of cowardice in face of, 180; contagion and, 22–4; defining attribute of gangs, 117; delight in, 144, 183; drug use and, 139; epitomizing feature of gangs, 172–3; everyday nature of, 173–5; explanations for, 184–6; expressive purposes of, 185–6; fatalism about, 182–3; frequency of at school, 199–200; functional purposes of, 185; gangs and, 171–86; gangs and in Thrasher, 5–6; in initiations, 174–5; key element in gang culture, 273–4; kinds of, 177–82; leaving gang linked to, 263–6, 269–70; potential of, 178–80; psychological reactions to, 184; racial at schools, 201; rates of in St. Louis, 173; retaliatory, 23, 179–80, 186; routine activity theory and, 185–6; school and, 198–204; serendipitous encounters with, 180–1; sex and, 177–8
voluntary desegregation program, and gang members, 191–2

Waldorf, Dan, 29
War on Poverty, and effect on gangs, 11–12
weapons, other than firearms, 176–7 (see also firearms, guns)
weed (see marijuana)
weekly compensation, from drug sales, 156

Yablonsky, Lewis, on violent gangs, 8